THE NEW

DRESS

DETECTIVE

Also by Ingrid E. Mida and also published by Bloomsbury

Reading Fashion in Art
Dressing and Undressing Duchamp

THE NEW
DRESS
DETECTIVE

A PRACTICAL GUIDE
TO OBJECT-BASED RESEARCH
IN FASHION, REVISED

INGRID E. MIDA

BLOOMSBURY VISUAL ARTS
LONDON · NEW YORK · OXFORD · NEW DELHI · SYDNEY

BLOOMSBURY VISUAL ARTS
Bloomsbury Publishing Plc, 50 Bedford Square, London, WC1B 3DP, UK
Bloomsbury Publishing Inc, 1359 Broadway, New York, NY 10018, USA
Bloomsbury Publishing Ireland, 29 Earlsfort Terrace, Dublin 2, D02 AY28, Ireland

BLOOMSBURY, BLOOMSBURY VISUAL ARTS and the Diana logo are trademarks of Bloomsbury Publishing Plc

First published in Great Britain 2015
This edition, fully revised and updated, published by Bloomsbury Visual Arts 2026
Copyright © Ingrid E. Mida, 2015, 2026

Ingrid E. Mida has asserted her right under the Copyright, Designs and Patents Act, 1988,
to be identified as Author of this work.

For legal purposes the Acknowledgements on p. vii constitute an extension of this copyright page.

Cover design: Charlotte Daniels
Cover image: Boy's cashmere frock with silk embroidery and tassels, c.1855.
Los Angeles County Museum of Art.(M.2007.211.88).

Bloomsbury Publishing Plc does not have any control over, or responsibility for, any third-party websites referred
to or in this book. All internet addresses given in this book were correct at the time of going to press. The author
and publisher regret any inconvenience caused if addresses have changed or sites have ceased to exist, but can
accept no responsibility for any such changes.

A catalogue record for this book is available from the British Library.

A catalog record for this book is available from the Library of Congress.

ISBN: HB: 978-1-3505-1732-5
       PB: 978-1-3505-1731-8
       ePDF: 978-1-3505-1733-2
       eBook: 978-1-3505-1734-9

Typeset by Typo•glyphix, Burton-on-Trent, DE14 3HE, UK
Printed and bound in India

For product safety related questions contact productsafety@bloomsbury.com.

To find out more about our authors and books visit www.bloomsbury.com and sign up for our newsletters.

This book is dedicated to my dear friend
Alexandra Kim
in appreciation of and in admiration for
her patience, kindness, grace and support

Contents

Foreword

Since 2015, when the first edition of *The Dress Detective* was published, it has been a source of great pleasure to hear about the different ways in which the book has encouraged people to engage in a deeper study of surviving dress objects, whether for family history, museum exhibition research or the making of reproduction clothing. Many of these readers highlight the value they have found in the *Slow Approach to Seeing*, the system Ingrid created to guide people through a careful and methodical approach to looking at items of clothing, with a belief that such study of object details would bring the researcher closer to understanding both the worn object and the wearer.

Much of what we wrote about in the first edition of *The Dress Detective* remains relevant today, but much has also changed, including the way in which the global pandemic severely limited access to collections, and the physical study of surviving garments and accessories has necessitated new ways of conducting research. Many new themes and directions for dress history have emerged, including an increasing recognition of the need to de-center the western fashion system and to highlight the clothing practices of those often overlooked, ignored and excluded. Ingrid's new edition of *The Dress Detective*, therefore, is especially timely and will ensure that the core beliefs and approach of the original book will be introduced to a new generation of dress historians and enthusiasts, as well as offering much new material to engage readers of the first edition.

The checklists created by Ingrid to aid the *Slow Approach to Seeing* which, with their insightful questions and prompts provide the bedrock of *The Dress Detective*, have been extensively revised and updated, to better reflect the many research avenues that might be opened up by a study of surviving garments and accessories. They are complemented by new versions of the chapters discussing each of the three research stages, Observation, Reflection and Interpretation, demonstrating how the study of dress objects can be integrated into different research journeys. And while this new edition continues to value the insights gained from an in-person study of dress objects, it also now offers a guide to studying collections virtually using digital object details and widens its consideration of primary source material, such as fashion journals and illustrated newspapers, to enrich the process of research.

The book contains a whole new suite of case studies, which intentionally interpret the carefully chosen dress objects, varied in artifact type and date, from a wide range of methodologies and research practices. They include the consideration of a deteriorating wedding dress as a springboard for artistic practice and a boldly patterned uniform jumpsuit as an exploration of fashion and identity. As Ingrid mentions in this edition, the new case studies form a complement to the original case studies, offering companion examples and possibilities for research outcomes. Generously illustrated, the new edition offers a visual feast, with dress objects ranging from sixteenth-century armor to contemporary designer outfits and showcasing the fashion and textile collections from a wealth of different of institutions including the Metropolitan Museum of Art, the Modemuseum Hasselt and Toronto Metropolitan University.

There is immense value in looking carefully and closely at items of dress, as a way of connecting people with the incredible, intimate and human narratives they reveal, imprints of lives lived and complex stories of wear. I have no doubt that this new edition of *The Dress Detective,* so beautifully written by Ingrid, will appeal to both a whole new readership and those readers already familiar with the first book's approach and insights. In doing so, I am sure it will inspire people to appreciate and connect with both the dress objects themselves and those who inhabited them.

Alexandra Kim

Acknowledgments

This book would not exist if not for the encouragement and support of many colleagues and friends. My deep gratitude is expressed to Frances Arnold, Bloomsbury Visual Arts Editorial Director, who suggested I write this book in 2023. She has been steadfast in her belief in and encouragement of my writing, and I am eternally thankful for her bottomless well of patience and for her unwavering support. I would also like to acknowledge my dear friend and esteemed colleague Alexandra Kim who stepped up as second author in the writing of the first edition of the book—when I was largely unknown. With this revised edition, Alexandra has been very gracious in allowing me to write this book and take full credit for having developed the *Slow Approach to Seeing* and the checklist-based approach to studying objects of dress. I have dedicated the book to her in recognition of her patience, poise, and kindness as a loyal and steadfast friend.

I offer my sincere appreciation to the many curators and collection managers who were so generous in allowing me access to their collections for the case studies. Special thanks to Sharon Takeda, Clarissa Esguerra and Rachel Tu at the Los Angeles County Museum of Art, Tarah Burke at Seneca College Fashion Resource Collection, Roxane Shaughnessy and Julia Brucculieri at the Textile Museum of Canada, and Eve Townsend at Toronto Metropolitan University Fashion Research Collection for welcoming me into their collection storage facilities. All were so munificent, not only in allowing me access to artifacts, but also in answering my queries and in their efforts to supply many of the beautiful images that accompany the case studies included in this book.

I offer my gratitude to Annette Becker and Ailie Pankonien at the Texas Fashion Collection at University of North Texas, Denise Birkhofer and Anna Jedrzejowski at the Image Centre at Toronto Metropolitan University, Karin Bohleke at Shippensburg University, Cole Bangia of Gzellig Studios for Seneca College Fashion Resource Collection, Neil Brochu at the Colonial Williamsburg Foundation,

Jasmine Bruno at the Victoria and Albert Museum, Sarah Casey at Lancaster University, Carolyn Cruthirds at Museum of Fine Arts Boston, Karolien de Clippel at Modemuseum Hasselt, photographer Tori Hopgood, Kate Irvin at RISD Museum, Kevin Jones and Christina Johnson at the ASU FIDM Museum, Sophie Jones at Art Resource, Nii Rie at the Kyoto Costume Institute, Dougald O'Reilly (grandson of Evelyn Wilkie), Lauren Stark at Royal Collections Trust, Martin Thompson at Bloomsbury, and Nicola Woods at the Royal Ontario Museum for their kind assistance in procuring the luminous images that populate this book.

A hearty thanks goes to the Rhode Island Historical Society for their assistance in accessing the family records related to the Spitalfields gown in Chapter 5. And special thanks to Christy Clark-Pujara, whose fascinating book *Dark Work: The Business of Slavery in Rhode Island* (New York University Press, 2016) opened my eyes to the history of slavery in Rhode Island and for her guidance in conducting more focused research in this area. I am also grateful to Clarissa Esguerra and Sharon Takeda for their generous time and assistance in reviewing my early drafts of chapters related to LACMA's artifacts, and of course, any remaining errors are my own. Thanks also to Pauline Wolstencroft at LACMA's Blach Art Research Library for permitting me to access an exceedingly rare copy of *The Cyclopaedia of the British costumes from the Metropolitan Repository of Fashions* (1823).

There are many others who contributed to this book in various ways including Alexa Greist, Curator, and R. Fraser Elliott, Chair, Prints & Drawings at the Art Gallery of Ontario, whose invitation to speak at the AGO sparked my interest in the story in the seams of the Garthwaite dress in Chapter 5. Thanks also to my anonymous peers who reviewed the initial book proposal and the draft manuscript since their thoughtful comments have made this a better book. The team at Bloomsbury from editorial, marketing, and production should all be commended for their attention to detail in making this a beautiful book. And I would also like to offer effusive thanks to Irene Gammel, Director of the MLC at Toronto Metropolitan University, for her ongoing support of my research.

There are many friends who nurture my soul. I offer special thanks to Alexandra, Carol, Guela, Jenny, Linda, Maura, Michelle, Sarah, and Tracy for your love, laughter and loyal friendship, which means more than you will ever know. My sons Mike and Jon bring me so much joy, and my little four-legged friend Floyd Le Frenchie reminds me to be present. And lastly, I must acknowledge the steadfast love and support of my husband Dan. Not only is he witness to my research joy, a patient listener and an outstanding proofreader, but it is his love that sustains me through the ups and downs of life.

An Introduction to Object-based Research in Fashion

Objects like a dress, a pair of shoes, or a painting thereof, hold stories—stories of the people, time and place in which these things were made, handled, owned or stored. As art historian Anne Smart Martin has noted, the objects we can touch, see and hold are "complex, symbolic bundles of social, cultural and individual meanings."[1] Unravelling the stories and layers of meaning in an object requires the skills of a detective in paying attention to the smallest of details, as well as devoting time, effort, critical thinking, and research to the task. This book is your practical guide to conducting object-based research in fashion.

Object-based research considers the relationship between objects made by humans and their meanings. As museologist Susan Pearce notes, objects have "lives which, though finite, can be very much longer than our own" and as such have the potential to "carry the past into the present by virtue of their real relationship to past events."[2] The 'material turn' in academia acknowledges that objects embody culturally constructed narratives and symbolic properties. Originating in the museum 'object lessons' of the Victorian era and borrowing from the traditions of anthropology, archeology, art history, and museum studies, the field of material culture studies has evolved over time and continues to evolve.[3] The material properties of objects hold evidence of how they were created, sold, used, altered, traded, or stored over time, and are thus able to transmit information which might otherwise be inaccessible through other means. And unlike the written accounts of history that favor the rich and powerful, ordinary objects such as clothing are viewed as "potentially more truthful."[4]

The material culture of fashion encompasses any physical object or space that relates to the design, creation, wearing and storage of clothing, accessories, and other forms of bodily adornment. This includes but is not limited to dresses (Figure 0.1), suits, waistcoats, shirts, skirts, trousers, undergarments, footwear (Figure 0.2), hats, gloves, jewelry, wigs, scraps of fabric, perfume bottles, wardrobes, sewing machines, and ephemera. Indeed, even the screens on which we view images of fashion can be considered part of the material culture of fashion. However, this book focuses on objects of dress—garments or accessories worn on the body— rather than the spaces, machines, or imagery related thereto.

OPPOSITE: Figure 0.1.
Mme. Grapanche, Dinner dress with bustle and train (silk), 1884–86, American.
Metropolitan Museum of Art (C.I.63.23.3 a,b).

Figure 0.2.
Shoes (brocaded and embroidered silk ribbons, silk satin ribbon, leather, and metal), c.1870, Europe.
Helen Larson Historic Fashion Collection, FIDM Museum Purchase with funds donated by Linda & Steven Plochocki, ASU FIDM Museum, (2017.5.48 a, b). Image courtesy of Arizona State University.

The word fashion can take on many different meanings depending on the context in which it is used. Within fashion studies, this term is typically used to describe the favored or prevailing mode of dress at any given period of time. And while it has become more common to use the words fashion and dress interchangeably, in this book, the word 'dress' is used to describe objects that were worn or used to adorn the body, and such objects may or may not have been 'in fashion' when they were worn.

Dress is distinctly different in material form and character than works of art and other objects of material culture, since dress has an intimate relationship to the body. In its use and wear, dress is subjected to the demands and whims of its owner, bearing the marks and strains of wear as well as the inevitable decomposition caused by light, moisture, pests and soiling. These marks and stains of living provide evidence of a personal history of a garment, and as fashion curator Amy de la Haye has observed: "more than any other medium, worn clothing offers tangible evidence of lives lived, partly because its very materiality is altered by and bears imprints of its original owner."[5]

Designed to be worn or adorn the body, garments and accessories not only incorporate functional elements but also embody symbolic and aesthetic qualities that echo the cultural norms of a particular time and place. Inherent in the design and production of clothing are technical choices reflecting the cost and availability of materials, such as the use of synthetic fabrics instead of natural fibers or the use of a zipper instead of buttons. An object of dress also embodies a multitude of design choices that may highlight or obscure certain parts of the body (Figure 0.3), reinforce or neutralize gender, or imbue political or social messages of belonging or difference. These symbolic and aesthetic qualities often echo the values of the people, the time, and the place in which that object was made and worn.

Figure 0.3.
Woman's Dress (Robe à la française and Petticoat), silk with metallic-thread lace, 1760–65, France or England. Los Angeles County Museum of Art (M.56.6a-b).

Many of the garments and accessories that form the core of museum and university dress collections were once part of someone's wardrobe. Within the institutional frame of the museum or university, an object of dress is set aside, protected, and preserved, and its biography is extended beyond its normal life cycle. In this way, an item from a personal wardrobe or a designer's archive may be transformed into an artifact of cultural significance. And while museums have recently endeavoured to be more inclusive in their collection practices, the bulk of institutional collections favor clothing and accessories worn by the elite of society and are thus not necessarily representative of what people wore at any given period of time (Figure 0.4).

Museum curators, dress historians, and collectors of dress were among the first to embrace the close study of objects of dress.[6] For many years, as dress historian Lou Taylor has documented, there was a notable divide between museum professionals and academics, such that the value of examining actual garments was little appreciated.[7] FIT Museum Director Valerie Steele wrote, "Because intellectuals live by the word, many scholars tend to ignore the important role that objects can play in the creation of knowledge."[8] Curator Alexandra Palmer echoed this sentiment when she wrote: "The seemingly old-fashioned museum-based approach of fashion studies, which begins with

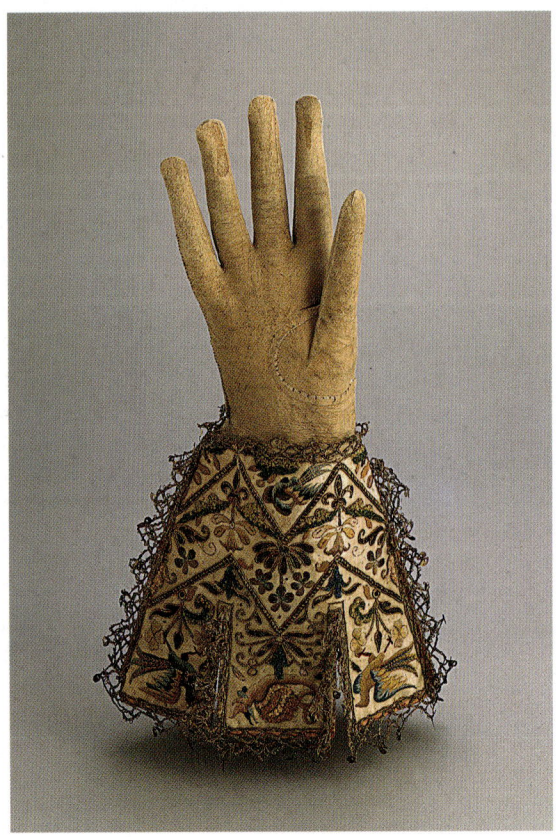

Figure 0.4.
Man's Gauntlet (leather, silk and gold metallic thread, silk satin; looped bullion embroidery), 1625–30, England.
Los Angeles County Museum of Art (49.45.1).

a description of the object, is a complex and underutilized approach for new scholars."[9] Cultural historian Giorgio Riello also noted the distinction between the object-centered approaches traditionally used by museum curators and dress historians (inductive approach) and the theory-focused approaches in fashion studies (deductive approach).[10] This book embraces a flexible hybrid approach in which the object remains central to the narrative.

The 'material turn' within fashion studies looks to the materiality (the physical properties) of dress as a method by which to expose and interpret the complex meanings and narratives embodied therein. A single garment, such as the silk dress (Figure 0.1) with the label of Mme. Grapanche (dates unknown) of 47 East 19th Street in New York represents the labor of many individuals, each of whom influenced its present form, including the weaver of the cloth, the designer herself, the seamstress, the person who fashioned the trim, the woman or women who wore the dress and saved it as a keepsake, and the collection staff who preserved it at the Metropolitan Museum of Art. The weight and texture of the cloth and other materials, the structure and proportions, the methods of construction, and the surface ornamentation offer clues that can be used to unravel time and tell a story that recalls, revisits, or reimagines the past in the present. That story might be told in a variety of formats, including a scholarly paper, a personal essay or history, a social media post, a reproduction, an artwork, or a work of fiction. For any of these formats, the material properties of the dress object can become the means by which to generate new forms of knowledge and/or inspire the creation of new objects.

When *The Dress Detective* was first published in 2015, the book filled a notable gap in the field by offering readers a step-by-step approach to object-based research with checklists that were designed specifically for dress artifacts. Recognizing that the motives for wanting to unravel the narratives behind the seams of a dress, a theater costume, or an accessory can be academic, professional or personal, this method has been designed to work for objects of dress that have been sourced from a museum, a university or college collection, a theater archive, or your personal wardrobe. Accordingly, the use of the term 'dress artifact' in the first edition has been supplanted by the use of 'dress object' or 'object of dress' for this book.

The New Dress Detective is intended as an aid to object-based research in fashion and related disciplines. This book will guide you through a step-by-step process of observing, reflecting, and interpreting the material traces of the past embodied in the things that have been worn on or adorn the body—such as a dress, a suit, an apron, an embroidered pocket, a pair of shoes or a piece of jewelry. For this edition, the checklists have been revised, and I have provided additional detail and guidance on what to look for and how to reflect upon and interpret findings. The interpretation phase has been reframed to acknowledge a range of outputs including creative practice. This edition further recognizes that there are circumstances in which the object cannot be handled or studied in person, and while this is less than ideal, it is still possible to craft a narrative about an object or engage with it through alternative modes of study.

The book begins with an overview of the phases involved in object-based research and introduces the *Slow Approach to Seeing* as a method of engaging with an object to see more. Subsequent chapters reveal and explain the three-phase approach to conducting object-based research with objects of dress. These chapters titled Observation, Reflection, and Interpretation provide tips and detailed annotations of the checklists included in the Appendices. And while it can be tempting to proceed directly to the checklists in the Appendices, there is much to be gained by reading the book from beginning to end if you wish to achieve optimal results.

This book references objects of dress that span several centuries in dress history. The seven case studies feature objects sourced from large and small institutions in North America and represent garments that might typically be encountered when using a museum or study collection. Each case study has a different focus. This includes explorations of the themes of identity and gender as embodied in objects of dress as well as the demonstration of an object biography, a wardrobe study, and creative practice.

The case studies feature an eighteenth-century Spitalfields silk gown, a man's dress ensemble (tailcoat and pantaloons) from the 1820s, a boy's frock dated to circa 1855, a homemade silk taffeta wedding gown and veil from 1927, a wool dress suit from Christian Dior Paris fall/winter 1958–59, a mass-manufactured 1976 CN Tower uniform, and an embroidered silk kimono with padded hem (*uchikake*) dated to the latter part of the Edo period (1603–1868). These new case studies, which supplement rather than replace the case studies in the earlier edition, articulate the methodological framework for the process, illustrate the use of the checklists, and show how evidence from the garment itself can be used to develop a narrative about an object or inspire creative practice. The 'Checklist for Observation' and the 'Checklist for Reflection' are included as appendices.

Although the focus of the book is primarily on western dress, the methodology also applies to non-western dress, and this has been illustrated with a case study about the language of the kimono (see Chapter 11). Fashion is a global phenomenon and in an ideal scenario, this book would have included case studies from institutions spanning the globe, but the limitations of time and budgetary constraints have narrowed the scope somewhat. Nonetheless, efforts have been made to reflect a range of objects and related images that reflect the global nature of fashion, feature women as makers and designers, and spotlight elite and everyday dress.

This book was written for a range of audiences, from novice scholars or museum interns unfamiliar with object-based research to instructors and museum professionals wanting a reference guide. Written in plain language, this book can also be used by anyone with a family heirloom or something in their wardrobe that they wish to examine more closely to unlock the stories embodied therein.

There is much that can be learned from object-based research, with possible outcomes as varied as the backgrounds, interests, and motivations of the readers of this book. Whether you are conducting a traditional form of scholarly research or engaging in an alternative form of making and knowing, the potential to reveal and unlock the narratives embedded in any dress object is constrained only by your imagination.

ENDNOTES

1   Anne Smart Martin, "Makers, Buyers, and Users: Consumerism as a Material Culture Framework," *Winterthur Portfolio* 28, no. 2–3 (1993): 141.

2   Susan Pearce, *Museums, Objects and Collections* (Leicester University Press, 1992), 24.

3   The history of material culture has been well documented elsewhere. See Leonie Hannah and Sarah Longair, *History through Material Culture* (Manchester: Manchester University Press, 2017). For additional information on the history of material culture research in fashion see Ingrid E. Mida, "Fashion and Materiality," Bloomsbury Fashion Central, 2021 DOI: 10.2752/9781474280655. BIBART2201

4   Jules David Prown, "Mind in Matter: An Introduction to Material Culture Theory and Method," *Winterthur Portfolio* 17, no. 1 (1982): 4.

5   Amy de la Haye, "Vogue and the V&A Vitrine", *Fashion Theory* 10, no.1–2 (2006): 135–136.

6   Some of the notable individuals who were pioneers in the field include: collector of dress Doris Langley Moore (1902–1989), museum curator Anne Buck (1910–2005), and costume maker Janet Arnold (1932–1998). See Ingrid Mida and Alexandra Kim, "A Brief History of Object-based Research with Dress Artifacts" in *The Dress Detective: A Practical Guide to Object-based Research in Fashion* (London and New York: Bloomsbury Visual Arts, 2015), 14–23.

7   See Lou Taylor, *The Study of Dress History* (Manchester: Manchester University Press, 2002). Also see Lou Taylor, "Fashion and Dress History: Theoretical and Methodological Approaches," in *The Handbook of Fashion Studies*, edited by Sandy Black, Amy de la Haye, Joanne Entwistle, Agnew Rocamora, Regina A. Root, and Helen Thomas, (London: Bloomsbury, 2013), 23–43.

8   Valerie Steele, "A Museum of Fashion is more than a Clothes-Bag," *Fashion Theory* 2, no. 4 (1998): 327.

9   Alexandra Palmer, "Looking at Fashion: The Material Object as Subject," in *The Handbook of Fashion Studies*, 268.

10 See Giorgio Riello, "The Object of Fashion: Methodological Approaches to the History of Fashion," *Journal of Aesthetics & Culture* 3, no. 1 (2011): 2.

1

HOW TO READ AN OBJECT OF DRESS

OPPOSITE: Figure 1.1.
The author studying artifacts at
the Textile Museum of Canada.
Photo by Julia Brucculieri.

Clothing is a form of material memory, carrying the imprints of its intimate relationship to the body. In observing and handling garments and accessories that were made and worn by others, it is possible to see, touch, and smell the past (Figure 1.1). The name or names of the people who made, sold, or wore these things might not be known, but their traces are there. Historic garments and accessories can also inspire the present, offering up design potential for reinterpretations of styles of the past; and as Christian Dior once said, "We invent nothing, we always start from something that has come before."[1]

All types of clothing and accessories that adorn the body, such as dresses, suits, waistcoats, lingerie, shoes, purses, hats, and jewelry, are artifacts of material culture. The material qualities of such objects not only provide evidence of the cultural and social history associated with a specific time and place but may also hold the stories of the person or persons that made (Figure 1.2), wore, owned or donated these things. As dress historian Linda Baumgarten noted, "All artifacts have individual stories to tell about their past lives if the clues can be deciphered."[2] Although a dress cannot be 'read' as easily as a text, every object of dress has a story—if you are patient and willing to spend time and effort unravelling the clues embodied therein. This chapter provides a brief overview of the overall framework, and subsequent chapters provide detailed guidance for each step.

Garments and accessories are distinctly different in material form and character from other objects of material culture, since objects of dress bear some relationship to the body that wore them. A dress can alter the silhouette of the body through its cut and construction; a floor-length silk taffeta skirt might rustle with movement; a luxurious cashmere sweater can invite touch; a hat (Figure 1.3) or a pair of shoes might add inches to a person's height. Garments and accessories fulfill a variety of functions in protecting, adorning, revealing, or concealing the body. The fact that dress is worn on the body also means that the actions of the body become imbued in the cloth or leather, especially at points of contact with body parts that move, such as the elbows and knees, or with the parts that leak or perspire. If a garment no longer fits or needs repair, it might have been mended, altered, or recycled into something else. Such marks provide evidence of a personal history in the object's biography. This intimate relationship to the body is central to unravelling the narrative of that object.

OPPOSITE: Figure 1.2.
Charles Frederick Worth, Fancy dress costume, 1870, France.
Brooklyn Museum Costume Collection at The Metropolitan Museum of Art (2009.300.1363a, b).

Figure 1.3.
Riding Hat (baleen and silk ribbon), c.1830, Great Britain.
Helen Larson Historic Fashion Collection, FIDM Museum Purchase with Funds raised by the FIDM Museum Fashion Council [2011–2015] and other generous donors, ASU FIDM Museum (2017.5.38). Image courtesy of Arizona State University.

The work of 'reading' an object of dress encompasses the gathering, assessment and interpretation of evidence from the object itself. To help you gather information in a systematic manner and ensure that nothing is forgotten, a checklist-based approach has been developed. These checklists are specific to objects of dress and are in this way distinct from the methodology articulated by Jules David Prown in 1981.[3] The practical and easy to use checklists—which have been revised since the previous edition of this book—present a series of questions or prompts that will help guide you through the process. Please note that the checklists are not meant to be read in isolation, and you are strongly advised to read the annotations of the checklists in the subsequent chapters in order to fully appreciate the nuances of each question and better anticipate what to look for. Whether the object comes from a museum or your wardrobe, the methodology is the same.

The process of conducting object-based research in dress is divided into three main phases, including:

1. **Observation**: Gathering and documenting information from the dress object
2. **Reflection**: Documenting initial thoughts and reactions, followed by the gathering of related contextual material in order to assess the evidence and determine next steps
3. **Interpretation**: Linking observations and reflections to create an academic or personal narrative for that object or to creatively engage with it in some manner.

These phases are described briefly below and are fully articulated in the chapters that follow.

1. OBSERVATION

The first step in analyzing an object of dress (or any object) involves close looking. To observe means to notice or see something, and the goal of this phase is to capture all the information presented by the object as it exists at that moment, recognizing that it may have changed or been altered since its initial creation. This phase of research is oriented around a question-based methodology that guides you through the examination and documentation of the evidence at hand.

The Observation Checklist has been designed specifically for objects of dress and moves from general to specific questions. The checklist includes a series of forty prompts or questions and includes taking measurements, describing the way the garment or accessory is cut and constructed, observing the proportions relative to the body, noting the type, color and texture of the materials used, discerning the nature of any surface design or ornamentation, identifying labels, logos and marks, documenting signs of use, wear and alteration, and gathering supporting material if available.

The goal of this stage of the process is to document enough factual information to be able to create a rich description of the dress object or artifact (Figure 1.4). This should be sufficiently detailed that a person who has not seen this object can create a mental picture of it, if this description was read aloud. The Observation Checklist and the questions have been extensively annotated in Chapter 3 and the checklist is included in Appendix 1.

The guiding principle for this phase of work is a method of looking called the *Slow Approach to Seeing* which will be explained in more detail later in this chapter. Like other slow movements that advocate patience, the *Slow Approach to Seeing*

Figure 1.4.
Cristobal Balenciaga, Silk gazar evening dress with cape, 1961.
Photo by Chicago History Museum/Getty Images.

promotes looking carefully and thoughtfully to appreciate all the evidence at hand. Objects of dress are particularly challenging to document since minute details can easily be missed or misunderstood, especially if you are inattentive or rushed because of time constraints.

In an ideal scenario, you would make detailed drawings of the front and back of the dress object. Making quick sketches or tracing and annotating printed photographs of the object are alternative modes of engaging in *slow seeing*. In every case, it is important to reduce distractions and make a mental shift to slow down, work methodically and carefully, and take the time to make detailed notes. The longer you look, the more you will see.

2. REFLECTION

After gathering evidence from the close study of an object, the next steps are not always obvious. The second phase of research, called *Reflection*, is designed to help you gather a full range of material that might enrich and support your understanding of the object that is the focus of your study. This typically includes the identification and study of related objects of dress from other collections, visual sources such as photographs and magazine covers (Figure 1.5) as well as textual sources, such as books, journals, letters and diaries.

The Reflection Checklist in Appendix 2 includes a series of twenty-five questions or prompts that have been divided into five parts: General, Personal Reactions, Sensory Reactions, Contextual Information, and Next Steps. These questions or prompts direct you to give due consideration to all the evidence gathered, document your personal reactions to the object, and identify and analyze related contextual material. This phase of the research is far more involved than the questions in this checklist may appear, especially since the gathering of related contextual material can be time-consuming. Also, please note that this phase of research often ends up being iterative rather than linear since each new piece of information may alter your understanding or lead to another discovery.

Although it was once considered inappropriate to invoke the personal while conducting research, today that no longer holds true. By pausing and reconsidering your experience of examining the object of dress and making written notes that are more personal in nature as to your sensory and affective responses, you may gain new insight into the object and your motivations for such research. Each of us has an innate knowledge of whether we might wear a garment, and whether it would fit or be comfortable on our body, and sometimes we are drawn to objects that appeal to us in some way.

Figure 1.5.
Model Stella Oakes wearing a Balenciaga ball dress of white satin with red taffeta bow. *Vogue* **(New York) Magazine Cover,**
November 15, 1952. Photo by Cecil Beaton/Conde Nast via Getty Images.

Figure 1.6.
Woman and her poodle,
each wearing a matching
leopard-spotted fur coat,
c.1945. Photo by Hulton
Archive/Getty Images.

While studying an object, you may experience a range of sensations or emotions, depending on your level of experience, the type and condition of the object, and the memories that such an object invokes for you. Although clothing is loaded with visual clues, the other senses might be stimulated as well, especially when a garment has an appealing texture or holds a lingering scent. A garment or accessory might also remind you of something you once wore or bought, or perhaps someone you once knew or loved who wore a similar style. In some cases, your personal reactions may alert you to shifts in cultural beliefs between the time in which the garment was created and the present. For example, being repulsed during the examination of a fur garment might signal attitudinal changes in contemporary society towards the wearing of fur (Figure 1.6).

A critical step in the Reflection phase is the gathering and analysis of other sources of contextual material. By seeking related objects and materials, you will better be able to assess and interpret the evidence gathered from the object itself. The identification and study of related objects—made by the same maker/designer, from the same period or from the same wardrobe—can provide additional benchmarks for comparison. If you are conducting a wardrobe analysis or are interested in the social history of the donor, identifying and studying garments worn by the same person can offer a rich source of data about a person's stylistic, color and material preferences as well as about their body size and stature.

Contextual material can come from a wide range of sources. Written records—including diaries, letters, and biographies; legal documents such as wills, inventories, and court records; and published texts such as newspapers, periodicals, illustrations and novels—can provide a range of insight into a person, place or time period. Visual sources such as designer sketches, photographs (Figure 1.7), magazine covers (Figure 1.8), fashion illustrations (Figure 1.9), patterns, and even exhibition photographs (Figure 1.10) allow you to not only see how that object of dress was worn and styled on the body but also gain insight into cultural values. Provenance files, if available, may include important information about the donor. There are many fertile sources of information for this stage of reflective analysis and the more widely you are able to search, the richer the outcome will be.

Figure 1.7.
Model wearing a blue wool coat by Zelinka-Matlick, over a green silk dress by Larry Aldrich. Published in *Vogue* (New York), January 1, 1961. Photo by William Bell/Conde Nast via Getty Images.

Figure 1.8.
Still-life of three leopard patterned handbags by Nettie Rosenstein, with jewels in the foreground by Schlumberger for Tiffany. *Vogue* (New York) Magazine Cover, October 1, 1958.
Photo by Richard Rutledge/Conde Nast via Getty Images.

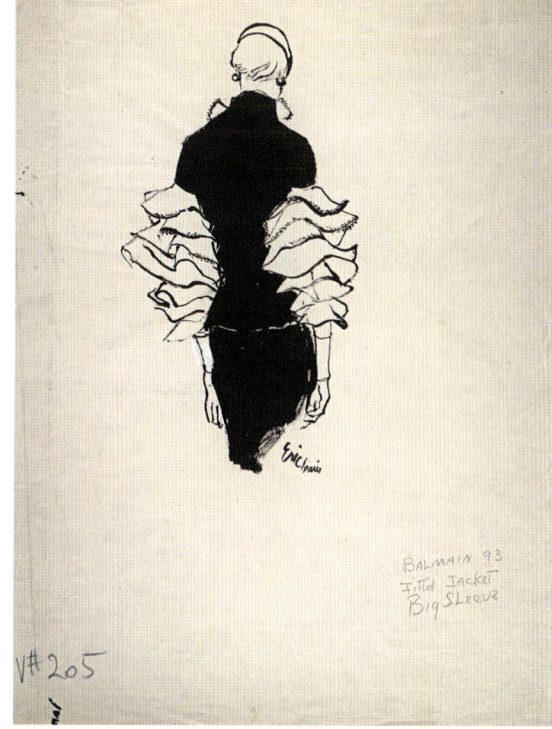

Figure 1.9.
Illustration of model wearing a black fitted jacket featuring muti-tiered 'lantern' half-sleeves by Pierre Balmain. Signed Eric/Paris by artist. Published in *Vogue* (New York), March 1, 1950.
Photo by Carl Oscar August Erickson/Conde Nast via Getty Images.

3. INTERPRETATION

The third phase of research is called *Interpretation*. In this phase, you synthesize the material gathered during the Observation and the Reflection phases of research and produce a narrative about the object in some form.

One object can have multiple interpretations depending on who is looking at it. Each of us comes to the table with different backgrounds, interests, skills and goals. A designer may seek to understand a particular construction technique or look for inspiration from the past; a collection manager documents objects for the catalog record; a conservator documents and assesses treatment options for a dress artifact prior to display; an anthropologist may strive to understand the cultural nuances of a garment worn within a distinct society; a historic interpreter wants to remake the clothing worn during a particular period; an author hopes to understand the nuances of wearing a corset or crinoline from the mid-nineteenth century; an art historian looks to analyze the accuracy of clothing rendered by an artist; or a scholar may seek to illuminate the politics of colonization by studying the link between the fashion for cotton chintz and the slave trade.

A single dress object can be used to develop a variety of outputs. This includes the traditional scholarly paper that uses the object to interpret or illuminate aspects of history or culture as well as alternative formats such as a personal essay, podcast or social media post. Other creative possibilities include the reproduction or reinterpretation of the garment in its entirety or in part, a finished artwork, a story of fiction, an exhibition (Figures 1.10 and 1.11), or a myriad of other creative outputs.

The Interpretation phase is the most creative and imaginative aspect of object-based research, and it is impossible to articulate a single prescription for this phase of research, since each researcher has different goals in undertaking this type of research. The seven case studies included in this book, and the case studies in the previous edition, present a mere sampling of the possibilities.

OPPOSITE: Figure 1.10.
Diana Vreeland shows off a one seam coat by Balenciaga at the Metropolitan Museum of Art, March 22, 1973.
Photo by Bettman/Getty Images.

Figure 1.11.
The Costume Institute of the Metropolitan Museum of Art's first exhibition devoted to designer Cristobal Balenciaga opened on March 23, 1973.
Photo by Nick Ackerman/WWD/Penske Media via Getty Images.

THE *SLOW APPROACH TO SEEING*

The guiding principle behind the careful examination of a dress object or artifact is the adoption of the *Slow Approach to Seeing*. There is a difference between looking and seeing, since you can look at something, but not really see all the subtle details therein. Seeing requires a commitment to careful observation and takes time. Like the fictional detective Sherlock Holmes, you have to make time to patiently observe the subtle clues that are embedded in an object of dress. This might include for example, a forgotten sewing pin left in a seam, a faint line from where a hem has been let down, initials embroidered into a lining, a pocket sewn closed, a missing stone in a piece of jewelry, an extra piece of fabric that has been inserted to add ease, or the use of an eighteenth-century textile in a nineteenth-century dress that points to its use as fancy dress. As I have argued elsewhere, it takes time, patience and effort to not merely look but to see and drawing facilitates this type of seeing.[4] For example, in drawing this ruby red velvet jacket by Christian Dior New York, details of construction including the unusual pockets became evident (Figures 1.12 and 1.13).[5]

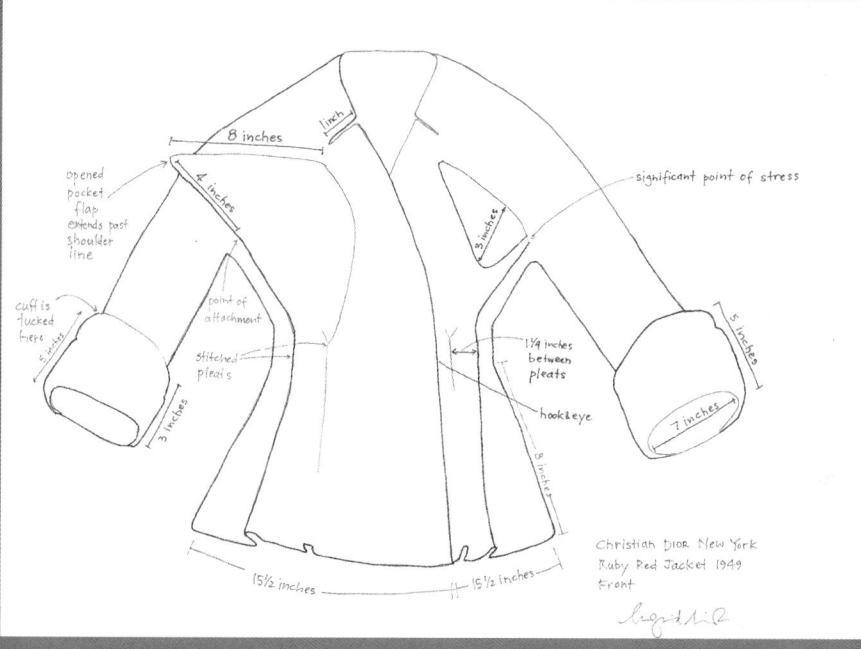

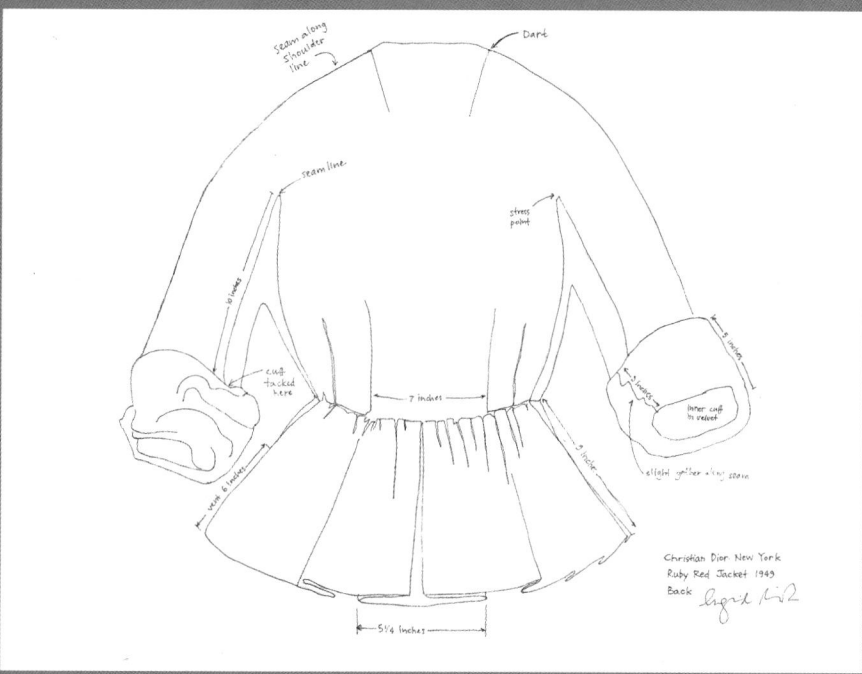

TOP: Figure 1.12.
Ruby Red Velvet Jacket by Christian Dior New York, fall/winter 1949–50 (front). Sketch by author.

BOTTOM: Figure 1.13.
Ruby Red Velvet Jacket by Christian Dior New York, fall/winter 1949–50 (back). Sketch by author.

Drawing helps you to see more, and each time you put pencil to paper, you embark on a path of discovery. Allowing sufficient time to draw will greatly aid your understanding, especially if you are a maker. As John Berger so eloquently wrote: "a line, an area of tone, is not really important because it records what you have seen, but because of what it will lead you to see."[6] In other words, it really does not matter if you have the skills to produce a highly technical rendition; you may also draw to record the path of your eye as you trace the contours of the object, through the folds, seams and textures therein.

Whatever your skill level, drawing will allow your brain to assimilate the information and see what might not be readily visible. If you are not willing to or do not have time to draw, look at the object as if you were drawing it, and/or trace over a photograph of the object. Although the checklists have been developed to help facilitate a systematic approach to close looking, this type of looking with care and attention—*The Slow Approach to Seeing*—requires a mental shift. To get the most out of your experience, make a commitment to slow down and work thoughtfully and methodically through the evidence at hand.

Before you begin, resolve to be mindful, especially if your time is limited. Turn off your notifications, free your mind of other distractions, and mentally commit to slow down and focus on the task. Take several deep breaths and be fully present. Fix your gaze on the object and study it for a few minutes before you do anything else. Let your eyes luxuriate over every small detail. If you decide to draw, let your pencil record the path of your eyes. Work through the checklist thoughtfully and systematically and pay attention to what seems irregular or unusual.

BEFORE YOUR RESEARCH VISIT

Since access to dress artifacts in museum or university collections necessitates a pre-arranged research appointment, knowing your objective will aid you in achieving your goals within the time constraints set by the institution. However, it is also possible that you might not know why you are initially drawn to something and/or the form of your output. If that is the case, begin the process, be alert to what you find, take note of what is most striking or unusual, and see where the object leads you.

In advance of visiting the research facility, gather your dress detective toolkit (see boxed material opposite). Read over the checklists and carefully review the annotated material in Chapters 2 and 3. Consider each question in relation to your research goals. Are you interested in the biography of the object, the designer, the type of garment, the methods of construction or embellishment, this period in history, theories of gender, sexuality or identity, cycles of production and consumption, a wardrobe study, remaking the garment, or something else? Given the broad spectrum of objects that might be encountered within the study of dress—from grass skirts to rubber boots—it may be appropriate to omit or adapt some questions to meet your specific situation. It is also helpful to do some reading and gathering of contextual material (about similar objects, the maker/designer, the period and/or the place of origin), in order to be better able to identify what is unusual or unique about the object you have chosen to study.

The Dress Detective Toolkit and Tips

The ideal dress detective toolkit includes:

1. A copy or copies of the Observation Checklist in Appendix 1
2. A notebook, sketchbook, or loose paper
3. Several sharpened pencils or a mechanical pencil
4. A cloth or flexible measuring tape
5. A magnification loupe (optional)
6. A camera with the ability to disable the flash (if permitted)
7. A small color chart for color calibration of images (optional).

Coming armed with sufficient paper and sharpened pencils is essential, since laptops, pens and cameras may or may not be permitted in certain facilities. Do not bring or use an eraser since this produces deleterious material that is detrimental to museum artifacts. A magnification loupe is helpful if you wish to study the textile weave. A color chart is useful if you have one, since the lighting in research facilities may distort the actual color of the object in your photographs. Turn off the notifications on your phone (by using airplane mode) so that you can stay focused on the task at hand.

Anticipate that your backpack, purse, coat and other accessories might be stored away from the study area, so have your toolkit organized for easy access. Avoid wearing clothing or accessories that might inadvertently damage a garment, such as dangling necklaces, rings or other jewelry that might get caught in a textile, or long scarves that might hang onto an examination table.

METHODS OF DOCUMENTATION

Documentation is a key element of research, especially since small details can be quickly forgotten or merge into a fog of general impressions. Take meticulous notes of your observations on the checklist itself, in a notebook or on your laptop, and include as much specific information as possible. ,

Ideally, the process of studying the garment or dress object should be conducted in a way that minimizes handling. This means that all measurements and drawings/photographs of the front should be completed *before* opening the garment to see the inside, and *before* turning it over to examine and draw/ photograph the back.

As explained earlier, drawing is a method of helping the mind to slow down and, in the process of doing so, take notice of small details, as well as to calculate the relationships of one part of a garment to another. Drawings or quick sketches are also useful as a place to record measurements, since it may later be unclear where the measurement began and/or ended. For many people, the idea of sketching may be daunting, yet the goal is not to create a work of art, but simply to aid the process of observation. A sketch need not be more than a quick line drawing, since this is a valuable method of recording key information and embracing the *Slow Approach to Seeing.*

If time permits, an annotated line drawing of the garment or object, both front and back, is ideal (see Figures 1.12 and 1.13). Translating the cut and construction of a dress object into lines on a page requires close attention, and an accurate drawing necessitates careful notation of each element, such as the cut of the bodice, the details of seams, the fullness of a sleeve-head relative to the wrist, the length of the skirt, or the attachment of trim. Many dress historians, including Norah Waugh (birth year unknown–1966), Janet Arnold (1932–98), and Jenny Tiramani in the United Kingdom, and Dorothy Burnham (1911–2004) in Canada, have used drawing as a method that guides their analysis of the cut and construction of garments.[7] Detailed drawings can also be fully rendered after the appointment.

Since most research appointments come with time limitations, it can be tempting to capture key features of the garment with photography. However, caution is advised in using only photography as a method of recording information, since so much more can be gained in the close observation and handling of the object (and there is always the danger of a technical failure with such technology). It is easy to snap photographs and think that sufficient information has been captured to later read the object, but it often can be difficult to remember or discern what part of the garment you have photographed. The exact location of a stain or a repair or other details might be forgotten unless you have made detailed notes and labelled your images before you forget. Photography is recommended as a memory aid and documentary tool, but not as the principal method of research since nothing can quite replicate the experience of seeing an object in person. In most institutions, flash photography is not permitted; and in some cases, professional photographs may be available for purchase. Be aware that publication of photographs of the artifact, online or print, usually requires additional written permission (and often payment of fees) from the museum, study collection or archive.

Many museums will provide gloves for the handling of collection artifacts, although in some institutions, gloves are not required. Always be sure to wash your hands prior to handling any museum artifact. There are some cases in which researchers are not permitted to handle the artifact at all, and then the supervising curator or assistant will handle the object during your visit. Always be sure to ask for help if you are unsure as to the policy and especially if the garment or accessory is fragile or unwieldy.

A DIGITAL ALTERNATIVE TO IN PERSON STUDY

To fully appreciate the material qualities of a dress object or artifact, you have to be present. This allows you to touch, feel, smell and hold the past in your hands and by so doing, you can be transported into the world of the persons that made, wore, or owned these things. And yet, there are circumstances in which it is impossible to study an object in person.[8] This could be because travel to the museum is prohibitive in cost, access is limited due to fragility of the object, or for other reasons. In 2020–22, when museums closed during the pandemic, many researchers, including myself, found themselves in situations where physical access to the object was impossible. And although this mode of research was challenging, such obstacles were overcome with creativity and collaboration.[9] As a result, this book acknowledges an alternative model of object-based research that does not require handling the object itself and encourages drawing as a means of echoing the sensation of touching.

Nothing really can compare to the experience of studying an object in person. Certain aspects of the object's materiality, including the measurements and relative dimensions, the texture and weight of the cloth or other materials, visible signs of wear and use, the scent (if any), and other small nuances may only be accessible by having physical proximity to the object. And yet it may still be possible to conduct an alternative form of object-based research if the museum or collection has digital images of the object available online and/or is willing to make images available, and if you are willing to draw or otherwise engage with the *Slow Approach to Seeing*.

In 2021, the Modemuseum Hasselt provided me with high resolution images of objects in their collection, including this celery-green satin-weave silk cocktail length gown with alternate bodice dated to 1955–56 by Pierre Balmain (1914–82) (Figures 1.14, 1.15 and 1.16). By carefully studying these (and other) images, reviewing the conservation report, undertaking related research and drawing, I was able to craft a narrative about this dress for a talk titled "Behind the Seams with The Dress Detective," delivered remotely in connection with the programming for their exhibition *Dress Codes* (October 1, 2020–May 9, 2021).

Figure 1.14.
Pierre Balmain, Celery-green silk cocktail dress, c.1958, France.
Modemuseum Hasselt (2020.0022 ab).

TOP: Figure 1.15.
Inside of bodice showing
signs of wear.

BOTTOM: Figure 1.16.
Detail of inside of skirt
showing that the hem
was shortened.

If you cannot study the object in person, I highly recommend that you make drawings using the images that are available to you, since drawing can be equated to a form of touching.[10] And it is this sensation that can be harnessed to facilitate the study of an object that you cannot physically access. Using images available online or via consultation with museum collection staff, print out the images and then draw from, trace on and/or annotate them. If the museum has photographed the object with a measuring tape in proximity to the object, it may even be possible to estimate measurements or approximate relative dimensions between parts. If high resolution images are available, it may also be possible to zero in on certain details that might not otherwise be visible by unaided sight (such as thread count or construction details).

Sometimes curatorial staff may also be willing to share conservation reports for an object. These reports typically include many of the details asked for in completing the observation checklist with detailed drawings and/or annotated photographs to document changes in the physical properties of the object or accessory. Such reports can provide extremely valuable information when you are unable to study the object in person.

Research is a journey of discovery. And while undertaking object-based research without being able to examine the object in person is challenging (see boxed material below), it is a feasible alternative, especially if you take time to draw.

Conducting Digitally Oriented Research of Dress Objects

1. What is your desired outcome for this project and how does the materiality of this object impact your research? Are you interested in recreating the object, writing an object biography, comparing this object to others like it, or exploring some other aspect?
2. Assess what information is available about the object. Does the collection portal offer multiple views of this object? Are there any photos of details such as closures, embellishments, or linings? Are the photos sufficiently high resolution in order to facilitate magnification? If only limited or low-resolution photos are available, consider whether it is possible to request additional photos from museum staff.
3. What information is available about the object itself in the catalog record? Does the object record include any measurements and/or provenance information?
4. Is it possible to request conservation reports related to the object from museum staff?
5. Are curatorial staff willing to answer your questions about the object that may arise from your study?
6. Has the object been documented elsewhere, including in books, newspapers, journal articles, videos, or social media?
7. How will you utilize drawing to enhance your engagement with the object?
8. What information cannot be accessed and how will you adapt your approach?

ENDNOTES

1   Christian Dior qtd. by Marie France Pochna, *Dior* (New York: Assouline, 2004), 80.

2   Linda Baumgarten, *What Clothes Reveal: The Language of Clothing in Colonial and Federal America* (New Haven and London: The Colonial Williamsburg Foundation in association with Yale University Press, 2002), 184.

3   I first developed an early version of the observation checklist in 2013 to aid students conducting object-based research in the Fashion Research Collection at Ryerson University (now Toronto Metropolitan University). Although the first edition of this book emphasized the similarities with Prown's methodology, the checklists were borne of and have been revised based on my experience in handling and documenting thousands of objects. I acknowledge Prown as being one of the first to write a general methodology for the study of material culture, but the methodology advocated here builds thereon in order to more accurately reflect the practical realities of fashion studies and also the inherent challenges of interpretation. See Jules David Prown, "Mind in Matter: An Introduction to Material Culture Theory and Method," *Winterthur Portfolio* 17, no. 1 (1982):1–19. See also E. McClung Fleming, "Artifact Study: A Proposed Model," *Winterthur Portfolio* 9 (1974): 153-168.

4   See Ingrid Mida, "The Curator's Sketchbook: Reflections on Learning to See," *Drawing, Research, Theory & Practice* 2, no. 2 (2017): 272–285.

5   For more on this Dior jacket, see Chapter 11 in the previous edition of this book. It was in drawing this jacket that I came to fully appreciate the complexity of its construction.

6   John Berger, "Drawing is Discovery," *Statesman and Nation* 46 (1953): 232.

7   See the Janet Arnold Patterns of Fashion series, including Janet Arnold, *Patterns of Fashion: Englishwomen's Dresses and their Construction* (London: Macmillan, 1972); *Patterns of Fashion 2: Englishwomen's Dresses and their Construction 1860–1940* (London: Macmillan, 1977); and *Patterns of Fashion 3: The Cut and Construction of Clothes for Men and Women 1560–1620,* (London: Macmillan, 1985). Also see Dorothy Burnham, *Cut My Cote* (Toronto: Royal Ontario Museum, 1997 [1973]).

8   For my book *Dressing & Undressing Duchamp*, I relied on conservation reports and collaboration with curatorial staff at the Museum of Israel in Jerusalem and at the Te Papa Tongawa Museum of New Zealand in considering the material evidence within the waistcoat readymades of Marcel Duchamp. See Ingrid Mida, *Dressing & Undressing Duchamp* (London: Bloomsbury Visual Arts, 2022).

9   In 2022, I also conducted object-focused research remotely, in collaboration with the curatorial staff of the Museum fur Kunst & Gewerbe Hamburg, in conjunction with the exhibition *Dressed: 7 Frauen – 200 Jahre Mode*. See Ingrid Mida, "Dress and Memory," in *Dressed: 7 Frauen – 200 Jahre Mode* (Hamburg: Museum fur Kunst & Gewerbe in conjunction with MK&G Hirmer, 2022), 16–17.

10 Ingrid Mida and Sarah Casey, "Drawing as a Creative Approach to Studying Dress Artifacts: A Case Study of John Ruskin's Clothing," *Costume* 54, no. 2 (2020): 202–221.

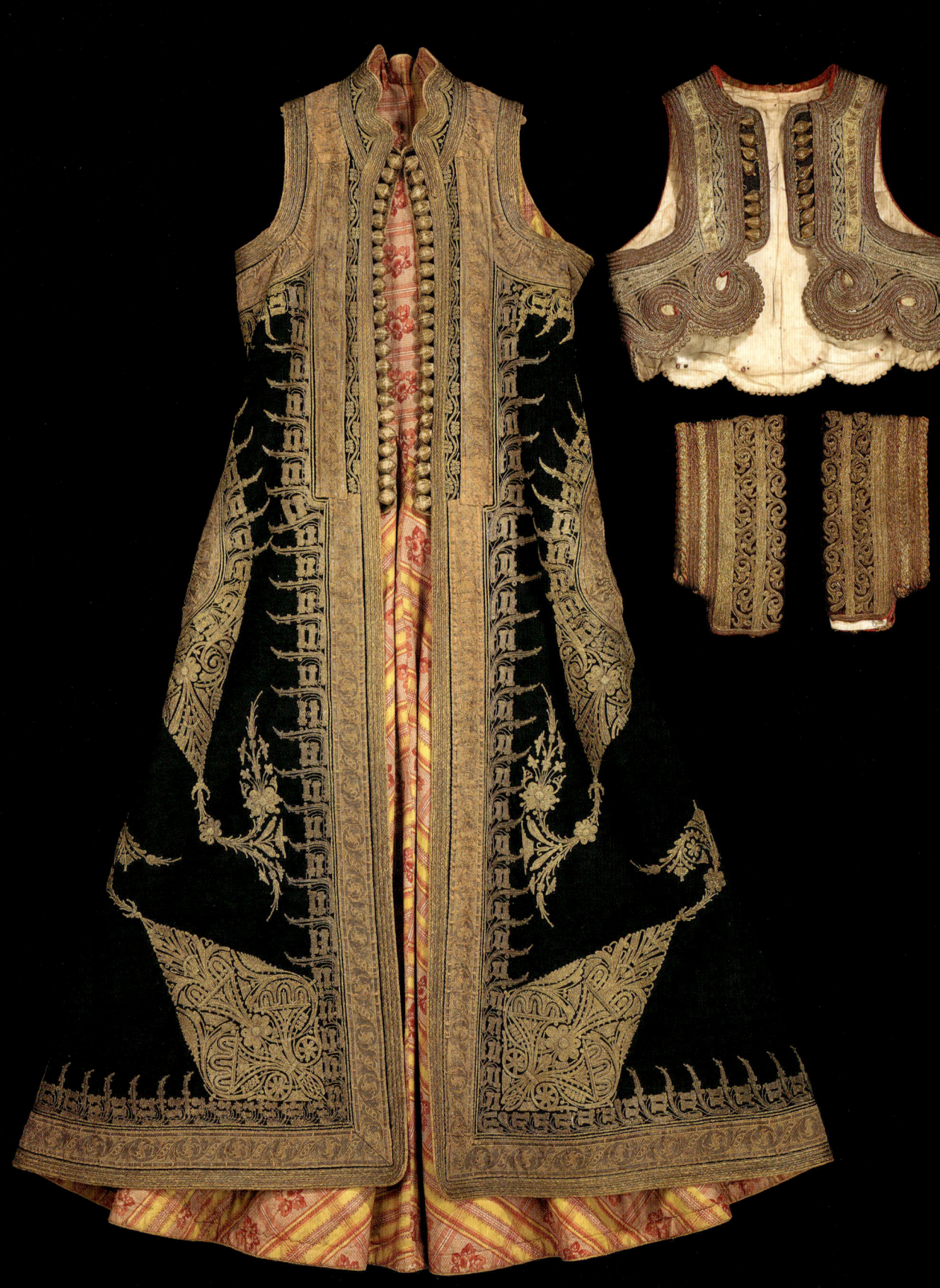

2

OBSERVATION

To observe something is to focus your attention upon it and look at it with sufficient care to understand and appreciate it as it exists at that moment in time. In the words of Maurice Merleau-Ponty, "to look at an object is to inhabit it, and from this habitation to grasp all things in terms of the aspect which they present to it."[1]

The first phase of your research journey is called *Observation*, and in this phase, the material properties of the object as it exists at the time of examination are documented, recognizing that it may have been altered or changed since its original conception. In this phase, you seek to identify the materials, the features of construction, and the details of embellishment, and also discern the marks and stains, the patches of wear, the repairs and other clues related to its use, wear or storage. Whether you want to tell the stories of the makers and/or persons who once wore, handled or owned that garment or accessory, illuminate an aspect of history, recreate or reinterpret the dress object, or use it as inspiration for a creative endeavor, you first must look closely at what is before you—close enough to feel as if you have inhabited it.

It can be hard to know where to begin and what to look for. To help you gather and document the evidence contained within the object itself, this book provides an Observation Checklist (Appendix 1). This checklist (which has been revised from the previous edition) includes forty questions and has been specifically designed for objects of dress, including accessories and costumes. In this chapter, each question has been annotated to provide additional information and tips on what to look for.

To improve your chances of achieving an optimal outcome, take care to consider each question on the checklist. In certain instances, some questions may be more relevant than others depending on the type of object selected and your research focus. For example, if you are seeking design inspiration, looking to recreate a garment or accessory, or undertaking conservation work, you may want to spend more time studying the aspects related to construction and materials, taking careful measurements and creating accurate, drawn-to-scale drawings on graph paper. If you are studying a garment worn by a known person, you may be more interested in measurements that reveal their height or size, signs of use and wear, and especially aspects that reveal their aesthetic and clothing preferences. If necessary, customize the checklist to suit your focus but think carefully about omitting questions; sometimes research ends up on a different trajectory than is initially anticipated and you may only have this one opportunity to view this object. Gathering more information than you think you will need allows for flexibility within your research journey.

It is strongly recommended that you carefully review this chapter prior to the research appointment and spend some time doing some preliminary research. Study the information available about that object on the collection portal, which may include certain measurements, identification of materials, and/or provenance information, and record this information on the checklist in advance of your visit. It can also be highly beneficial to identify similar or related objects on the collection portals of public museums with large dress collections such as the Metropolitan Museum of Art or the Victoria and Albert Museum so that you become familiar with that category of object. Such efforts will improve your efficiency during your research visit and will benefit the outcome.

During your appointment, embrace the *Slow Approach to Seeing* and make detailed notes and sketches to record your observations. As discussed in the previous chapter, drawing facilitates seeing by allowing the eye to slow down to see small details that might otherwise go unobserved. Even a quick and messy sketch is better than none at all, especially if you are not permitted to handle the object. In my experience, the objects that I have taken the time to draw are ones that I remember. Impressions can be fleeting and easily forgotten, and careful documentation is time well spent.

Work methodically, always being careful in handling the object to minimize damage. At the end of the appointment, take a few minutes to review your notes and double check that you have all the information you need. And as soon as possible after your research visit and while your impressions are still fresh, use the information gathered during your appointment to write a fulsome description that captures all the relevant information about that object. The goal is to write something that is so rich with descriptors that you could read it out loud to someone who has not seen the object and they would be able to visualize it in their mind's eye.

The Observation Checklist has been divided into three parts in order to help organize this phase of your research journey. The four preliminary questions in Part I should be documented prior to your research appointment. Part II includes thirty-three questions that are to be answered during your examination of the object, and there are five sections: General; Construction; Textile and Materials; Marks, Labels and Logos; Use, Alteration and Wear. Part III includes three questions related to the gathering of supporting material and the documentation of your initial impressions before you leave the facility or very soon thereafter.

While the Observation Checklist has been designed with space for notes and sketches, it may be useful to have extra paper or a digital tablet on hand. Ideally, you will use terms that are specific to dress and fashion and a fashion dictionary can be helpful in clarifying the precise terms used to describe types of collars, sleeves, skirts, and other features.[2] Measurements of key parts of the garment, costume or accessory are encouraged to the extent that these measurements will provide useful information. If you are not permitted to touch the object during the study appointment, the collection manager can usually provide or assist in collecting this type of information.

PART I: PRELIMINARY QUESTIONS

This brief section includes four questions that should be answered before beginning your study of the object. Unless the object comes from a personal wardrobe or private collection, such information is usually necessary to secure a research appointment.

1. Identify the object of dress for study. If applicable, record the description provided by the institution including the associated collection accession number(s).

What is it that you wish to study? Is it a dress (Figure 2.2), skirt, apron, blouse, suit, waistcoat, shirt, ceremonial robe, cravat, tie, hat, pair of shoes, parasol, ballet costume, or something else worn on the body? If this object comes from a museum or university collection, it will usually have an accession number or other form of identification. Note this number carefully as this information is needed for museum staff to locate the object within collection storage. If the museum has an online collection portal, note down the description and any other information provided on the website, including any related provenance information such as the name of the donor.

2. What decade or general period does the garment or accessory belong to?

If the object is associated with a museum or university collection, an assessment as to the date or period of origin will likely have been made when the artifact was accepted into the collection (Figure 2.3). If the artifact has been given a very broad or no date attribution, this might become the focus of your investigation and it may be appropriate to gather and assess evidence related to the silhouette, materials, techniques used in construction, and alterations in relation to other garments with documented date attribution. Even if the artifact has been assigned a date attribution, this can be subject to error and a close study may reveal undocumented alterations or other evidence that points to the need to update the record.

3. Why are you interested in this particular object?

What is the focus of your interest in this object? Do you have a specific research question you want to answer? Are you interested in the maker, owner, or materials associated with this object? Do objects of dress from a particular time period in history interest you? Are you wanting to recreate this object or use it to inspire an artistic or literary project? Does this object spark a memory?

There are many reasons for wanting to study a particular object. This might include documenting the object for a museum catalog entry; learning more about a certain type of object or the work of a particular designer; wanting to recreate or reinterpret a garment; unraveling the sartorial history of the owner/donor; verifying

Figure 2.2.
Silk and organza dress with imitation-pearl glass beads, 1830s, England.
Los Angeles County Museum of Art (M.2007.211940a-b).

the material qualities of a dress in a painting or photograph; seeking to unravel
the cultural beliefs from a particular period of time; and/or finding inspiration for
creative work. You may not even be conscious of why you are drawn to something,
but clarifying your motivations will help make the most of the limited time in research
appointments. As well, be mindful that you may discover evidence that ultimately
leads you in an entirely new direction from what you initially identified as your goal.

4. Does the collection have any other comparable objects of dress from the same period that might be helpful to your study? If so, list them here for follow up.

Studying an object in isolation may lead to erroneous conclusions, especially for
garments or other objects that pre-date industrial manufacture. Most museums or
study collections have other objects from the same period and these other objects
may aid your research by providing useful comparisons in terms of construction,
materials, and ornamentation. Identifying such objects in advance is necessary if you
wish to have them made accessible to you during your research appointment.

PART II: AT YOUR RESEARCH APPOINTMENT

General:

In this section, the questions are designed to be broad in scope, offering an overview of the key identifying features of the garment or accessory. The idea is to take note of initial impressions before becoming overly concerned with the details.

5. What type of dress object is it? Who was it designed to be worn by? Male, female or gender-neutral? Child, teen, or adult? Was it designed with a specific purpose in mind (fancy dress, wedding, mourning, maternity wear, sportswear, work uniform, or theater costume)?

Define the object in broad terms, such as a woman's dress, a man's suit, or a child's frock. If it is obvious, note whether it was intended to be worn for a particular purpose such as a wedding (Figure 2.1) or theater costume (Figure 2.4). Note that the gender associated with a particular garment may signal the cultural beliefs for a specific time and place. For example, in the mid-nineteenth century, young boys and girls were often dressed in similar frocks until about ages four to seven (see Chapter 7).

Figure 2.4.
Embroidered Jacket from Theatrical Ensemble for a Female Role, eighteenth century, Qing dynasty (1644–1911), China.
Metropolitan Museum of Art (30.76.20).

6. Does the dress object have multiple parts or removable elements such as an alternate bodice or waistcoat, or detachable collars or cuffs? If so, list the components that make up the ensemble and note whether any parts are missing.

Some objects of dress are made up of multiple parts, such as footwear, a man's three-piece suit (Figure 2.5), or a boy's dress ensemble (Figure 2.6). Each component of the ensemble should be studied methodically. If a part is missing, this may be a clue to the object biography, since certain items of clothing wear out at different rates or may have been recut and recycled into other garments.

Figure 2.5.
Man's three-piece Suit (Coat, vest and breeches), c.1770, Italy. Los Angeles County Museum of Art (M.83.200.1a-c).

Figure 2.6.
Boy's dress ensemble
(wool, silk), 1869,
American.
Brooklyn Museum
Costume Collection
at The Met
(2009.300.656a–d).

7. What materials have been used to make this garment, costume, or accessory?

Objects of dress can be made of or incorporate a range of materials. Garments are typically made of textiles that can be easily shaped to conform to the body such as silk, wool, cotton, linen, canvas, leather, or synthetics but they may also incorporate or be made of other materials such as metal (Figure 2.3), paper (Figure 2.7), fur (Figure 2.8) or wood. With contemporary garments, information from the label may provide detailed textile composition. Accessories may be made of cloth or hides but might be made of or incorporate a wide range of materials such as felt, fur, plastic, metal, rubber, baleen (see Figure 1.3) or even gemstones.

8. What are the dominant colors and/or patterns?

Use basic color terms—red, yellow, blue, green, black—adding descriptors such as *ruby red* or *emerald green* to clarify the shade. Color is perhaps one of the most difficult aspects of dress to record objectively, since each person sees color differently, and it can be difficult to find a color term which is both precise and universal. Specify the dominant color first, and then identify the pattern, if any, such as floral, tweed, stripe, or polka dots.

Figure 2.7.
Maxi bridesmaid jumpsuit of Reemay spun polyester and floral-printed paper, produced by DHK Industries Inc., 1965–69. University of North Texas (2006.008.002).

Figure 2.8.
Shannon Rodgers, Black wool dress with leopard fur, 1960–65. Texas Fashion Collection, College of Visual Arts and Design, University of North Texas (2007.003.010).

9. What are the most unusual or unique aspects of the garment or accessory that first attract your attention?

Note your initial impressions of the most striking features. Often these elements were intended by the designer/maker to alter the body's silhouette or create visual impact (Figure 2.9).

Figure 2.9.
Balenciaga, Babydoll style dress of champagne-colored chantilly lace, 1965. Texas Fashion Collection, College of Visual Arts and Design, University of North Texas (1975.003.023).

10. Are there any obvious signs of fragility that require special care in handling?

Historic dress can often be incredibly fragile (see chapter 8), and even conscientious handling can cause additional, irreparable damage. Care should be taken with every object to ensure its preservation for the future and, if handling is permitted, ask for help when needed. Work systematically during your examination to gather all the evidence from the front of the object before opening of the interior or handling to examine the back.

Construction:

Careful examination of the details of construction can yield important information, especially when wanting to recreate that object. Such details are also invaluable in dating artifacts, as well as presenting clues as to the cultural beliefs related to gender and identity, since the structure of a garment can emphasize certain parts of the body. Anomalous details that depart from typical modes of construction for a particular period should be carefully documented as these details may be clues to the remaking or reuse of a garment. In this regard, it is useful to be aware of the developments in technology that altered construction practices, such as the adoption of sewing machines and lightweight steel hoops in the mid-nineteenth century.

11. Engage in the *Slow Approach to Seeing* to generate a detailed description of the object of dress. You may wish to draw the object or specific details to enhance your ability to see. Consider the front, back, side, and/or detail as appropriate.

If possible, draw the object of dress as it appears before you—capturing the key aspects of its construction. For example, in the case of an evening gown, draw the bodice, sleeves, details of the neckline, skirt and train, if applicable. If this is not feasible because of time constraints or other reasons, consider making a quick sketch or annotating a printed photograph or digital image of the garment or accessory.

Find a systematic way of working to ensure that all major components of the dress object have been considered and recorded, such as working from the outside in, starting at the top and working downwards, or from left to right. Follow your inclination but work methodically. If you are permitted to handle the dress object, feeling it gently may reveal hidden details, such as padding, interfacing, or metal weights that help the garment hang as it was intended.

12. Record relevant measurements as appropriate in metric and/or imperial measurements. For accessories, use your judgment to record key measurements. Annotate your drawings as appropriate.

Record relevant measurements in imperial and/or metric units in the table below. Please note that not all measurements will be relevant to your research but be sure to include measurements that give a sense of scale (such as waist or bust measurements). Label your drawings as appropriate. If your goal is to recreate the object, other measurements will likely be necessary.

Object Part	Imperial Measurement	Metric Measurement
Overall length		
Chest/Bust		
Waist		
Hip		
Front neck to hem		
Front waist to hem		
Length of zipper or opening		
Size of buttons		
Sleeve length		
Inseam measurement		
Outside trouser leg measurement		
Dress hem circumference		
Trouser leg circumference		
Armhole circumference		
Neck or collar circumference		
Height of collar		
Center back neck to hem		
Back waist to hem		
Width across back		
Underarm to underarm at back		
Other		
Other		
Other		
Other		
Other		
Other		
Other		
Other		
Other		
Other		

It can be challenging to take accurate measurements. Use a soft, flexible tape measure and ensure the garment or accessory is placed on a flat surface while measuring. Take your time and if possible, record the measurements in both imperial and metric which will aid in checking for accuracy.

For measurements related to girth such as bust, waist, and hip, it is usual to take measurements from the inside of the garment. This step can reveal important information that can be helpful in gauging the previous owner's body size or assessing the object in relation to comparable objects.

If the garment or accessory is one that only takes form when wrapped on the body, such as a sari or an obi, focus on the dimensions of the textile.

13. Does the structure of the garment or accessory give shape to or add emphasis to one part of the body? If so, how does it accomplish this? Consider the use of pleats, darts, placement of seams, and other construction techniques in shaping the body.

Throughout history, certain parts of the body have been given different emphasis. For example, the fashionable *Jean de Bry* coat of the 1790s emphasized a man's shoulders, while the enormous *gigot* or leg-of-mutton sleeves of the 1890s provided emphasis to a woman's shoulders and comparatively diminished her waist (Figure 2.10).

Figure 2.10.
Wool Sweater, c.1895, probably American.
Brooklyn Museum Costume Collection at The Met (2009.300.1111).

14. Was the object made with the aid of a machine, by hand, or incorporate a combination of these methods? What types of stitches have been used? Has the same thread or wool been used throughout? Is the stitching consistent in quality?

The patenting of the Singer sewing machine in the USA in 1851 was a pivotal moment in terms of clothing production, since prior to its introduction all garments were hand sewn. Studying the quality of the stitching and the thread color facilitates identification of alterations, since repairs may be made in different grades or colors of thread. Identification of the type and quality of stitches used in hand stitching—such as running stitch, backstitch, overcast stitch—provides evidence of the maker's skill, and variations in quality can also reveal subsequent alterations or repairs. If the garment or accessory is handmade by knitting, crocheting or some other technique, note the type and quality of the stitches.

15. How is the garment, costume or accessory closed or fastened? How many closures are there? Are these closures original to the dress object? Document the details such as ornamentation of buttons or manufacturer's stamps and take measurements of the fastenings if relevant to your research. For a costume, is there evidence that indicates it was made to be worn by different performers?

Does the object of dress have a side/back/front zipper, or metal/plastic/ self-fabric buttons, or other types of closure such as fabric ties, lacing (Figure 2.11), drawstrings, hooks and eyes, or snaps? Fastenings such as buttons are sometimes stamped with the manufacturer's name which can then be used to narrow or confirm a date or period of manufacture. Sometimes buttons or zippers may be used as ornament.

Certain types of closures relate to specific periods. For example, metal zippers became popular in the 1930s as a sign of modern construction. It is also important to pay attention to whether the fastening is original to the garment or accessory since their constant use means that they are susceptible to damage and therefore may have been replaced. The type of closure—such as the double row of buttons on fall front breeches, pantaloons or trousers—can be helpful in dating a garment. In costumes worn for performances, a double row of hooks and eyes may reveal that more than one performer wore it.

Figure 2.11.
Back view of corset (cotton sateen, quilted with cotton
twill and cotton plain-weave tape),1830–40, England.
Los Angeles County Museum of Art (M.63.54.7).

16. Are there any front, side, flap, or hidden pockets? Are the pockets functional or merely decorative? If the pockets are visible, are they embellished in any way? Have any objects been left inside the pockets?
Pockets can be a design element of the garment itself (Figure 2.12) or concealed within, including inside a waistband, placket, seam, or coat tails (see Figure 6.5). If possible, look inside the pocket to assess whether it was functional and to discern whether it was ever used. Sometimes pockets have initials or other identification marks therein. And on occasion, items once belonging to the original owner such as a handkerchief, a theater ticket, or lipstick may have been forgotten, found at the time of donation and documented in the catalog record.

Figure 2.12.
Afternoon dress (silk),
1874, American.
Brooklyn Museum
Costume Collection
at The Met
(2009.300.777a–c).

17. Are the pattern pieces cut straight on the grain? Are there any remarkable features in the construction, such as pinking, bias cut, piecing of fabric, or use of nontraditional materials or structural elements?

Study the main pattern pieces to identify their orientation relative to straight of grain (the threads going parallel to the selvedge of the fabric). Identify any exceptional features of the dress object's design. This might include the use of pinking, bias cut (Figure 2.13), piecing of fabric, or other unusual elements.

Figure 2.13.
Bill Blass, Gingham plaid taffeta dress with bias cut full skirt, 1955–65.
Texas Fashion Collection, College of Visual Arts and Design, University of North Texas (1998.035.003).

18. How are the seams finished? Is the fabric selvedge visible in the seams, and has this been incorporated into the cutting or construction of the garment?

The finishing of seams is indicative of the care taken by the maker. And if present, the selvedge—the self-finished edge of the fabric—can reveal valuable information about the textile. For example, if both selvedge edges are retained within the construction of the garment (as was the case in an eighteenth-century petticoat Figure 2.14), this allows for the measurement of the finished width of the fabric which may be used to confirm the dating. The selvedge can also reveal the care with which the garment was cut, particularly if the selvedge is used decoratively as a finishing element.

Figure 2.14.
Selvedge edge used in seams of silk petticoat, 1750s.
Textile Museum of Canada (T94.0412). Photo by author.

19. Is the object of dress reinforced in any way using interfacing, padding, boning, metal hoops, or wire reinforcements? If so, describe in detail and note how this affects the drape and shaping.

Tailored garments often have buckram (a coarsely woven stiffened cotton or linen cloth) or some type of interfacing to help create body, shape and structure; this might not always be readily visible but can often be felt. Bodices and dress corsets may have boning to shape the body and create a smooth line (Figures 2.15 and 2.16). The addition of padding (wool, cotton, or other materials) at the shoulders or hips, and hoops or wire reinforcements at the hips or buttocks may be used to create a distinctive silhouette. Note that padding on one side of a garment may suggest a physical asymmetry or other irregularity in the wearer's body that the maker sought to conceal.

Figure 2.15.
Valentino, Red crepe strapless floor-length gown with
inner corset and boning, 1965.
Toronto Metropolitan University Fashion Research
Collection (1997.04.009).

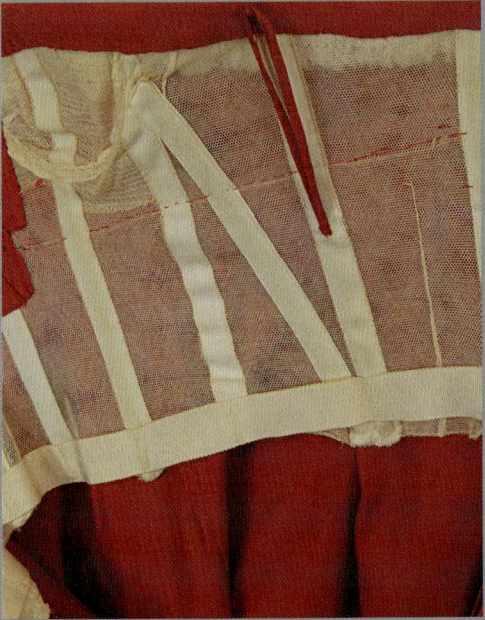

Figure 2.16.
Inner corset with boning inside
Valentino gown.

20. Is the dress object fully or partially lined? What materials have been used in the lining? Is the lining original to the garment or accessory?

Linings may be helpful in revealing the history of a garment or accessory. For example, the inside of a waistcoat dating to 1789–94 revealed an old green striped silk waistcoat that was used as the lining (Figure 2.17). It is common for linings to be replaced or altered over time as they are subject to greater wear than other elements. The quality of the lining fabric (silk, satin, polyester) may also offer clues about the economic status of the wearer. On occasion, the lining may have been cut out, exposing hidden aspects of construction (Figure 2.18).

21. Has any material been subsequently added or removed?

Alterations to the original design can reveal aspects of the object's biography. For example, the addition of a length of material at a waistband may have been needed to accommodate changes in weight. Children's garments may have been designed to be let down to anticipate the child's growth or have been cut down from an adult's garment. See, for example, Chapter 5 on the refashioning of an eighteenth-century gown and Chapter 7 on the remaking of a woman's jacket into a boy's frock. If something seems atypical or unusual, document it carefully and make a note to follow up with further study.

Figure 2.17.
Waistcoat, 1789–94, France. Los Angeles County Museum of Art (M.2007.211.1078).

Figure 2.18.
Interior of green silk embroidered coat, 1770s. Textile Museum of Canada (T94.0392). Photo by author.

Textiles and Materials

The choice of materials used to create a garment, costume or accessory affects the shape and appearance of the object itself (Figure 2.19). Typically, garments are made from textiles, but other materials such as fur, feathers, metal, leather, paper or wood might be used. Garments may also have other elements added to the textile such as gelatin or plastic sequins, glass beads imitating pearls (Figure 2.2), gemstones, and silk or wool embroidery. Accessories might be made of materials ranging from metal to plastic. Since most garments are made of cloth, some of the questions specific to textiles may not apply if you are studying an object made of other materials, such as a pair of wooden clogs, a jeweled bracelet, or a hat made of baleen (Figure 1.3). In such cases, focus on observing and recording details about the nature and quality of the materials and how that has influenced design choices.

**Figure 2.19.
Zhandra Rhodes,
Peignoir set of medium
blue with pale green and
pink print polyester. Fine
plain weave fabric (challis
appearance) with print
of wavy green bands,
groupings of seashells
and scattered "Zandra
Rhodes" signature, 1973.**
Texas Fashion Collection,
College of Visual Arts
and Design, University
of North Texas
(1984.011.189).

Knowledge of the unique characteristics of the materials used in creating a garment or accessory can greatly assist with your close analysis and there are various online resources and toolkits that can aid in the identification thereof. For textiles, see The DATS Textile Resource or The Fiber Reference Image Library at The Museum of Fine Arts Boston.[3]

When recording textiles, there are two main elements to consider. The first element is the identification of the fiber or fibers used to make the fabric. Sometimes this will be relatively straightforward. Before the widespread adoption of synthetic textiles (see boxed material below), such as rayon in the 1930s, the majority of all clothing would have been made from wool, silk, linen, or cotton. These natural fibers could be combined to produce a vast array of fabric blends that differed in weight, finish, and appearance. Although it can be difficult to work out exactly which fibers have been used in a mix of natural fibers and in synthetic blends, record your best guess as to the main fiber.

Synthetic Textiles

Artificial silk was first developed in France during the First World War. DuPont purchased the rights and marketed the textile under the name "Fibersilk". In response to resistance from consumers, the textile was renamed and remarketed by DuPont as "rayon" in 1924.[4] This word combined "ray," to connote the sheen of silk, and "on," to suggest a fiber such as cotton. DuPont undertook intensive promotional campaigns including advertisements in *Harper's Bazaar* to promote rayon as a fashionable and easy-to-care-for alternative, and the company has continued to research and develop innovative textiles, introducing Dacron in the mid-1950s, and Lycra in 1959. The use of synthetic fibers has increased expotentially since 1975, when synthetic fibers represented less than half (44 percent) of the 24 million metric tons of global textiles produced.[5] Not only has the total volume of textiles produced globally increased exponentially, but the relative percentage of synthetics has increased dramatically as well. In 2022, 113.8 million metric tons of textiles were produced globally, of which natural fibers (wool and cotton) represented 23 percent (25.2 million metric tons) and synthetic fibers (polyesters, polyamides, viscose, rayon) represented 77 percent (87.6 million metric tons).[6] As this data indicates, acknowledgement of the environmental harms posed by synthetic fibers has not blunted the demand for them.

The second main element of the fabric to note is its weave structure. This is the way that it is created on the loom, whether in a preindustrial hand-operated loom or fully mechanized process. It reveals the way in which the threads cross over and provides the finished fabric with much of its final character. Common weave structures are plain weave, twill weave (with its distinctive diagonal ribs), and satin weave (with a smooth surface). All these weaves can be made using a variety of fibers, so although people often talk about satin as if it was always made of silk, a satin weave could equally be made from a synthetic. A magnifying loupe is a very helpful tool in studying the weave of a fabric. As noted above, there are many useful fabric dictionaries and toolkits that can help guide you through the different types of weave structure, and provide you with the most common terminology.[7] Be aware that names for different types of fabric can change over time, and from place to place (for example, what is known as '"calico" in the United Kingdom is called "muslin" in North America).

22. List the textiles and/or materials and their associated colors used in creating this dress object, including the lining (if present). If possible, note whether the materials used in making this object are natural or man-made.

Just like clothing, textiles have come in and out of fashion. For example, for much of the eighteenth century, floral-patterned textiles were much in demand (see Chapter 5). The identification of the dominant textile or material provides important clues as to the date(s) associated with a particular object. However, be aware that a textile may predate the style of the garment since—prior to the twentieth century—garments were often restyled to conform to prevailing fashions (see Chapter 5) or recycled (see Chapter 7). It can also be helpful to consider the relevance of innovations in textile design or manufacturing processes in identifying textiles, such as the introduction of aniline dyes in the 1860s which made purple, apple green, and other bright shades of silk fashionable.

Garments can also be a combination of textiles or a combination of cloth with other materials like leather or fur. If this is the case, consider how the other fabrics and/or materials have been incorporated into the design and construction. For example, in a Kenzo jacket from 2004, the designer Antonio Marras incorporated an array of textiles from synthetic velvet to tweed to create a patchwork effect (Figure 2.20). This piecing of the fabrics, in a patchwork-like pattern, resembles the technique of *boro*—in which clothing or bedding is created from an assortment of worn-out garments, old futon covers and other household textiles (Figure 2.21). The word *boro* in Japanese means 'tattered rags', and although this technique was once regarded as a sign of thrift and economy, such garments have in more recent years come to be considered fashionable and chic.

Figure 2.20.
Antonio Marras for
Kenzo, Kimono-style
Jacket, autumn/winter
2004.
Toronto Metropolitan
University Fashion
Research Collection
(2009.01.686).

Figure 2.21.
Cotton kosode using
boro technique,
1900–30, Japan.
Textile Museum of
Canada (T2007.12.3).

23. Record your perception of the relative quality of the materials. If relevant to your research, note the thread count of the textile.

Materials are subject to fashion trends like anything else, and this information can be useful in dating, and in discerning the relative cost of an object. Typically, the finer the quality, the greater the cost.

For textiles, identify the fibers used and the type of weave, if possible. A magnifying loupe can aid with this step, but blended fabrics that incorporate an ever-increasing range of complex synthetics can make it difficult to identify the precise nature of the fibers in contemporary clothing. For contemporary fashion, often the only way to discern the precise fiber is to read the accompanying care label, which typically identifies the material content in terms of percentages.

24. Does the textile or other material incorporate a floral design, stripe, plaid, check, brand logo, family crest, or other form of patterned ornamentation? How has this been created (woven into the fabric, embroidered, stenciled, painted, or by manipulation)? How has the maker dealt with the pattern at the seams?

Design elements can be created using a variety of methods. For example, a patterned textile might be woven into the cloth (Figure 2.22), created through surface techniques such as embroidery (Figure 2.23), beadwork, painting, block printing, or achieved in a novel way such as the weaving of ribbon (Figure 2.24). Brand logos are sometimes woven into the cloth, such as the distinctive tartan-check pattern associated with the Burberry brand. Family crests may be woven into custom-made textiles for kimonos or other garments.

Taking note of how the pattern or ornamentation is handled at the seams may offer evidence of the maker's skill (Figure 2.25). For example, in order to match complex patterns at the seams, especially plaids and checks, a maker has to carefully lay out the pattern pieces and not only does this require extra fabric, but the maker must have the appropriate knowledge and skills.

Figure 2.22.
Silk waistcoat with
woven floral motif,
c.1747, British.
Textile design by Anna
Maria Garthwaite and
woven by Peter Lekeux.
Metropolitan Museum of
Art (C.I.66.14.2).

Figure 2.23.
Linen dress or coat
embroidered with
floral motifs in wool,
mid-eighteenth century,
American.
Metropolitan Museum of
Art (54.124).

Figure 2.25.
Detail of back bodice showing handling of pattern at the seams in woman's silk taffeta dress, c.1855, France.
Los Angeles County Museum of Art (M2007.211.767).

OPPOSITE: Figure 2.24.
Todd Oldham, Midriff top of woven multicolored ribbon, 1994.
Texas Fashion Collection, College of Visual Arts and Design, University of North Texas (2021.013.001).

25. Has the dominant material been subjected to a finishing process, such as block printing, painting, bleaching, pressing, or glazing?

The type of finishing process may reflect certain fashions in textiles such as the fashion for painted silks (Figure 2.26) and glazed chintz in the eighteenth century.

Figure 2.26.
Painted silk dress (*Robe à la française*),1740s, British.
Metropolitan Museum of Art (1995.235a, b).

26. Does the object have any form of applied decoration, such as sequins, appliqué, trim, leather, lace, beadwork, fur, decorative buttons, ruffles, pleated bands, bows, or gemstones? If so, describe in detail. Are there signs that any such decoration has been removed or lost?

Forms of embellishment come in and out of fashion (Figure 2.27) and may offer clues as to the dating of the object or the identity and aesthetic preferences of the wearer (Figure 2.28). Are there any signs that any such decoration has been added, removed or lost? Look for small pinholes, stitch marks, or use of different color threads.

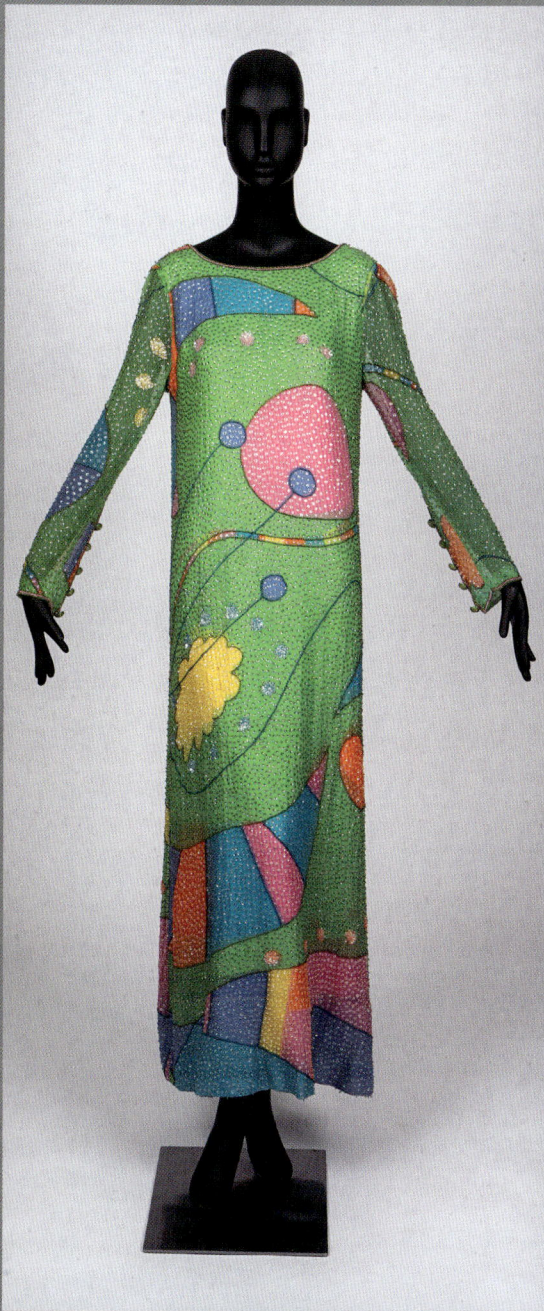

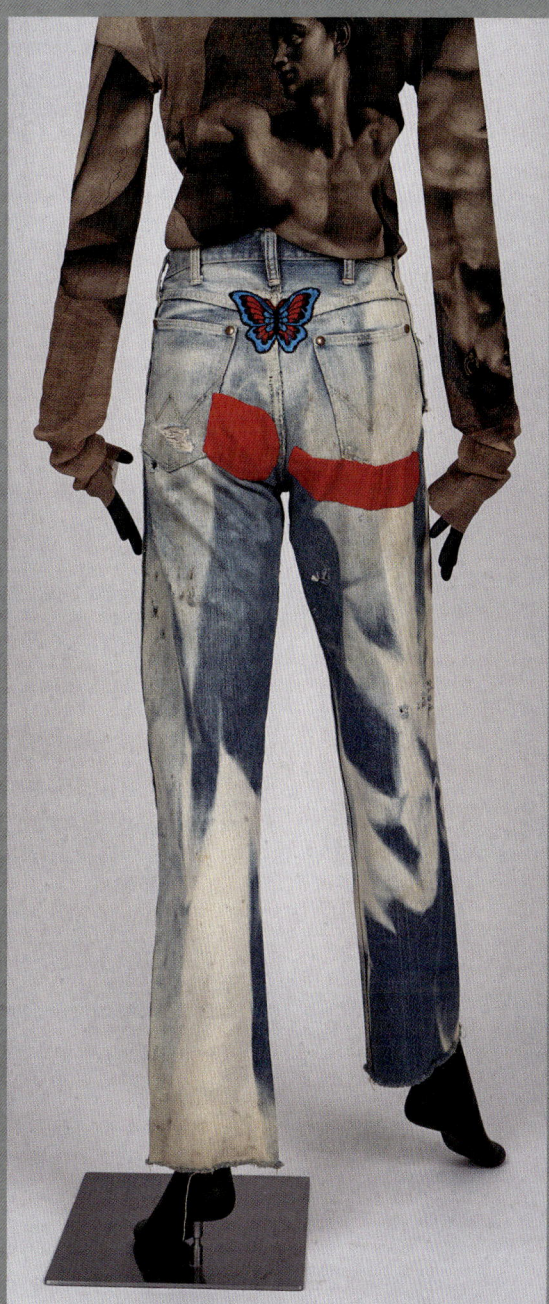

Figure 2.27.
Hanae Mori, Silk chiffon sheath dress embellished with clear sequins and beads, 1973.
Texas Fashion Collection, College of Visual Arts and Design, University of North Texas (1979.108.008).

Figure 2.28.
Men's Wrangler jeans of blue denim cotton; sun and chlorine bleached with added red velvet and butterfly patches, 1960s.
Texas Fashion Collection, College of Visual Arts and Design, University of North Texas (2006.007.136).

27. Has any fabric been added or removed? Are there any parts missing? Has the maker used piecing?

Noting what has been added or is missing can offer significant clues to the object's story. When a lining has been removed, the details of construction are easier to discern (see Figure 2.18). If there are small areas of wear or damage, it may be possible to see the interfacing or other details that might otherwise be hidden; if this is the case, be careful not to cause further damage. At times, a garment may have been partially unpicked in anticipation of reuse. In the past, when textiles were very valuable, the use of piecing was not uncommon, especially in skirts and linings (Figure 2.29). See also Chapter 7, where a boy's frock was recut from another garment and the piecing is barely discernable.

Figure 2.29.
Silk Jacket with pieced lining, late eighteenth century, France.
Metropolitan Museum of Art (2010.151).

28. Has the textile or other materials faded or otherwise changed in color with the passage of time?

Look under collars, pocket flaps, or other parts that have not been subject to fading from light to identify the original color of the fabric. Leather can fade or crack, depending on the conditions of storage.

Marks, Labels and Logos

Labels, logos, maker marks, and laundry marks offer significant clues to the identities of the brand, maker(s), or wearer. Designer Charles Frederick Worth (1825–95) is said to have been the first designer to use a label with his signature in his creations. Early in the twentieth century, designers such as Paul Poiret (1879–1944), Gabrielle 'Coco' Chanel (1883–1971), Jeanne Lanvin (1867–1946) and Madeleine Vionnet (1876–1975) used labels as a means of branding their garments and protecting their designs, and the use of the label as a brand marker has continued ever since. Some labels are designed to designate authenticity, with elements like number sequences or holograms offering the buyer assurance that the item is not a counterfeit copy. Labels can also aid in defining textile content, size, care requirements, and place of origin (Figure 2.30).

Finding a tailor's mark, designer label or store label provides information about the maker and the way in which the garment was acquired. Labels or marks of ownership come in different forms, and occasionally, one might find the name of the owner embroidered or handwritten in a garment. In contemporary clothing, the label is often sewn into the back neck facing (Figure 2.31). Maker labels might also be found in a seam or waistband. Be aware that unscrupulous sellers of vintage garments may sew a designer label into a garment that was not actually made by that label in order to achieve a higher price-point at resale. The potential for counterfeit goods has increased exponentially over time such that close attention to the smallest of details is needed in order to be able to assess authenticity.

Figure 2.30.
Designer labels inside Hanae Mori cocktail dress, 1960s.
Texas Fashion Collection, College of Visual Arts and Design, University of North Texas (1980.010.002).

29. Is there a marking inside the dress object that indicates the specific owner, such as embroidered or inked initials, a nametag, or a laundry mark?

Quality tailors and dressmakers often included a label with the client's name inside the garment. Owners may have added a laundry mark or personalized a garment (Figure 2.31). Uniforms may have nametags, and costumes typically include a label with the name of the theater or ballet company and/or a tag that lists the names of the performers who wore the garment.[8]

Figure 2.31.
Embroidered name (E. L. Hughes) on petticoat, 1890s.
Toronto Metropolitan University Fashion Research Collection (1986.09.101).

30. Is there a maker mark, label or brand logo? Note the placement of the logo and/or label, and document any information recorded thereon or related thereto, especially if the label records a couture number or season.

The maker of a garment may have labeled, stamped or marked it in some way (Figure 2.32). For clothing that predates the mid-nineteenth century, maker's marks may be concealed in a lining or pocket (see Figure 2.18). For contemporary garments, look for the clues as to dating, such as a number or season, and assess whether the label is consistent with the designer's *oeuvre*. Couture garments sometimes have handwritten labels with a name and/or a number assigned to the piece. Department stores sometimes insert an additional store label into clothing, and if the retailer has since gone out of business, this can offer clues as to the last possible year of sale for the garment or accessory.

The font as well as the text of a maker's mark or label can be invaluable in helping to provide the social and cultural context for a dress object. Font styles can be a useful guide to the dating of a label, especially since they relate closely to changes in graphic design. Label designs and logos used by major designers and stores often changed over time and have been well documented on various sites such as the Vintage Fashion Guild.[9] Consider whether the logo or mark might be used as a clue to date the object. Also carefully assess whether the label or logo and the quality of the product is consistent with other known examples from that maker, store or brand.

Figure 2.32.
Hattie Carnegie label with thumbprint inside opera-style cape of black long-hair colobus monkey fur, 1930. Texas Fashion Collection, College of Visual Arts and Design, University of North Texas (1973.001.064).

31. Is there a label or other mark such as a custom stamp that identifies where the garment or accessory originated?

Contemporary clothing typically includes a label that identifies the country of origin. Historic garments that crossed borders may have custom stamps. For example, a man's chintz banyan dated to the mid-1750s (Figure 2.33) includes several custom stamps and numbering sequences (Figure 2.34) that offer clues as to the journey of this banyan through time and across continents.

Figure 2.33.
Banyan (cotton),
c.1750, India, probably
Coromandel Coast for
the western market.
Los Angeles County
Museum of Art
(M.2005.42).

Figure 2.34.
Stamps inside banyan.

32. Are there any care or size labels? Have any labels been cut off or removed?

Care labels are a relatively recent development in clothing manufacturing regulations and appear most commonly in contemporary garments. Sizes differ by country and are another relatively recent regulatory requirement. If there is evidence of labels having been cut off or otherwise removed, this offers clues as to the wearer's preferences in terms of comfort since labels can cause friction against the skin.

Use, Alteration and Wear

In this section, questions prompt you to consider the way in which the owner(s) of the garment, costume or accessory might have worn and/or altered the object. Here, the focus is on observing how the dress object may have changed over time, from its initial design and construction to its current state. Such clues are often very significant in the revealing the biography of the object, and if this is relevant to your research interests, pay close attention to the questions in this part. Be alert to the fact that garments from the eighteenth century were often altered. Such is the case with a gown linked to Queen Marie Antoinette (1755–93) through its attribution to Marie-Jean 'Rose' Bertin (1747–1813); although the train is original, the dress skirt and bodice were restyled in the 1870s, and the bodice has been relined (Figure 2.35).

Figure 2.35.
Robe en fourreau or robe à l'anglaise or grand habit (court dress), embroidered satin with ribbon appliqués, sequins, faceted glass stones mounted on silver facings, and silver filé; fitted, boned bodice. 1780s, altered in 1870s, France. Attributed to Marie-Jean "Rose" Bertin (French couturière, 1747–1813). Royal Ontario Museum (925.18.3a-b).
Courtesy of ROM (Royal Ontario Museum), Toronto, Canada ©ROM.

Be aware that some dress artifacts in museum or study collections may have undergone conservation treatment that might involve the addition of material to support fragile areas, and/or to lessen the visual impact of areas of loss (see Figure 11.6). These treatments are usually designed to be both reversible and subtle, but this depends on the preferred conservation methods in use at a particular point in time, as well as the skill of the person doing such work.

33. Is the object soiled in any way (such as dirt or perspiration stains)? Where are these stains located? Mark the areas of soiling on your drawing(s).

The marks and stains of wear are telling signs of how an object of dress was used and worn. Examine the back of necklines, under the arms, shirt cuffs, and crotch area for stains. Study closures like buttons, zippers, lacing, and waistbands of fitted garments for signs of strain. Examine areas that are affected by movement of the body such as shoulder seams, elbow creases, trouser seats, and knees. Look for soiling at the hems of long skirts, the edges of trouser cuffs, inside hat brims, and on the fingers of gloves. The absence of any marks of wear may suggest that the garment or accessory was rarely or never worn. In the case of the eighteenth-century embroidered doeskin vest shown below (Figure 2.36), the visible signs of perspiration under the arms and on the back of the neck indicate that this vest was much worn.

Figure 2.36.
Vest (doeskin and silk), c.1750, American or European.
Metropolitan Museum of Art (C.I.43.90.12).

34. Does the object show other signs of use or wear such as friction, splitting, or fraying? Have seams ripped, silk split, or fabric decomposed? Is there evidence of insect or pest damage? Mark these areas of use and damage on your drawing(s).

Certain parts of a garment are subjected to the strains of movement. Look at the underarms, around the neck, over the joints (hips, knees, elbows), around fastenings, between the legs of trousers, and at the hem. Look at any applied decoration to see if there are signs of tears pulling on the original fabric caused by the decoration. Are there pin marks from jewelry or stitching? Have fibers worn thin in areas that are heavily rubbed, such as elbows, the seat of trousers and skirts? Does one elbow or shoulder show signs of rubbing, for example from a shoulder bag or something else (like horse reins)? Footwear will show signs of wear in the soles, the heel may be worn unevenly from the wearer's style of movement, and there may be scuff marks from heavy wear. Accessories such as a hat or a glove may take on the shape of that body part.

Small irregular holes in clothing or accessories made of natural fibers, especially wool, may indicate damage created by pests such as clothes moths, silverfish, or mice. Such pests are particularly attracted to untreated food or drink stains.

35. Is there any evidence of alteration, repair, or conservation work? If so, mark this on your drawing or annotated photograph. Where is this evident and how has this impacted the original object? If the object of dress has been altered or repaired, is the work of the same quality as the original construction?

Have patches, gussets, false hems, or pieces of fabric been added to extend the life of the garment or accessory? Where has the garment been let out, taken in, or recut? Look for hems that have been let down (see Figure 1.16), seams that have been let out, or additional pieces of fabric that have been inserted to accommodate an expanding figure. Have any sections been cut away?

In each case, consider the quality of the work as this may reveal the purpose of the alteration or repair. Work done by museum conservators will typically be documented in the object file. If you are permitted access to a conservation report, valuable information can often be found therein.

36. Are there any other indications that the garment or accessory has been altered from its original form? Has the object been dyed to alter its original color? Have trim or other forms of embellishment been unpicked or removed?

Look for fold lines, uneven seams, and pinholes that may reveal areas of alteration or removal of trim. If possible, examine any parts of the garment, costume, or accessory that have not been exposed to light, such as the fabric under a pocket flap or inside seams, to identify changes from the original color.

PART III: BEFORE YOU LEAVE

Supporting Material

Sometimes institutions have other material associated with an object, such as letters, bills of sale, photographs of the wearer, notations as to the occasions on which the garment was worn, or perhaps even an oral history recorded with the donor. Although such information may not have been available or recorded at the time the item was accepted for donation, it is always worth asking the collection manager if any supporting material exists, since such information can be extremely helpful in revealing the biography of an object. If the former owner was a known person, there may be related material elsewhere (see for example Chapter 9).

37. Does the collection have any provenance records or conservation reports related to this object that you might be permitted access to? Has the object been exhibited before? Is the donor a known person?

Record the name of the donor and any related information, if available. If the object has been exhibited or loaned out to another museum, there will generally be conservation reports for the object which often contain helpful information. If you are permitted access to such records, take note of prior conservation work, loans and exhibitions of the artifact, and other information related to the object. In the case study about an eighteenth-century Spitalfields silk gown (see Chapter 5), my curiosity about the provenance of the gown—which referenced Rhode Island—led to some important discoveries.

38. Are there any photographs of the garment or accessory being worn or mounted for display?

Photographs are useful in illustrating how the garment, costume or accessory was worn and styled. Certain articles of clothing are given shape by the body and thus it can be helpful to see the garment as it was worn or mounted for display. Does the collection have photographs showing the garment being worn by the owner? (See Figures 2.37 and 2.38). Is the collection manager aware of any related images from the runway, on display in an exhibition, or published elsewhere such as in a fashion magazine, exhibition catalog, or scholarly journal?

**Figure 2.37.
Hanae Mori, Evening
gown, 1967.**
Texas Fashion Collection,
College of Visual Arts
and Design, University
of North Texas
(2015.002.001).

Figure 2.38.
Photo of Joyce Shoop
(donor) wearing Hanae
Mori evening gown at
the Tokyo car show, 1967.

39. Does the collection have any other material (including related objects such as garments, tags, or original packaging, letters or other information) associated with the object that might aid in your research?

The owner may also have provided other related material including diaries, letters, or bills of sale that may aid your research. If conducting a wardrobe analysis, consider whether there are other garments from the same donor that may be relevant to your research. Tags and packaging can serve as rich contextual material about the artifact under examination, as well as offering clues as to whether the garment was actually worn. For example, the retailer's paper price tag in this Victor Costa maxi dress (Figure 2.39) not only reveals the original price of the dress (Figure 2.40) but also suggests that it was probably never worn.

Initial Impressions:

40. What is most notable, unexpected, intriguing, or puzzling about this object of dress? Does anything seem atypical or spark your interest?

Before you leave the collection facility, review your notes to make sure you have not missed anything. Also take a few moments to document what you found most interesting or unusual about the object, including your initial thoughts, impressions, and emotional reaction to the experience. It is important to try and capture this information as soon as possible because specific details are often quickly forgotten. This information will be helpful for the next phase of research.

ENDNOTES

1   Maurice Merleau-Ponty, *Phenomenology of Perception* (Florence: Routledge, 2002), 79.

2   See for example, Charlotte M. Calasibetta, Phyllis G. Tortora, and Bina Abling, *The Fairchild Dictionary of Fashion* (New York: Fairchild, 2002). Also see Valerie Cumming, C.W. Cunnington, and P.E. Cunnington, *The Dictionary of Fashion History* (London: Bloomsbury, 2022).

3   There are a myriad of helpful resources related to textile identification available on The Dress and Textile Specialist (DATS) website, including: "Identifying Fibres and Fabrics," accessed November 7, 2024 at https://dressandtextilespecialists.org.uk/wp-content/uploads/2021/08/Identifying-Fibres-and-Fabrics.pdf. See also the Fiber Reference Image Library, Museum of Fine Arts Boston, accessed December 11, 2024 at https://cameo.mfa.org/wiki/Fiber_Reference_Image_Library

4   Carmen Keist, "Rayon and its Impact on the Fashion Industry at its Introduction, 1910–1924." *Graduate Theses and Dissertations* (Paper 11072), 2009. Iowa State University, Available at: http://lib.dr.iastate.edu/etd/11072.

5   "Global production volume of textiles 1975–2022", Statista, Accessed November 8, 2024 at https://www.statista.com/statistics/263154/worldwide-production-volume-of-textile-fibers-since-1975/

6   *Ibid.*

7   See resources listed in Endnote 3.

8   See Ingrid Mida, "A Gala Performance Tutu", *Dress* 42, no. 1 (2016): 35–47.

9   Vintage Fashion Guild Label Resource, accessed November 8, 2024 at https://vintagefashionguild.org/resources/labels/

3

REFLECTION

OPPOSITE: Figure 3.1.
Unknown maker (Wasco tribe,
Native American), Dress of tanned
leather, glass beads, shell, bone, elk
teeth and brass thimbles. Belt of
leather with glass beads and metal
studs with awl case, c. 1870.
Metropolitan Museum of Art
(2019.456.1a, b).

To reflect is to give serious thought or consideration to something. In this second phase of research, information from other sources is gathered to facilitate your analysis and interpretation of the evidence gathered from the object itself. No object exists in isolation, and this is the step that will help deepen your understanding of this object in relation to the time and place in which it originated. As dress historian Linda Baumgarten so eloquently noted, "A surviving artifact is full of evidence, not just about its original manufacture, but about its continuing history as well."[1] After gathering evidence from the object itself, the second phase of the research journey requires reflection on what that evidence means. The Reflection Checklist includes twenty-five questions and is divided into five sections: General, Sensory Reactions, Personal Reactions, Contextual Material, and Next Steps. This chapter provides an annotated version of the checklist in Appendix 2 and will help you prepare for the final phase of research, *Interpretation*.

Work carefully through the Reflection Checklist and be sure to allow sufficient time for the gathering and analysis of contextual material. Please note that some parts or sections may be more relevant than others depending on your research goals, especially if you are engaged in creative practice. Nonetheless, be open to what you might discover during this phase of research. Makers may want to dive into the process of recreating, but it may be prudent to first consider related contextual information. And while some questions might initially seem to be unrelated to your research objectives, take care to review each question carefully since the questions are designed to prompt you to think expansively.

Research is not necessarily a linear process, and progress often happens in fits and starts. You may have started with a specific goal or research question, but you may change your focus as you assimilate and analyze the evidence. You may discover that you have additional questions about the object or the time period and need to undertake additional research. It is wise to anticipate that the natural flow of the research process will be more iterative than linear. There are many layers of complexity inherent in this stage of research and this phase will require an investment of your time, patience, and imagination.

I. GENERAL

1. What was remarkable, surprising, strange, or striking about the object of dress? What questions come to mind?

Take note of what you found most interesting or unusual during your close study. This is a highly personal response and there is no 'right' answer. Identifying what questions first come to mind can help direct your focus as you assimilate the evidence. For example, if you are a maker, you may have questions about the order of construction or a technique of embellishment. Often it is something that sparks interest that propels further research, and this can be useful in directing your next steps. For example, the pattern of the textile used in this luxurious silk doublet

(Figure 3.2) does not follow the cut of the garment, which raises the question of whether it was constructed from silk previously pinked for another use.

In the case of the 'Scare a Crow' wrap made of raffia by Todd Oldham (Figure 3.3), the name assigned to the garment and the incorporation of unusual materials may prompt questions about the designer's intent. Follow your instincts as to what is most interesting to you.

Figure 3.2.
Silk doublet, early 1620s, France.
Metropolitan Museum of Art (1989.196).

Figure 3.4.
Embroidered silk mantua with train, worn by Helen Slicher on her wedding on September 4, 1759. Rijksmuseum (BK-1978-24).

2. Why has this object survived? What does this reveal about the economic or personal value ascribed to this object?

Garments and accessories worn for special occasions such as weddings may have been lovingly preserved by families through the generations before they are donated to museums (Figure 3.4). Objects with high economic, aesthetic, or inherent value are more likely to survive. It is important to remember that museum collections are not necessarily representative of what people actually wore at any given period of time, and clothing worn by the laboring classes or historically marginalized communities is often underrepresented. Consider whether this may apply in your case.

OPPOSITE: Figure 3.3.
Todd Oldham, "Scare a Crow" wrap of woven black raffia with long fringe, spring 1994.
Texas Fashion Collection, College of Visual Arts and Design, University of North Texas (2021.013.023)

3. Is the manner of construction consistent with the dating of the dress object? Was the garment or accessory created from another? What is the condition of the object relative to its age? Are there clues that reveal how the garment or accessory was worn, altered, or stored? What might this reveal about the person(s) who wore, owned, or handled this object?

Having a knowledge of dress history and developments in technology can be helpful here in terms of assessing the accuracy of the dating of the garment or accessory relative to the manner of construction. For example, the identification of machine stitching in a garment said to be from the eighteenth century may signal its alteration for wearing as fancy dress in the latter part of the nineteenth century. Review the evidence of use, alteration, and wear. Is it consistent with the object's age and condition? Is there anything anomalous?

Was another garment recycled to create this object? In times past, textiles were valuable commodities, and recycling was far more common than it is now (see Chapters 5 and 7). Some contemporary designers have embraced the recycling of textiles in fashioning new looks (Figure 3.5).

Figure 3.5.
Cape made from antique obi (silk brocade embroidered with cranes and floral motifs) with label Kobayashi/Tokyo, 1970s, Japan.
Texas Fashion Collection, College of Visual Arts and Design, University of North Texas (1973.001.049).

4. Does the catalog record for this object accurately reflect what was observed? Was anything noted that seems to be inconsistent with the written record?

Catalog records can be subject to interpretation and error. Prior to the digitization of museum records, curatorial staff had less information about comparable objects at their fingertips. If something seems anomalous, it may be a signal to investigate further.

5. Does this object come from a culture different than your own, or a historically marginalized community? Would it be helpful to engage the assistance of a person from that community in your research?

In recent years, there has been a greater awareness of the need to adopt practices which are reflective of the values of inclusion and belonging. If the object you are studying is from a culture that is different from your own or a historically marginalized community, it may be prudent to seek to involve people from that community in your project in some way. For example, the use of glass beads, shell, bone, elk teeth, and brass thimbles on the dress created by an unknown maker of the Wasco tribe (Figure 3.1) reflects the traditions and culture of these indigenous people from south Oregon.[2] As well, if the garment or accessory only takes form when wrapped around the body (such as an obi or a sari), it can be difficult to discern how to properly wear such items and it may be wise to seek guidance unless you have worn this type of item yourself.

II. SENSORY REACTIONS

Cloth is a sensual material, offering a non-verbal experience that invokes a range of senses, including sight, sound, smell, and touch. By being aware of the full range of possible sensory reactions that may be taking place on a subconscious level, you can reflect on your personal experience as well as acknowledge the implicit judgments in play during the course of research.

6. What is most visually striking about this object? Does the color of the textile or the motifs therein have symbolic or cultural meaning? Does the object incorporate stylistic, religious, artistic, or iconic references? Does the garment, costume, or accessory represent a life transition?

Clothes speak for us—communicating aspects of identity without words. Consider what captured your attention first and reflect on the significance thereof. Does the garment or accessory give emphasis to a certain part of the body, reference a previous period in history, or invite an emotional response? Does the design incorporate symbolic motifs or take inspiration from nature, religion, or other artists? For example, Yves Saint Laurent adapted Piet Mondrian's painting motifs in designing the Mondrian dress for fall/winter 1965–66, and Alexander McQueen incorporated religious iconography into his Angels and Demons collection for fall/winter 2010–11. With non-western garments and accessories, certain motifs may have auspicious meanings, such as the use of bats in a Qing Dynasty woman's ceremonial robe (Figure 3.6) as a symbolic message of good fortune (the word for 'bat' (*fu*) sounds like the one for happiness).

For garments worn to important life events like presentation at court, weddings, or funerals, certain aspects of the garment have specific meanings. For example, in western cultures, black is associated with death and mourning, while in many eastern cultures, white carries that association. A garment may also have been designed with a specific function in mind, such as the linen waistcoat with open righthanded sleeve fastened with bows worn by King William III which facilitated ease of access after he broke his collarbone falling from his horse (Figure 3.7).

Figure 3.6.
Women's ceremonial robe in silk with metallic thread embroidery, c.1700–50 (Qing dynasty), China.
Metropolitan Museum of Art (43.119).

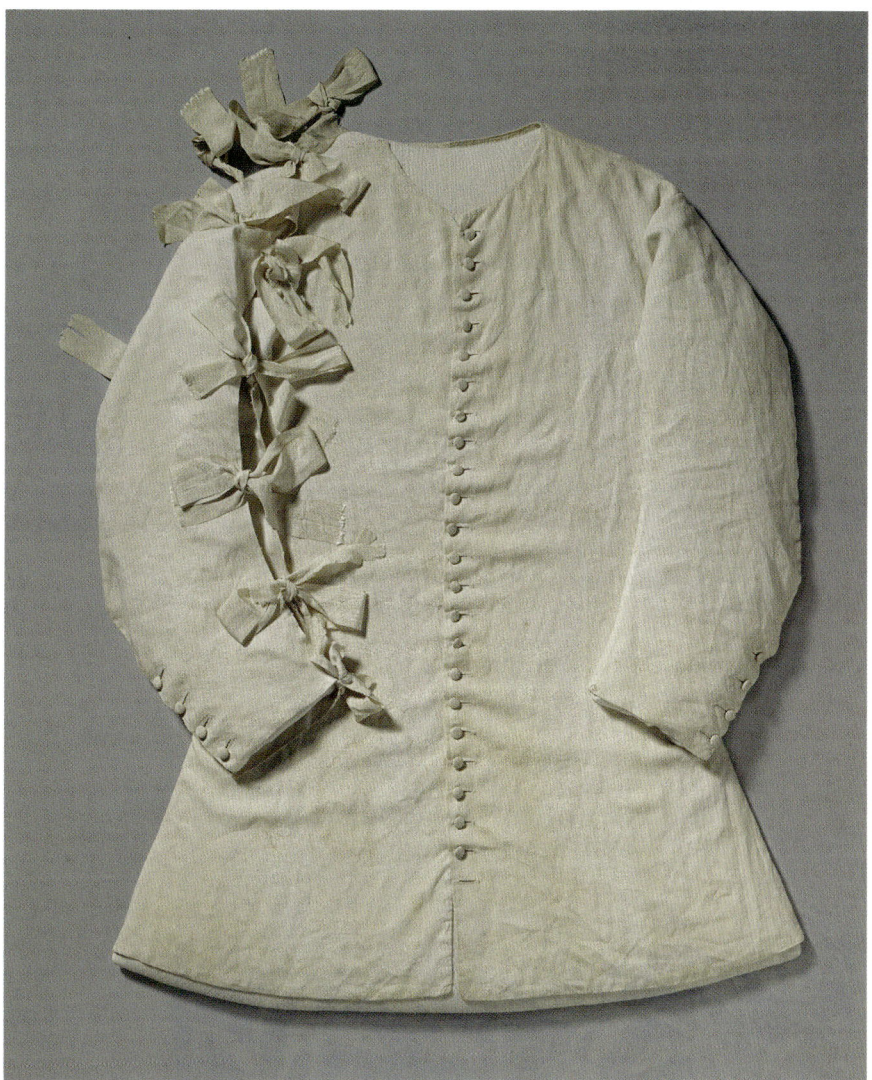

Figure 3.7.
Linen sleeved waistcoat with bows, worn by King William III of England, before 1702.
Rijksmuseum (NG-NM-1105).

7. Is the garment or accessory stylistically consistent with the period from which it came? Does it seem to reflect the influences of that period or diverge from it?

Textiles were once so valuable that many garments that survive from the eighteenth century and prior have been altered in some way.[3] For example, the exquisite ivory silk faille used to construct this *robe á la francaise* gown was fashionable in the 1740s, but the gown's silhouette dates to the 1770s (Figure 3.8). Moreover, the individual preferences of the wearer may override prevailing fashion, and if there is an anomaly, this may be a signal that further investigation is needed.

8. What is the texture and weight of the cloth or other materials used to construct the garment or accessory?

As dress historian Joanne Eicher points out, "textures provide clues about the person and cultural setting of time and space."[4] Is the texture soft and luxurious, or hard and unyielding? Does the texture reflect the value associated with that material, such as the sumptuous velvets worn by the elite during the Italian Renaissance?[5]

Has the texture of the material(s) changed over time? For example, once-soft, supple leather may become hard and cracked if not stored in optimal conditions for preservation. Would the garment or accessory feel pleasant against the skin, or cause itching or chafing? Would any part of the garment touch or drag along the ground, such as a train or cloak?

If you are a maker and plan to create a reproduction, you may wish to consider this question in relation to the types of materials available today. Will you be able to source comparable materials?

9. Would a person wearing this garment or accessory make noise and draw attention to themselves?

Consider the tinkling of the brass thimbles with the clinking of the shells in the dress shown in Figure 3.1, the click of a stiletto on the floor, the swish of silk against the legs of a woman wearing a long dress, the snap of a parasol when it opens, or the flutter of a fan (Figure 3.9). What sensations would this impart for the wearer and for those nearby? What messages are conveyed through these sounds?

10. Does the garment or accessory emit an odor? Can the origin of the odor be identified?

Certain textiles, such as linen and wool, have their own distinctive scent.[6] Our noses can also detect the scent of perfume, sweat, body odor, animal scents, dirt, moth balls, and other smells embedded in a garment, and these aromas of the past can cause a visceral reaction. What does this lingering smell reveal about the owner or how the garment was stored?

OPPOSITE: Figure 3.8.
Robe à l'anglaise (silk), c.1747, altered 1770s, England.
Metropolitan Museum of Art (2014.138a, b).

Figure 3.9.
Folding Fan with representation of a Royal Fireworks display (ivory and paper), 1781, France.
Metropolitan Museum of Art (59.13.7).

III. PERSONAL REACTIONS

Given that we are drawn inherently to objects that appeal to us in some way, it is important to reflect on what attracted you to a particular object, and what you initially hoped to learn or discover. When we look at a garment or accessory on display in a museum, we know intuitively whether or not we would wear it, and whether or not it would fit our body. This phenomenon can be used to consider our personal reactions to our object of study. The following questions explicitly invite you to imagine wearing the garment, costume, or accessory and reflect on your personal reactions.

11. Does this garment or accessory spark a memory or hold emotional resonance for you?

We are often attracted to things that have personal resonance for us. Does this object remind you of someone or something else? Can you identify a personal connection that could be acknowledged in your research? Does this resonance reflect an interest in the person who wore it, the maker, or some other aspect of its object biography? How might you harness this connection in your project?

Having a personal and emotional connection to something can be a powerful motivator for research. For example, Bethan Bide embraced the memories of her grandmother as a way to reconsider the evidence embodied in selected 1940s garments in the Museum of London and disrupt conventional narratives related thereto.[7]

12. Would the garment or accessory fit your body? Are you the same gender and size as the person who wore or owned this object? Would you wear this garment or accessory if you could? Is the style and color appealing to you? What would it be like to wear this garment or accessory? Would it be tight or loose on your body? Would it cause any discomfort?

Your answers to these questions reflect your personal preferences and taste. And even without taking detailed measurements of a garment, you may have a sense of whether the garment would fit and how it would feel on your body. If you are a maker and are creating a reproduction to wear, you will want to consider how you will adapt the measurements taken from the garment so that the replica will fit your body with the desired amount of ease.[8]

13. Does the design of the object emphasize status, sexuality, or gender roles? What does this communicate about cultural values of the time in which the object was made and worn?

Identifying areas of divergence makes us alert to our own time and perspective. For example, being repulsed by a dress artifact in some way—by its appearance, its texture, the way it is cut or fit to the body, or some other aspect—may be a clue to a shift in cultural beliefs or values. For example, although monkey fur was considered fashionable in the 1930s (Figure 3.10), it might now invoke repugnance. Strong reactions may also occur with a dress or accessory that we would not wear because it does not appeal to us aesthetically. Such gaps can reflect changes in society's cultural stance and aesthetic preferences.

By engaging with the object on a personal level, your values, stylistic preferences and cultural shifts become more readily evident and allow for further reflection on how cultural beliefs related to sexuality, gender, status, and identity have shifted over time and across cultures.

If you are recreating an object of dress or using it as inspiration for something altogether new (such as a theater costume), this step can allow you to reflect on whether you wish to emphasize or exaggerate certain aspects to make a point.

**Figure 3.10.
Hattie Carnegie,
Opera-style cape of
black long-hair colobus
monkey fur, 1930.**
Texas Fashion
Collection, College of
Visual Arts and Design,
University of North
Texas (1973.001.064).

IV. CONTEXTUAL INFORMATION

Objects of dress do not exist in isolation. Their place in dress history is marked by what came before, what came after, and what others were making and wearing at the time. And it is important to note that items of dress may or may not have been fashionable at the time they were worn. The context—the circumstances that formed the setting for the creation, the marketing, the wearing, and the retention of that object of dress—help to delineate the scope by which it can be fully understood and assessed.

Contextual material—text and imagery relating to the object itself, the maker, and/or the owner—will aid in the assessment and interpretation of the clues revealed within the object itself. This work is essential in order to appreciate how a garment or accessory was actually worn and accessorized. For example, although a Japanese kimono might seem to be relatively straightforward in construction, it is only one of several layers and accessories that fashion the body. As well, certain garments such as kimonos and saris may only take form when wrapped around the body, and in such cases, related imagery can be extremely helpful in understanding how such garments were worn (Figures 3.11 and 3.12).

With the widespread digitization of visual and textual material, ready access to historical records (both text and images) is much easier than in the past. Nonetheless, be aware that the terminology for garments will not be consistent across institutions, disciplines, and time. For example, a waistcoat might also be described as a vest or a gilet, even within the same museum collection. A women's jacket dating to the eighteenth century might be described as a bed jacket, bodice, or waistcoat. As well, some museum portals are not searchable via Google or other search engines and their collection portals must be searched separately. And of course, not all historic records have been digitized and, in some cases, old-fashioned sleuthing in a dusty archive might be necessary.

Be forewarned that this phase of research is multi-faceted, and it is wise to allow sufficient time to undertake this step, as gathering this material will greatly facilitate your understanding of the time period and aid in developing your interpretation.

Figure 3.11.
Suzuki Shin'ichi,
Photograph of Two
Japanese Women in
Traditional Dress, 1870s.
Albumen silver print from
glass negative with applied
color (25.2 x 19.9 cm.)
Metropolitan Museum of
Art (2005.100.505.1,19b).

Figure 3.12.
Sikh bride and her two bridesmaids, 1994.
Photo by Viviane Moos/Corbis via Getty Images.

14. If you were permitted access to the provenance record for the artifact, what does this information reveal about the owner and their relationship to the object?

The donor's name may be a significant piece of information in crafting a biography of an object, especially if that person was a notable collector, philanthropist, or public figure. For example, the Mexican coin purse shown in Figure 3.13 was once owned by Elizabeth Morrow (1873–1955), who collected this and other objects between 1927–30 when her husband, Dwight Morrow Sr., served as US ambassador to Mexico. Upon her death, this purse and other objects in her collection were donated to the Brooklyn Museum by Anne Morrow Lindbergh (wife of aviator Charles Lindbergh) and her siblings.

Figure 3.13.
Coin purse (glass, linen, silk, metal), 1790, Mexican.
Brooklyn Museum Costume Collection at The Met (2009.300.1901). Gift of Dwight W. Morrow, Jr., Constance Morrow Morgan, and Anne Morrow Lindbergh, 1956.

If available, photos of the donor wearing the garment can offer visual references to how they accessorized and styled the garment. Some museum records may include information from the donor about where they purchased the garment or accessory, when it was worn, what it meant to them, or why they kept it. However, memories can fade or be distorted with time. If the object of dress was donated by a person who wishes to remain anonymous, or if there are no records of provenance, other individuals may have worn something similar (see, for example, the uniform in Chapter 10).

15. If the museum, study, or private collection has other garments that are similar, how do these other garments compare to your object of study? If the garment or accessory was worn by a known person, are there other objects from that person's wardrobe that can be accessed for study? Depending on your research focus, you may wish to study garments that were made by the same designer/maker, come from the same period, from the same wardrobe, or were made for a specific purpose (such as maternity wear like Figure 3.14). If you are a maker, studying comparable examples of similar objects may serve to deepen your knowledge of construction techniques.

If the object was once worn or owned by someone whose life has been publicly documented in some way, there may also be objects of relevance to your study in the same or other collections. For example, Mona Campbell, the woman who donated the Dior dress ensemble considered in Chapter 9, not only donated other garments and accessories to the Seneca College Fashion Resource Collection but also donated a number of Dior gowns to the Royal Ontario Museum. If multiple garments and accessories from the donor's wardrobe have survived, assess how the object of your study relates to the donor's wardrobe as a whole.

Figure 3.14.
Balenciaga, Maternity
ensemble (top and skirt
with elastic waist) of
black silk faille, 1950.
Texas Fashion
Collection, College of
Visual Arts and Design,
University of North
Texas (1981.022.025).

Figure 3.15.
Male Court Doll
(carved and painted
wood dressed in silk and
linen), c.1780, France.
Los Angeles County
Museum of Art
(M.85.229a-c).

16. Do other museums have similar objects? Can you identify similar objects in online collections of dress? How do these objects compare?

Answering this question will help you determine the rarity and uniqueness of the object under study. Many museum collections around the world—including the Metropolitan Museum of Art in New York, the Los Angeles County Museum of Art, the Victoria and Albert Museum in London, and the Rijksmuseum in Amsterdam as well as many university and college collections—have online collection portals. However, due to database limitations, many of these collections can only be searched via the institution's portal.

What information can you learn from these other collections? Consider the number of similar garments in other collections and the type of information that is available, including exhibition catalogs and other references to specific books and/ or journal articles.

A museum may also have related objects that are relevant to your study. For example, in researching the dissemination of fashions for men's clothing in the eighteenth century, it may be helpful to study a fashion doll (Figure 3.15) from that period.

17. Are there any significant historical events that occurred around the time that the object was made that may be relevant to the object biography?

It may be helpful to identify and reflect on notable historical events that occurred around the time the object of dress was worn or used. For example, the 'Make-do and Mend' campaign in Britain (Figure 3.16) had a significant influence on clothing practices during the 1940s. Pandemics, times of conflict (such as the French Revolution, the First and Second World Wars), economic downturns (the Great Depression), and technological developments (such as the invention of the sewing machine and the washing machine) are notable examples of significant moments in history that influenced what people wore and the types of garments that have survived.

18. How are similar garments or accessories represented in fashion plates, photographs, illustrations, paintings, or other forms of visual media? What does this reveal about the social context of the time? How was this object worn and accessorized?

In seeking related material from contemporaneous visual sources, you will gain a fuller appreciation for how the garment was accessorized, styled and worn. Visual imagery can include drawings (Figure 3.17), paintings (Figure 3.18), fashion plates (Figure 3.19), illustrations (Figure 3.20), portrait photographs (Figure 3.21), satirical prints (Figure 3.22), and pattern books. For contemporary fashion, an array of imagery can be sourced, from runway shots and videos, photographs in fashion magazines and social media. Image aggregation services such as Getty Images can also be useful in gaining an appreciation for the wide scope of imagery available.

It is important to carefully assess in each case whether the artist has presented an idealized version of what was actually worn at the time.[9] Although Belgian artist Alfred Stevens (1823–1905) was known for his accuracy in depicting dress (Figure 3.18), other artists (such as James Jacques Tissot 1836–1902) were known to reuse or refashion gowns in their works.[10] Looking at a wide array of sources from any given time period can help to counteract an artist's distortions or biases. See, for example, the various depictions of women wearing similar styles of gowns from the 1870s, as shown here in Figures 3.17 to 3.24 inclusive.

Identifying visual references that include similar garments may also provide social context. For example, fashion plates from the nineteenth century often illustrate women engaged in drawing, needlework, visiting, shopping (Figure 3.19), or playing musical instruments. With satirical prints, you may be alerted to prevailing societal attitudes (Figure 3.22) and/or what not to wear and extremes to be avoided.[11]

Depending on the object of your interest and your research focus, it may be prudent to go beyond the most obvious types of visual referents such as paintings or photographs. In seeking out less studied visual sources such as sheet music (Figure 3.23), sculptures (Figure 3.24), or even the illustrations accompanying design patent applications, you may be able to gain new insights and generate new knowledge.[12]

OPPOSITE: Figure 3.16.
War-time poster: *Go Through Your Wardrobe—Make-do And Mend,* **c.1942, Britain.**
Photo by Donia Nachshen/Imperial War Museums via Getty Images.

Figure 3.17.
Alfred Stevens, *A Standing Young Lady Taking Off Her Gloves*, undated (1876 or after).
Pen and brown ink over graphite (33 × 24.5 cm).
Metropolitan Museum of Art (2014.106).

OPPOSITE: Figure 3.18.
Alfred Stevens, *After the Ball*, 1874. Oil
on canvas (95.9 x 68.9 cm).
Metropolitan Museum of Art
(146.150.2).

LE MONITEUR DES DAMES ET DES DEMOISELLES

Paris, Rue de Richelieu, 92

Étoffes et Nouveautés de La Ville de St Denis, Faub^g St Denis. 91-97.

Ceinture Régente de Mmes De Vertus Sœurs, r. de la Chaussée d'Antin, 27.

Lait Antéphélique de Candès & Cie B^d St Denis 26.

1872

Figure 3.19.
A. Bodin, "Shopping", *Le Moniteur des Dames et des Demoiselles*, 1872. Rijksmuseum.

Figure 3.20.
An illustration of a woman working at a Sholes & Glidden typewriter invented by Christopher Sholes. Published in the periodical "Scientific American" on August 10, 1872.
Getty Images.

Figure 3.21.
The daughter of typewriter inventor Christopher Latham Sholes is seen with one of her father's early typewriters.
Getty Images.

THE COMING RACE.

Doctor Evangeline. "By the bye, Mr. Sawyer, are you engaged to-morrow afternoon? I have rather a ticklish Operation to perform—an Amputation, you know."

Mr. Sawyer. "I shall be very happy to do it for you."

Dr. Evangeline. "O, no, not *that*! But will you kindly come and administer the Chloroform for me?"

Figure 3.22.
George du Maurier, "The Coming Race," 1872. Cartoon showing the patronising attitude women in the medical profession could expect from male colleagues.
From *Punch*, London, September 14, 1872. Oxford Science Archive/Print Collector/Getty Images.

Figure 3.23.
Sheet music cover image of the song "Dolly Varden Galop," 1872, United States.
Photo by Sheridan Libraries/Levy/Gado/Getty Images.

Figure 3.24.
Albert-Ernest Carrier-Belleuse, *Girl in a Straw Bonnet*, **c. 1868–70.**
Terracotta with wood base.
Metropolitan Museum of Art (1987.87).

19. Has this object, or others like it, been referenced in documents such as published diaries, letters, magazines, novels, or other forms of written material like inventories, wills, or legal documents? What does this reveal about the material practices or the cultural beliefs of that time?

Sources for textual references include newspapers, magazines, novels, and other published sources such as etiquette manuals. Personal writings such as memoirs, letters, and diaries can offer illuminating information about a person or a period. Archival material such as ancestry records, legal documents (wills, inventories, patents, and criminal proceedings), and a myriad of other documents can also offer alternate sources of information related to fashion. For example, in Barbara Burman and Ariane Fennetaux's study of tie-on-pockets, they analyzed the proceedings of London's Old Bailey criminal court from 1674 to 1913 to recover the information about the material practices of women from the lower socioeconomic class.[13]

Textual references like novels and plays may include clues as to the cultural attitudes related to dress in the time period under consideration. As well, letters and memoirs may also include specific references to dress. For example, author Virginia Woolf (1882–1941) often wrote about clothes not only in her diaries, but also in her fiction and non-fiction works.[14] In her autobiographical work *Moments of Being*, Woolf recalled her first memory of her mother and mentions the specific colors and patterns of a dress her mother wore, writing that she "can still see purple and red and blue [flowers] ... against the black [background]; they must have been anemones."[15]

Be aware that textual sources are valuable sources of information but are also subject to manipulation and error. Keep this in mind especially when using personal writing and novels.

20. Are there similar objects (such as fashion dolls) or related ephemera (advertisements, fashion photographs, packaging, and other print material) available for sale on online vintage retailers, auction sites or eBay? What does this information reveal about the perceived value and rarity of this object?

These sites can offer a window into what people consider valuable or collectible (Figure 3.25). Some of the world's leading art auction houses, including Christie's and Sotheby's, as well as several specialty auction houses—such as Kerry Taylor Auctions in London, and Karen Augusta Auctions in New York—hold regular sales of fashion collectibles. Studying their auction catalogs and websites can be another source of contextual information and alert you to the value assigned to similar objects. The proliferation of online vintage retailers also facilitates comparison for more saleable items.

Figure 3.25.
Barbie dolls dressed in outfits designed by Yves Saint Laurent, from the collection of Barbie
aficionado Billy Boy.
Photo by Pierre Vauthey/Sygma/Getty Images.

21. If the designer/maker of the garment or accessory is a known person, what information is available about them? How does this object fit into their *oeuvre*? Has the maker written an autobiography, recorded an oral history, or been profiled in magazines or journals?

Many prominent designers including Pierre Balmain (1914–82), Christian Dior (1905–57) and Elsa Schiaparelli (1890–1973) published their autobiographies during their lifetimes (Figure 3.26). And while such accounts must be read with a degree of skepticism, this material can offer rich insight into a designer's life and work. If the name of the maker is unknown, seeking out related information about contemporaneous designers or makers may be helpful.

22. Have other scholars written about this type of garment or accessory in scholarly books or peer-reviewed journals? If so, list these sources and assess how this work might be used to interpret this object.

Reading the work of other scholars can save valuable time and enhance your ability to reflect on and understand the uniqueness of this object and its place in history.

Figure 3.26.
Fashion designer Elsa Schiaparelli at her desk, March 6, 1936.
Photo by Sasha/Hulton Archive/Getty Images.

V. NEXT STEPS

23. Consider the cultural values of the time in which the object of dress was made and how these values are reflected in the design, use and survival of the object. How do these values inform your understanding?

Every object embodies the cultural values of the time in which it was created. Such values may privilege displays of wealth in the form of luxurious textiles embellished with lavish embroideries or other forms of ornamentation, or the creation of silhouettes that emphasize or disguise the female form (see Figure 3.4). If relevant, reflect on the societal constructions of propriety and morality in relation to class and gender and how that might have impacted the wearing and survival of this object.

24. After studying the object and the related contextual material, what patterns have emerged? What questions remain? What interests you most about this object now?

Consider the material evidence you have gathered from the object in relation to the contextual material you have compiled. What patterns have emerged? How does this object differ from others of its kind? Are you able to make any conjectures as to its uniqueness? What is most interesting about this object?

25. List your anticipated next steps.

Research is rarely linear. The focus of your interest may have shifted, and this is normal. Consider what evidence you gleaned from the object itself in relation to the contextual material you have gathered so far. What is the most meaningful piece of evidence to you? Will you be recreating this object or taking inspiration from it? Or will you produce a traditional form of scholarly output such as a research report or article? Perhaps this research inspired an alternative form of creative output such as a story, an artwork, or an exhibition. Reflect on what form your output might take. How will you document and share this new knowledge with others?

Depending on your goal for this project and your progress so far, you may need to undertake additional work before you are ready to proceed to the next phase. If you are unfamiliar with the norms of the culture from which this object originated, additional research or collaboration with a person from that community might be needed. If you are a maker, you may need to research the availability of comparable materials, enhance your understanding of certain construction techniques, or other technical processes. If you are an artist, you may want to consider the medium and format of your intended presentation. Creating a list of definable tasks and setting attainable targets for their completion not only helps in managing anxiety and stress, but also makes it more likely that you will attain your goal.

ENDNOTES

1   Linda Baumgarten, "Altered Historic Clothing," *Dress* 25 (1998): 42.
2   See "History of The Wascoes" in *Confederated Tribes of Warm Springs*. Accessed December 12, 2024 at https://warmsprings-nsn.gov/history/
3   For more on this topic, see Carolyn Dowdell, "'No Small Share of Ingenuity': An Object-Oriented Analysis of Eighteenth-Century English Dressmaking," *Costume* 55, no. 2 (2021): 186–211.
4   Joanne B. Eicher, "Dress, the Senses, and Public, Private and Secret Selves," *Fashion Theory* 25, no. 6 (2021): 780.
5   See for example, Length of Velvet (silk and metal thread), late 15th century. The Met (12.49.8). Accessed December 12, 2024 at https://www.metmuseum.org/art/collection/search/219394
6   Eicher, "Dress, the Senses," 782.
7   Bethan Bide, "Signs of Wear: Encountering Memory in the Worn Materiality of a Museum Fashion Collection," *Fashion Theory* 21, no. 4 (2017): 449–476.
8   For more on this topic, see Elaine McKay, *19th Century Patterns for the Modern Body: A Step-by-Step Guide* (London: Bloomsbury Visual Arts, 2025).
9   Ingrid E. Mida, "Artists & Wardrobes" in *Reading Fashion in Art* (London and New York: Bloomsbury Visual Arts, 2020), 22–39.
10 *Ibid.*
11 For more on this topic, see Ingrid E. Mida, "Men's Fashions and Satirical Prints in 1799: James Gillray and Elegance Democratique," *Costume* 58, no. 2 (2024): 159–179.
12 Jean L. Parsons and Sara B. Marketti, "The 'Perfect Dress,'" *Dress* 49, no. 2 (2023): 119–135.
13 Barbara Burman and Ariane Fennetaux, *The Pocket: A Hidden History of Women's Lives,* (London: Yale University Press, 2019).
14 Carolyn Abbs, "Writing the Subject: Virginia Woolf and Clothes," *Colloquy text theory critique* 11 (2006): 209.
15 Virginia Woolf, "A Sketch of the Past," *Moments of Being* (San Diego: Harcourt Brace, 1985), 64.

4

INTERPRETATION

OPPOSITE: Figure 4.1.
Ingrid Mida,
My Mother/Myself #1, 2010.

Research is a journey of discovery. As anthropologist Tim Ingold has pointed out, "In its literal sense, research is a second search, an act of searching again."[1] In undertaking object-based research in fashion, the object—a dress, a suit, a corset, a costume, a pair of shoes or a piece of jewelry—becomes the central focus of your inquiry. *Interpretation* is the process by which you bring together the *Observation* and *Reflection* phases of research to generate new forms of knowledge and/or a creative output. This phase of the process is both imaginative and highly creative, requiring you to assimilate the evidence, to find patterns, to make conjectures, and to produce a written narrative and/or an alternative output such as a reproduction, an artwork (Figure 4.1), a literary work of fiction or poetry, or an exhibition.

One object can be interpreted in a myriad of ways and thus it is difficult to definitively articulate the course of action for this phase. Makers may seek inspiration from historic dress or focus on techniques of construction or embellishment; art historians might concentrate on the aesthetic qualities of the garment or how fashions are depicted in paintings and other media; sociologists might be more interested in the function of the garment in the wardrobe of its owner; and others might be interested in processes of production and consumption. Whether you are planning to recreate an object, curate an exhibition, or write a scholarly paper using theory as a lens of analysis, in this last phase you must bridge the gap between what you observed and the contextual material you have gathered and determine what this means. Your aim is to generate new knowledge and/or create something new.

At the core of the interpretative phase of research is the development and consideration of what the evidence from the garment represents in terms of a specific research question or goal. Harnessing your experience, skills, and strengths, and knowing your motivations can be helpful in narrowing down your focus. What led you to study this object and what did you expect to see or learn? What did you discover that was surprising or interesting to you? What are you wanting to accomplish?

Fashion does not exist in isolation. Each object of dress originated and existed in a specific time and place. Some of the questions that you might consider in telling the story of the object include: how do the material qualities of this object reflect the values of that time, place, and culture in which it was made? What has happened to this object since it was first created? How does that history inform your understanding of its material presence as it exists today? If the garment or accessory was worn by a known person, what does the material evidence reveal about that person in relation to their aesthetic preferences, body dimensions, and expressions of gender, sexuality, wealth, race, or other aspects of their identity?

I want to emphasize again that research is rarely linear. This means that as information is gathered and assimilated from different sources, you may need to adapt your approach. In analyzing information and making connections, you may also come to appreciate that a certain detail is more relevant than you anticipated, or you may find that there are gaps in your knowledge that lead you to search again. This type of curiosity is encouraged. As Ingold points out, "curiosity and care go together, in the attention we pay to things", since these words share the same etymological root (from the Latin *curare*).[2] With each new discovery, not only is your understanding of the object enriched, but the story you can tell becomes more compelling.

USING FASHION THEORY IN INTERPRETING RESULTS

Compared to other disciplines, fashion, as a cultural phenomenon, is a relatively recent field of independent study. The journal *Fashion Theory: The Journal of Dress, Body and Culture,* which defines fashion as "the cultural construction of embodied identity," was launched in 1997 to offer a forum for critical analysis and scholarship. However, there is no singular theorist or central framework to describe fashion phenomena, since fashion intersects with disciplines that examine the full range of human activity. Within the field of fashion itself, the scope is also broad, including elements of design, production, merchandising, display, and consumption. The absence of an overarching framework can be confusing and confounding to the novice scholar but also presents an opportunity to be more imaginative and creative in interpreting results.

If you have been asked to produce a scholarly paper, this phase of research typically involves translating evidence gathered during observation into a nuanced argument using theory. Theory—the set of ideas or the framework used to explain a particular phenomenon—can seem highly abstract and impenetrable, but at its core, theory represents one learned person's opinion that has come to be generally accepted by other scholars over time. And as Giorgio Riello explains, theory can be thought of as the abstract ideas on "how fashion takes shape, how it penetrates the world, reproduces itself and conditions the social and the power relations between individuals and society."[3] Theory can be used to generate meaning from an object of fashion.

Theory comes in and out of parlance as scholarship develops over time, and since fashion studies is interdisciplinary, a broad range of theoretical perspectives can be harnessed to generate meaning. Knowing which theorist to draw upon is highly dependent on the research project at hand and cannot be prescriptive. However, if you remember that theory is a lens by which to interpret your object, it makes the process seem much less intimidating. It is not possible within the limited scope of this book to summarize all the major theorists whose work intersects with fashion, and if you will be undertaking a theory-based analysis, introductory scholarly texts such as *Thinking through Fashion: A Guide to Key Theorists* may be helpful.[4] As Agnes Rocamora and Anneke Smelik explain in their introduction to this book, the use of theory can enrich our understanding of the dynamics of fashion by giving "us the means to achieve the critical distance necessary to a full understanding of its layered complexity."[5]

The aim in using theory to interpret an object of dress is to illuminate the materiality of the evidence gathered from the object itself and create a well-reasoned argument in support of your underlying research question. It is wise to anticipate that this process will be iterative, requiring multiple attempts to reflect and reconsider the evidence in the artifact against the evidence obtained from other objects, in textual sources or imagery. As Ingold reminds us, when we research, we must search again.[6]

ALTERNATIVE MODES OF INTERPRETATION

There are many ways to generate knowledge. Although traditional forms of scholarship have long privileged text-based outputs, in recent years alternative modes of learning and knowing—such as making, doing and wearing—have also been recognized as valid forms of knowledge generation. Dress historian and maker Hilary Davidson has described this shift as the "embodied turn" in fashion studies, which has led to the acceptance of "experimental and interpretative processes in re-enactment or material reconstruction."[7] For example, in the process of reconstructing what was believed to be Jane Austen's silk pelisse, Davidson generated evidence that supported the provenance of the pelisse as having once belonged to Austen and also gleaned information from the replica about her physical stature.[8] In describing the process of making, Davidson concludes that the act of reproduction is "an even deeper form of 'slow looking' because the maker must confront practical problems that cannot be avoided and must be solved before the project can progress."[9]

The drafting of patterns and the recreation of historic garments can lead to an embodied understanding of technical processes of design and construction used in the past. For example, conservator Betty Kirke sought to better understand the use of the bias cut in garments designed by Madeleine Vionnet (1876–1975). In her careful study and remaking of garments designed by Vionnet, Kirke was able to illuminate aspects of the designer's creative process and method, including Vionnet's use of the grid in cutting and sewing, as well as her focus on the natural female body in motion.[10]

Exhibitions of fashion typically foreground objects as a means by which to tell a story. And although exhibition making is not often acknowledged as creative practice, considerable imagination, research and collaborative effort is required to tell a story using objects. In the 2014 fashion exhibition *Charles*

James: Beyond Fashion at the Costume Institute at The Met, the secrets underpinning the construction of twenty-six iconic garments designed by James were unlocked with the use of X-radiography. In the exhibition, video animations adjacent to the garments allowed viewers to more easily appreciate James's design preferences, including the elimination of darts and seams and the use of asymmetry and draping.[11] Similarly, in the exhibition *Balenciaga: Shaping Fashion* at the Victoria and Albert Museum (May 27, 2017 – February 18, 2018), the innovative methods used by Balenciaga were documented during a collaborative project between curators and students from the London College of Fashion.[12] During this project, the students used the *Slow Approach to Seeing* and the methods developed in the first edition of this book to study and document select garments by Balenciaga with the aim of deconstructing the designer's methods of design and construction.[13]

In making and doing as a form of research, the sensorial and tacit experience of the body is acknowledged as a method by which to create new forms of knowledge. In Ellen Sampson's book *Worn*, the artist and researcher spotlights wearing as a research method and argues that the maker and wearer become entangled in the wearing of clothing since the wearer encounters the maker's choices, practices, and accidents in the experience of wearing that garment. In documenting her personal experiences of wearing shoes in a wearing diary, Sampson foregrounds the sensorial experience and feelings evoked, and as she explains, this research method "binds the subject and object" and "also produces sensory knowledge."[14] Sampson argues for wearing as a way of thinking.

Drawing and other forms of artistic outputs can also serve to generate knowledge. As Sarah Casey and Gerry Davies explain in the introduction to their book *Drawing Investigations*, the value of drawing is "not simply in finding optical equivalence, as in the mechanical reproduction of a camera," but rather in "its inherent capacity to synthesize observation and idea."[15] Casey is a UK-based artist and scholar who has used drawing to 'draw' out meaning from a variety of extant objects, including Queen Victoria's underwear.[16] She and I share an affinity for drawing, and in 2018 we undertook a joint project to study the clothing of the art critic and polymath John Ruskin (1836–1900). This work culminated in an exhibition titled *Ruskin's Good Looking* (February 8 – April 7, 2019) featuring Casey's drawings and held at the site of his former home— Brantwood Museum in the Lake District. In his lectures at Oxford University, Ruskin advocated for drawing to see and also argued that drawing was an instrument for gaining knowledge rather than an end in itself.[17] Our work on this project confirmed that a dress detective conducting object-based research and an artist wanting to produce a mimetic representation of that thing undertake similar processes of close looking, and this type of engagement has the potential to generate new knowledge about those garments.[18] In the exhibition, the form and materiality of Casey's finished artworks underlined the haunting beauty and spectral presence that exists within clothing, prompting visitors to reflect on the survival of these garments and the transience of life. As Ruskin himself observed:

> *The whole function of the artist in the world is to be a seeing and feeling creature; to be an instrument of such tenderness and sensitiveness, that no shadow, no hue, no line, no instantaneous and evanescent expression of the visible things around him, nor any of the emotions which they are capable of conveying to the spirit which has been given him, shall either be left unrecorded, or fade from the book of record.*[19]

In embracing alternative forms of studying objects and harnessing the tacit knowledge gained by drawing, making, or wearing, researchers focus on the material properties of fashion as a means by which to unlock and articulate narratives of the past.

THE CASE STUDIES

Dress objects are complex composites of material and cultural values. Reading a dress is like reading a painting: both can be undertaken with care and precision, but the interpretation is ultimately subjective. The guidelines established in this book are intended to assist in the gathering of evidence, but ultimately it is up to you to be rigorous and imaginative in interpreting what you find.

The following seven case studies illustrate how evidence from a garment can be used to articulate the cultural narratives and personal stories that are embodied in these objects. These selections reflect a representative sample of garments that might be available for study from a museum or study collection and are oriented around certain themes. And, as was mentioned in the introduction, the new case studies, while longer and more nuanced, do not replace but are additive to the ones published in the first edition of this book.

Chapter 5 traces **the biography of an object**—an eighteenth-century silk gown from the collection of the Colonial Williamsburg Foundation in Virginia. This gown is an exceptional example of a floral-patterned textile made of the highest quality silk woven in Spitalfields, England. The textile, or possibly a ready-made version of the gown, was shipped to the United States and was worn by at least two women from one family in Rhode Island. Although this dress is deceptively pretty, there is a compelling story behind the seams and folds that connects this object to the slave trade.

Chapter 6 considers a dark blue wool tailcoat and a pair of cream silk pantaloons dating to the 1820s from the collection of the Los Angeles County Museum of Art in California. These two garments represent key pieces in a man's dress ensemble from that time, and will be analyzed in relation to the infamous figure of **the dandy** in the first part of the nineteenth century.

Chapter 7 addresses the topic of **fashion and gender** as exemplified by a mid-nineteenth century boy's frock from the collection of Los Angeles County Museum of Art. Recut from another garment, this beautiful child's dress dates to a time period in which young boys and girls were dressed the same. This garment has no distinguishing marks or features which definitively categorize it as having been made for or worn by a boy. This ambiguity raised the question as to what advice mothers were given on dressing young children in relation to societal norms during this period in history.

Chapter 8 is a case study highlighting the role of **creative practice** in relation to a silk wedding gown and veil dated to 1927 in the Fashion Research Collection at Toronto Metropolitan University. Although the fragile condition of this wedding ensemble precludes handling, this garment offers the opportunity to consider the poignancy of embodied memory and the ravages of time. This case study presents several alternative interpretations, including both theoretical and creative outputs.

Chapter 9 focuses on **fashion and glamour** in relation to a green wool belted dress and matching jacket designed by Yves Saint Laurent for his fall/winter 1958–59 collection for Christian Dior Paris. This couture dress ensemble, now housed in the Seneca College Fashion Resource Collection in Toronto, once belonged to a woman who was born into a life of wealth and privilege and who became CEO of a large Canadian conglomerate at a time when few women held such positions. One of many designer garments donated by her to this study collection, this chic Dior dress ensemble illustrates the role of fashion in crafting a glamourous public persona.

Chapter 10 considers **fashion and identity** with a case study of a mass-manufactured striped cotton blend jumpsuit uniform worn by female employees at the CN Tower in Toronto, Canada in 1976. Given by an unknown donor to the study collection at Toronto Metropolitan University, this uniform facilitates a discussion about the relationship between uniforms and fashion, and between uniforms and identity.

Chapter 11 is a case study about **the language of the kimono**, specifically an embroidered silk *uchikake* (outer kimono) from the collection of the Textile Museum of Canada in Toronto. The symbolic qualities of this ceremonial robe worn by a bride during the Edo period are unraveled to reveal a story about the family's hopes and dreams for their daughter.

The case studies in this book are offered as examples of how the checklists may be applied to a range of dress objects. Several of these chapters are subtitled with the three distinct stages of object-based research: Observation, Reflection, and Interpretation. However, it should be noted that this format may or may not be appropriate for a scholarly essay, and you may prefer to present your analysis in a more fluid and integrated manner.

    Each of these objects could have been interpreted in any number of ways, and I recognize that my interpretation is a reflection of my background and interests. I offer these case studies as examples of how to apply the methodology advocated in this book, but please do not feel constrained by what is here. Whether you adopt a conventional form of object-based research or engage with alternative forms of making and knowing, the potential to reveal and unlock the narratives embedded in objects is limited only by your own ingenuity. Research is a journey of discovery and that is part of the fun.

ENDNOTES

1   Tim Ingold, "Art, science and the meaning of research," *Research in Arts and Education,* no. 3 (2018): 1–9.

2   *Ibid,* 7.

3   Giorgio Riello, "The object of fashion: methodological approaches to the history of fashion," *Journal of Aesthetics & Culture* 3 (2011): 1–9.

4   Agnes Rocamora and Anneke Smelik, eds., *Thinking Through Fashion* (London and New York, I.B. Tauris, 2016).

5   *Ibid,* 3.

6   Ingold, "Art, science and the meaning of research," 1–9.

7   Hilary Davidson, "The Embodied Turn: Making and Remaking Dress as an Academic Practice," *Fashion Theory* 23, no. 3 (2019): 329–62.

8   Hilary Davidson, "Reconstructing Jane Austen's Silk Pelisse, 1812–1814." *Costume* 49, no. 2 (2015): 189–223.

9   Davidson, "The Embodied Turn," 330.

10   Anne Bissonette. "Doing History with Objects: Betty Kirke and Madeleine Vionnet," *Fashion Theory* 19, no. 3 (2015): 281–314.

11   The video animations created for the exhibition of "Charles James: Beyond Fashion" at the Met (May 8–August 10, 2014) can be viewed online. Accessed December 6, 2024 at https://www.metmuseum.org/exhibitions/listings/2014/charles-james-beyond-fashion/animations

12   See the video about this project at the Victoria and Albert Museum, "Learning from the Master" https://www.vam.ac.uk/articles/learning-from-the-master. Accessed March 21, 2025.

13   Susanne Baldwin, "An Object-based Research Study of Archive Pieces Incorporating Digital Technology," *Art, Design & Communication in Higher Education* 17, no. 1 (2018): 25–32.

14   Ellen Sampson, *Worn: Footwear, Attachment and the Affects of Wear* (Bloomsbury Visual Arts, 2020), 39.

15   Sarah Casey and Gerry Davies, *Drawing Investigations: Graphic Relationships with Science, Culture and the Environment* (London and New York: Bloomsbury, 2020), 4.

16   Sarah Casey, "Hidden Drawers," 2009–2013, accessed December 6, 2024 at https://www.sarahcasey.co.uk/hidden-drawers. Other projects by Casey involving clothing are also featured on her website.

17   John Ruskin, *The Elements of Drawing, with a New Introduction by Lawrence Campbell* (New York: Dover Publications, 1971 [1857]), 13.

18   Ingrid Mida and Sarah Casey, "Drawing as a Creative Approach to Researching Extant Garments: A Case Study Involving John Ruskin's Clothing," *Costume* 54, no. 2 (2020): 202–221.

19   John Ruskin, *The Stones of Venice*, III, *The Fall* (New York: Cosimo, 2007 [1886]), 37. See also John Ruskin, 'Lecture 1, Inaugural', in *Lectures on Art, Delivered Before the University of Oxford in Hilary Term, 1870* (Oxford: Clarendon Press, 1870), 20.

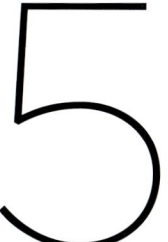

5

THE BIOGRAPHY OF AN OBJECT

An Eighteenth-Century Spitalfields Silk Gown

Clothes are some of the most intimate and compelling of all objects because of their close connection to the body. As dress historian Linda Baumgarten observed, clothing may be "stretched out and shaped by the body that wore it, wrinkled by years of use, soiled from two-hundred-year-old perspiration", and these traces are what make clothing "the most intimately human of the surviving decorative arts." [1] And while these marks and stains of living hold the stories of the person or persons that wore that piece of clothing, a careful study of a garment or accessory can also reveal other aspects of its story, including its design, use and successive lives. This is what the cultural anthropologist Igor Kopytoff has described as the "biography of the object," which charts the trajectory of an object through time. [2]

This case study considers a floral-patterned silk gown dated to the eighteenth century (Figure 5.1). The pattern for the textile was initially drawn on paper in the mid-1720s, woven into lengths of silk in Spitalfields, England, and shipped to the United States as a textile or possibly as a ready-made gown. This beautiful gown was worn by three generations of women from a Rhode Island family and stored by their descendants until 1951 when it was acquired by the Colonial Williamsburg Foundation. In 2023–24, the dress was displayed in the exhibition *Making Her Mark: A History of Women Artists from 1400–1800* at the Baltimore Museum of Fine Art (October 19, 2023 – January 7, 2024) and at the Art Gallery of Ontario (March 27 – July 1, 2024). It was at the AGO that I encountered the dress displayed behind glass (Figure 5.2). Even though I was unable to handle it, this dress has a compelling story to tell—one that not only links a multitude of women, but one that also highlights the role of textiles in global trade and the history of slavery.[3]

OBSERVATION

This eighteenth-century silk gown is made of a sumptuous floral-patterned brocaded silk lampas (Figure 5.1). A pattern of interwoven floral vines and brocaded flowers has been woven in light green, light blue, and coral silk threads on a cream-colored ground. The gown, in its current state, has a front-closing fitted bodice with rounded tabs at the centre front, elbow-length fitted sleeves, and an attached skirt. The low-cut squarish neckline has been trimmed with a narrow band of pinked edge self-fabric ruching. The full, floor-length skirt is finely pleated at the waist with extra fullness at the sides and the scalloped-edge pinked opening reveals a reproduction rose pink silk petticoat.

According to the catalog record for this gown, the bodice and sleeves are lined in linen and the skirt is unlined.[4] The dimensions of the textile used in this gown are consistent with Spitalfields silks of that period, measuring 21 inches (53.3 cm) wide with a vertical repeat of 18 inches (45.7 cm).[5] The length of the gown (shoulder to hem) measures 54 inches (137.1 cm), and the dress waist measures a slim 22 inches (45.7 cm). The museum has assigned a date for the initial construction of the gown as 1726–28, and in Linda Baumgarten's article "Altered Historic Clothing," she described the alterations to this dress as follows:

OPPOSITE: Figure 5.2.
Silk gown on display during the exhibition *Making Her Mark: A History of Women Artists 1400–1800* at the Art Gallery of Ontario (March 27 – July 1, 2024).
Photo by author.

Figure 5.3.
Front bodice detail of gown on display. Photo by author.

The gown is made of imported English silk dating from 1726–28 but is now in the style of the 1770s or early 1780s. Faint impressions of folds and piecing indicate that its bodice was changed from a stomacher-front to an edge-to-edge closure. The sleeves were narrowed by taking in the seams and elongated with pieces set in at the elbows. The back bodice has old folds from the pleats of a sack back.[6]

Even when displayed behind glass, the alterations to the dress front, back and sleeves are readily apparent to the naked eye. It is obvious where additional fabric has been inserted at the bodice front, bodice back and the sleeves, since the pattern of the textile does not line up well along the seams where the additional fabric was inserted (Figures 5.3 and 5.4). The stitching at the back of the bodice also shows considerable puckering. While no obvious stains or other marks were visible on the dress on display, the lining of the gown likely has soiling at the underarms and neckline.

Figure 5.4.
Back bodice detail of gown on display.
Photo by author.

REFLECTION

The vibrancy of this gown—even after three hundred years—is a testament to the high quality and enduring beauty of the silk textiles woven in Spitalfields, England. The ravages of time and use mean that relatively few such garments exist, and there are only a handful of extant garments and textiles (Figure 5.5) that have been linked to the work of English textile designer Anna Maria Garthwaite (b.1688–90 – d.1763).[7]

An extant silk gown of floral-patterned silk designed by Garthwaite (Figure 5.6) in the collection of the Victoria and Albert Museum presents a notable comparable. Like the case study gown, this gown has been altered and the record notes that "the last conversion in the 1780s to the style of that time was quite clumsily executed, suggesting that perhaps the gown had been handed down to a maid."[8] A notable difference is that the textile used for this gown is an exact match to a design on paper for a 'Mr. Gregory' (dates unknown) in Garthwaite's hand, dated to April 22, 1744.[9]

The case study gown has a date attribution of 1726–28 for the textile and 1775–85 for the alteration of the gown. If Garthwaite designed this textile in the 1720s, this gown may be one of the earliest surviving silks from her career. This presents the following research questions: What evidence links the gown to Garthwaite? Who wore and altered the gown?

LEFT: Figure 5.5.
Skirt panel, 1749, England. Designed by Anna Maria Garthwaite, woven by Daniel Vautier in Spitalfields. Photo by Heritage Art/Heritage Images via Getty Images.

OPPOSITE: Figure 5.6.
Gown, floral patterned silk designed by Anna Maria Garthwaite, 1744 (woven), 1745–50 (made), 1780s (altered). Victoria and Albert Museum (T.264-1966).

INTERPRETATION

Drawing on the notion of an object biography, this interpretation traces this floral-patterned silk gown through its various life stages as a textile design, piece of cloth, gown, and museum artifact, bringing together the stories of multiple women who designed, made, wore, altered, housed, and handled the dress.

The Textile

The floral pattern used to weave the silk textile for this gown has been attributed to the English textile designer Anna Maria Garthwaite.[10] Unlike most textile designers of the time, Garthwaite had no training and experience as a weaver, and it is not known what prompted her to pursue textile design as a career.[11] Like most young women of the upper and middle classes, she and her two sisters would have been encouraged to learn the genteel arts of drawing, embroidery, and paper cutting.[12] An intricate paper cut dating to 1707—when Garthwaite was a teenager—not only demonstrates her incredible focus, skill and imagination, but also presages the rhythms of her botanical designs for silk (Figure 5.7).

Figure 5.7.
Anna Maria Garthwaite, Papercut on a vellum backing (32 x 40 cm including frame), 1707.
Victoria and Albert Museum (E.1077-1993).

Garthwaite's earliest textile designs date to 1726, two years prior to her move to Spitalfields, the centre of the textile weaving industry in England, where she established herself as a highly competent silk designer.[13] During her thirty years of work as a textile designer, Garthwaite generated several hundred textile designs on paper, many of which include dates, annotations and the names of the weavers to whom they were sold.[14]

During the first half of the eighteenth century, fashions in textiles changed more rapidly than the cut of women's clothing, and textiles incorporated novelty by varying the colors, the motifs, and the size of the pattern. In Natalie Rothstein's documentation of eighteenth-century textile designs in her book *Silk Designs of the Eighteenth Century*, she credits Garthwaite's success to "her understanding of the medium" and knowing "what was necessary for each type of fabric and how not to waste silk."[15] Garthwaite's designs were drawn in pencil on paper (often on gridded paper) and colored in with watercolor or gouache. Each design was created for a specific weaver and in most cases, Garthwaite took care to note the name of her customer on the design itself, as she did for the textile used to create the gown shown in Figure 5.6. My close examination of a selection of Garthwaite's designs revealed her painstaking efforts; often there were faint pencil lines that have not been filled in with paint, pieces of paper pasted over sections to cover mistakes, and extra strips of paper added to extend the length of the paper.[16]

Many of Garthwaite's early designs from 1726 until about 1729 consist of semi-naturalistic flowers painted in pale blues, greens, and an orange yellow on a light-colored ground. Rothstein notes that the pattern of the silk textile used in the Colonial Williamsburg gown is similar to but does not match the designs by Garthwaite numbered 5970:6, 5970:10 and 5970:26 (Figures 5.8, 5.9, 5.10).[17]

Figure 5.8.
Anna Maria Garthwaite,
Textile Design 1726–28.
Watercolor on paper
(57.2 cm x 25.4 cm).
Victoria and Albert
Museum (5970:6).

Figure 5.9.
Anna Maria Garthwaite,
Textile Design 1726–28.
Watercolor on paper (29
cm x 25.4 cm).
Victoria and Albert
Museum (5970:10).

Figure 5.10.
Anna Maria Garthwaite,
Textile Design 1726–28.
Watercolor on paper (33
x 23.5 cm).
Victoria and Albert
Museum (5970:26).

Given how carefully Garthwaite documented her designs on paper during the course of her career, it is noteworthy that there is no exact match to the woven textile used in this gown. Rothstein notes the close parallel between the hand of Christopher Baudouin (1662–1724) and Garthwaite's drawings from this time, but she does not comment on the absence of a close match for this dress.[18] To my eye, the textile design of the woven silk in the gown is denser and more intricate than other surviving early designs on paper in Garthwaite's hand, and it is within the realm of possibility that the silk design originated from the hand of another, possibly her peer Baudouin or the Huguenot designer and weaver James Leman (1688–1745).[19] And yet it is also possible that Garthwaite did not initially document her work with the same rigor as she did in later years. On one of her early designs, she wrote "This was sent to London with the rul'd paper before I came up,"—evidence that she was working and selling her designs while still living in Yorkshire.[20] Garthwaite's close relationship with her brother-in-law, the apothecary Vincent Bacon (1702–39), may have been helpful in establishing her connections to the silk weavers of Spitalfields, since silk designers worked independently and on commission.[21]

Spitalfields silk weavers, like Garthwaite's customers Simon Julins (c. 1686–1778) or Daniel Vaultier (dates unknown), were members of the London silk weavers' guild—known as the Weavers' Company. This male-dominated organization not only lobbied against imports of printed calicoes, but also established membership standards that dictated the number of looms and apprentices that a weaver could have working at any given time.[22] In the early part of the eighteenth century, raw silk was imported by silk brokers from Turkey, the Levant region, Italy, India, China or Bengal.[23] The process of transforming the raw silk into dyed silk thread suitable for weaving was typically carried out by a silk mercer, although some master weavers preferred to undertake this work themselves. Once the appropriate colors of silk thread had been acquired, the loom was set up according to the textile design—a process that could take up to five or six weeks.[24] In general, Spitalfields silks typically measured 19 to 21 inches wide (48.25 to 53.3 cm), while lengths varied according to the order.[25] The work progressed slowly at a rate of about one yard (0.9 metres) a day.[26] William Hogarth's illustration of apprentices at their looms suggests that some found the work tiresome (Figure 5.11).

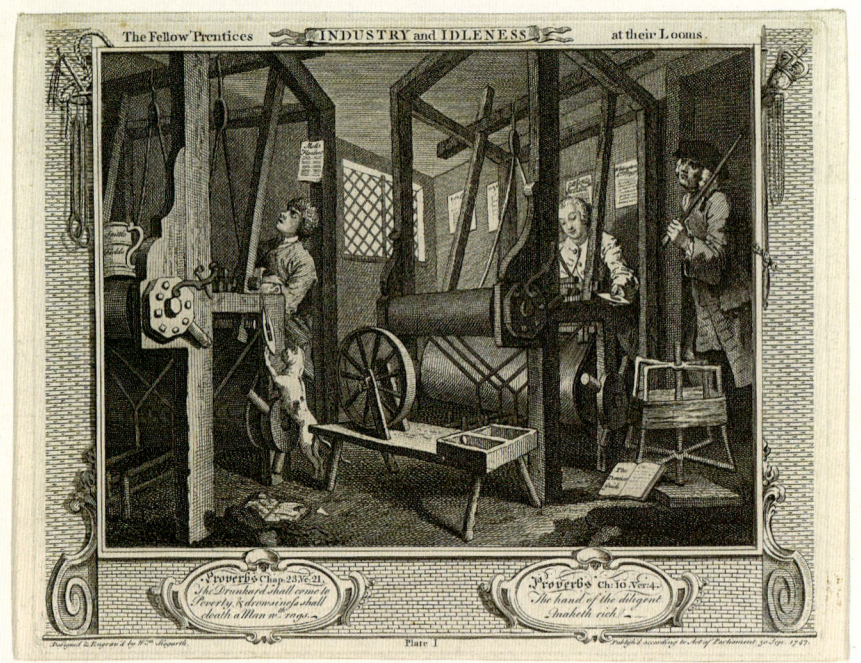

Figure 5.11.
William Hogarth, *The Fellow 'Prentices at their Looms' (Industry and Idleness, plate I)*, 1747. **Etching and engraving (26.4 x 34. 2 cm).**
Metropolitan Museum of Art (9.11.9).

The Gown

After the silk lengths had been woven to order in Spitalfields, such textiles were sold as lengths of cloth (or sometimes made up as ready-mades) and transported to the American Colonies by wooden ship. Regular trade routes transported all sorts of goods from Britain, including clothes, jeweled swords, harpsichords, and gunpowder; and as Rothstein notes, "the merchants who controlled this trade were the aristocracy of the Colonies."[27] Textiles, including silks but also wool, linen, half silk (silk blended with linen), and imported printed cottons, were among "the most important goods British manufacturers exported to the colonies, both in terms of quantity and profit."[28] Colored silk damasks were Garthwaite's most popular designs in the Colonies. Extant examples of gowns and banyans made with such fabrics can be found in various American museum collections, including this gown made of a green silk damask (and matching shoes) dated to 1743–45 and attributed to Garthwaite (Figure 5.12).[29]

Figure 5.12.
Spitalfields green silk damask gown, c.1775. Textile dated to 1743–45
and attributed to Anna Maria Garthwaite.
Metropolitan Museum of Art (1994.406 a-b).

Flowered silks were only produced to order, and generally limited to four pieces woven from a single design.[30] In the 1720s, two types of floral-patterned silks were popular: an ornate baroque-style pattern of florals woven with silver or gold threads, as well as a more delicate and naturalistic pattern of the 'meadow silk' type.[31] Floral-patterned silk on a light ground, like that used to make the case study gown, was a very popular choice for weddings for much of the eighteenth century, and such silk was also incredibly expensive—almost double the cost of a plain silk.[32] A woman wearing a dress like this beautiful floral-patterned Spitalfields silk not only signaled her wealth but also her affinity for the natural world at a time when the scientific community was seeking to document the range of botanical species around the globe.

It is in Rhode Island that the story continues, since the Colonial Williamsburg Foundation acquired this dress in 1951 from a Rhode Island family. Like many objects and garments that are lovingly saved by families for decades, or in this case centuries, specific details and information about the circumstances of how and when something was acquired gets increasingly muddled with time. According to family lore, this dress was worn by Sarah Wickes (1700–86) for her wedding to Colonel Benoni Waterman (1701–87) on the 11th of February 1725 in Warwick, Kent, Rhode Island. However, the date of the Wickes–Waterman wedding points to an anomaly. If this silk was designed by Garthwaite, Sarah Wickes could not possibly have worn this gown as her wedding dress, since this date predates Garthwaite's career as a textile designer. Perhaps Sarah Wickes acquired the silk after her marriage and had it made up into a gown to wear to some other formal event. The name of the maker or makers has been lost to time, even though the imprint of her/their hand(s) live(s) on (Figure 5.13).

Figure 5.13.
Geertruydrt Roghman, Two Women Sewing, Plate 1 from Five Feminine Occupations, 1640–47, Engraving (21.2 × 16.5 cm).
Metropolitan Museum of Art (56.550.2).

In its original incarnation in the 1720s, the gown may have had a shape and silhouette like this rare unaltered gown made of a dark-colored Spitalfields silk woven in a fashionable lace-like pattern (Figure 5.14).[33] Another style that was popular during the 1720s was the *robe volante* or sack back gown (Figure 5.15).

Figure 5.14.
Spitalfields silk gown (unaltered), c.1725, British.
Metropolitan Museum of Art (C.I.64.14).

Figure 5.15.
Robe volante **(silk), c.1730, French.** Metropolitan Museum of Art (2010.148).

The case study gown may have been worn (and altered) by Sarah's daughter, Mary Waterman (1726–65), who married Captain Thomas Greene in 1758. It was a second marriage for her husband, and Mary, who was thirty-two years old at the time, may have decided to have her mother's gown remade in the style of that period since the textile pattern was still fashionable.[34] Mary did not live to see her daughter Sarah Greene marry Sargent Caleb Hill Jr. in 1784, but Sarah's grandmother—Sarah Wickes Waterman—was still alive, and perhaps she encouraged her granddaughter to have the dress altered to wear to that event.

The gown was last altered in the 1770s or 80s with pieces of fabric inserted to transform the open front bodice into a closed front, remove the cuffs, lengthen the sleeves and open the skirt front. Such alterations would have helped the gown to more closely align with the fashions of that period. It is also obvious that Sarah Greene was very slight in frame, because even with the addition of fabric to the bodice, the waist of the dress measures only 22 inches (55.9 cm). As noted earlier, the alterations lack finesse, and it may well have been Sarah or perhaps a servant who fashioned the adjustments. It is readily apparent—even without close examination—that the pattern of the textile does not match up in the places where additional fabric has been added (see Figure 5.4), even though there should have been sufficient fabric from the transformation of the dress from a sack back style and opening of the skirt front to match the pattern at the seams. As well, the seams at the back of the bodice show puckering, and the lack of refinement suggest a lack of skills or work done in haste. Sarah likely wore this dress for her wedding and perhaps as her best dress for a few years, before the radical change in dress styles in the 1790s rendered it unfashionable.

Many bridal ensembles are carefully stored as a material memory of a significant life event. This particular gown—having been worn by several women from the same family—held emotional poignancy for the family and was lovingly stored and passed down through the generations until the Colonial Williamsburg Foundation purchased it from the family in 1951. The museum's catalog record identifies the provenance of the gown as being linked to Warwick, Rhode Island. This information sparked my curiosity, since I would have expected such a sumptuous gown to have a provenance linked to a major metropolitan centre such as New York City or Boston. After undertaking additional research, I was surprised to learn that Rhode Island was actually one of the busiest hubs of the slave trade in North America.[35]

Textiles and the Slave Trade

Weddings connect families. When Sarah Wickes married Colonel Benoni Waterman in 1724, she became a member of one of the most prominent families in Rhode Island. The lineage of Sarah's husband Benoni can be traced to two of the founders of Rhode Island—Richard Waterman (c.1605–73) and Roger Williams (c.1606–83).[36] Williams, who attended Cambridge University, left England to seek religious freedom and "purchased land from the Narragansett Chiefs, Canonicus and Miantonmi," in what is now known as Providence, Rhode Island.[37] Williams shared his purchase with twelve others, including Richard Waterman, and this new colony grew through its acceptance of settlers of all religious backgrounds. Benoni's father—John Waterman (1666–1728)—was the first to make his family's residence in Old Warwick, a town that sits along the Narragansett Bay.

The husband of Sarah Wickes—Benoni Waterman—was born in Warwick and held various civic and military positions in Kent and Providence Counties. He lived his entire life on the family homestead, which was situated in a region that was well-suited to agriculture, with rich soil, moderate temperatures and easy coastal access. Many of the farmers in this area engaged in commercial farming operations that bred livestock such as horses, cattle, and sheep, manufactured cheese and other dairy products, and also cultivated crops such as corn, flax and tobacco for export to markets in the West Indies and southern colonies.[38] As historian Christy Clark-Pujara has documented, Narragansett farmers rarely performed manual labour themselves, but instead relied on enslaved peoples in order to achieve commercial levels of production of agricultural goods.[39] Farmers "initially relied on indentured Native Americans but replaced them with enslaved Africans," and "by 1740 the Narragansett Country had the highest concentration of enslaved people in the colony, many of whom came directly from Africa."[40]

Although it is not clear whether Benoni ran a commercial farming operation on his homestead, he was involved in the shipping trade with his brother.[41] The vessels owned by brothers Benoni and Resolved Waterman often conducted business in Surinam, South America, a key port in the Transatlantic Slave Trade involving the trade of rum, sugar, molasses and other goods in exchange for captive Africans.[42] Several historic documents point to the brothers' involvement in the Transatlantic Slave Trade. For example, a document titled "Forreign [sic] Vessels Entred [sic]" into Surinam lists two vessels captained by Resolved Waterman docking in Surinam on at least two occasions, with the Sloop Rotterdam entering on March 18, 1745, and the Sloop Mary on July 12, 1745.[43] The cargos of other ships included in this manifest list beef, hog's lard, rum, brandy, sugar, and tobacco as well as slaves.[44] As well, there is documentation that the Waterman brothers transported slaves at least once, when the Sloop Recovery captained by Resolved Waterman transported about fifty slaves between Rhode Island and other American ports in November 1731.[45] And, given that the demand for sailors was so high, it is also likely that the brothers had enslaved men working on their ships.[46] This family was part of an economic network that benefited from the business of slavery, since "by 1730, most trades and professions in Rhode Island were tied in one way or another to slaveholding and slave trading."[47] When Benoni Waterman died on July 14, 1784, his will listed three slaves as his property, who were bequeathed to his wife and granddaughter Sarah Hill.[48]

Benoni Waterman, his wife Sarah, and their descendants benefitted from the unpaid labor of enslaved people in their home, on the homestead, and through their involvement in shipping goods for the Transatlantic Slave Trade. And while Warwick, Rhode Island might seem like a small town in comparison to larger centers such as Boston and New York City, the lifestyle of the Rhode Island elite was not only "elaborate and leisurely" but also "attempted to emulate the English countryside and manor homes."[49] In this context, the beautiful Spitalfields floral-patterned silk gown (Figure 5.16) worn by Sarah Wickes Waterman (and perhaps her daughter Mary and/or her granddaughter Sarah) is symbolic of this family's status as one of Rhode Island's elites.

Figure 5.16.
Side view of case study
silk gown.

Summary

In tracing the biography of this gown from the hand of Anna Maria Garthwaite (or possibly another textile designer) through to the family in Rhode Island that owned the gown, an additional layer to the story has been unraveled. In focusing on a single line in the catalog record which revealed the provenance of the dress as originating from Warwick, Rhode Island, I was able to trace the family to the slave trade—linking it to innumerable unnamed enslaved persons who worked in the Waterman family home, in the family's homestead, on their ships, or who were traded for the goods that were transported on their ships. As it turns out, this is not just a pretty dress.

ENDNOTES

1   Linda Baumgarten, *What Clothes Reveal: The Language of Clothing in Colonial and Federal America* (The Colonial Williamsburg Foundation & Yale University Press, 2002), 52.

2   Igor Kopytoff, "The Cultural Biography of Things: Commoditization as a Process," in *The Social Life of Things,* ed. Arjun Appadurai (Cambridge: Cambridge University Press, 1986), 90.

3   I presented my initial research on this dress during my lecture "Making Her Mark: Art and Fashion" at the Art Gallery of Ontario on June 22, 2024.

4   Alexandra Kim was able to view the dress in the conservation lab at Colonial Williamsburg in November 2024, and confirmed the presence of the linen lining in the bodice. Also see the catalog record, accessed February 15, 2024 at https://emuseum. history.org/objects/65868/gown

5   Typical widths of English silks from the period measure 19–21 inches. See Natalie Rothstein, *Silk Designs in the Eighteenth Century In the Collection of The Victoria & Albert Museum, London With a Complete Catalogue* (London: Little Brown Company, 1990), 27.

6   Linda Baumgarten, "Altered Historic Clothing," *Dress* (1998): 49.

7   Garthwaite's birth year is given as 1690 in the *Oxford Dictionary of National Biography*, but other sources show it as 1688. Extant examples of garments linked to Garthwaite's textile designs can be found in various dress collections, including the Metropolitan Museum of Art in New York, the Boston Museum of Fine Arts, the Victoria and Albert Museum in London, and the Fashion Museum in Bath.

8   See the object description as noted for this gown with textile attributed to Anna Maria Garthwaite, 1744 (woven), 1745–50 (made), 1780s altered, Victoria and Albert Museum (T.264-2966). Accessed March 25, 2025 https://collections.vam.ac.uk/item/O79606/gown-anna-maria-garthwaite/

9   See Anna Maria Garthwaite, Design on paper for Mr. Gregory, April 22, 1744, Victoria and Albert Museum (5982.10). https://collections.vam.ac.uk/item/O92305/design-garthwaite-anna-maria/

10 See the catalog record accessed February 15, 2024 at https://emuseum.history.org/objects/65868/gown

11 Rothstein, *Silk Designs in the Eighteenth Century*, 33–35.

12 See Ann Bermingham, *Learning to Draw: Studies in the Cultural History of a Polite and Useful Art* (New Haven and London: Yale University Press, 2000).

13 Rothstein, *Silk Designs in the Eighteenth Century*, 33–36.

14 These textile designs are housed in the Prints & Drawings Collection of the Victoria & Albert Museum and are accessible online.

15 Rothstein, *Silk Designs in the Eighteenth Century,* 34–35.

16 I examined numerous examples of Garthwaite's designs in the V&A Prints and Drawings Study Room in June 2023.

17 Rothstein, *Silk Designs in the Eighteenth Century*, 118.

18 *Ibid.,* 117.

19 See for example the designs for woven silk with similar colors and motifs from the 'Liddiard Set' in the V&A Museum collection, including designs by James Leman E.4468–1909 from 1718–19, and E.4487–1909 from 1721. Also see the unattributed textile design dating to 1719, E.4517–1909.

20 Rothstein, *Silk Designs in the Eighteenth Century*, 117.

21 Zara Anishanslin, *Portrait of a Woman in Silk: Hidden Histories of the British Atlantic World* (New Haven: Yale University Press, 2016), 56.

22 *Ibid.,* 115. The guild was also active in pursuing legislation to protect the industry from the importation of cotton chintz from India.

23   Gerald B. Hertz, "The English Silk Industry in the Eighteenth Century," *The English Historical Review* 24, no. 96 (October 1909): 711. Rothstein notes that the warp of the textile, which had to take greater strain, was typically sourced from Italy or China, while the weft was often sourced from Persia via Turkey. Rothstein, *Silk Designs in the Eighteenth Century*, 18.

24   Rothstein, *Silk Designs in the Eighteenth Century*, 27.

25   *Ibid.,* 16, 22.

26   *Ibid.*, 27.

27   *Ibid.*, 23.

28   Anishanslin, *Portrait of a Woman in Silk*, 83.

29   Extant examples of garments linked to Garthwaite can also be found in the Boston Museum of Fine Arts in Massachusetts, and other dress collections in the United States.

30   Rothstein, *Silk Designs in the Eighteenth Century*, 22.

31   Aileen Ribeiro, *Dress in the Eighteenth-Century* (New Haven: Yale University Press, 2002), 41.

32   *Ibid.*, 23.

33   For more on lace-patterned silk, see Rothstein, "1720–32 Lace Patterns" in *Silk Designs in the Eighteenth Century*, 40–42.

34   When the museum acquired the dress from the family in 1951, there were two other objects linked to it, including a yellow quilted petticoat backed with wool and dated to the 1750s, as well as a pair of silk damask shoes with leather soles, dated to the 1750s based on the label inside the shoes (made by John Hose in Cheapside London). These dates seem to correspond more closely with the marriage of Sarah Wickes daughter, Mary Waterman, in 1758.

35   See Christy Clark-Pujara, *Dark Work: The Business of Slavery in Rhode Island* (New York: New York University Press, 2016). My thanks to Dr. Clark-Pujara for her helpful suggestions on how I might research the family and its relationship to the slave trade.

36   Benoni Waterman was the son of Captain John Waterman (ca. 1666–1728). His father John was the grandson of Richard Waterman and Roger Williams.

37   Kay Kirlin Moore, *Descendants of Roger Williams*, Book I (Baltimore: Gateway Press, Inc., 1991), viii.

38   Clark-Pujara, *Dark Work,* 26.

39   *Ibid.*, 26-27.

40   *Ibid.*

41   Dorothy Higson White, "Waterman Line" in *Descendants of Roger Williams*, Book I (Baltimore: Gateway Press, Inc., 1991), 14.

42   "Historical Note," Benoni and John Waterman Family Papers, Rhode Island Historical Society. Accessed August 10, 2024 at https://www.rihs.org/mssinv/Mss787.htm. My thanks to the research staff at the Rhode Island Historical Society for their assistance in accessing the relevant family records.

43   Export Cargoes Manifests 1775-90, Volume 1, p. 13. Accessed August 14, 2024 at https://sosri.access.preservica.com/uncategorized/IO_dd4fcad0-e6bb-437c-8bcd-72be86bee39a/

44   *Ibid.* There are also other handwritten manifest lists on this site with evidence of the transportation of slaves to/from Rhode Island ports by other captains. This includes: 256 slaves transported on the Sloop Rembrance [sic] in April 1774; 2554 slaves on the Sloop Florida on April 1774; 2000 slaves on the ship Unity on April 1776; 7000 slaves on the Schooner Sally on May 1776; and 'about 180' slaves on the Sloop Two Brothers on May 1776.

45   See The Trans-Atlantic Slave Trade Database, Intra-American Database Downloads. Accessed August 14, 2024 at www.slavevoyages.org

46   Clark-Pujara, *Dark Work*, 49.

47   *Ibid.*, 19.

48   Higson White, *Descendants of Roger Williams*, 14.

49   Clark-Pujara, *Dark Work*, 27.

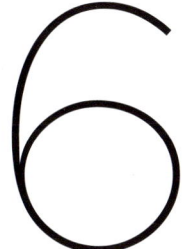

6

FASHION &
THE DANDY

A Man's Tailcoat
and Pantaloons,
circa 1820s

In the early nineteenth century, men's fashions turned away from the artifice of the colorful silk embroidered suit of the previous century and instead embraced a more practical and restrained look inspired in part by English country riding dress.[1] The textile of choice for the coat became wool, which could be cut and shaped to give emphasis to the masculine ideal of a lithe, muscular form.[2] This aesthetic ideal will be considered in relation to a man's tailored dark blue wool tailcoat and cream silk pantaloons dating to 1825–30 with a British provenance, from the collection of the Los Angeles County Museum of Art (Figure 6.1). In the 1820s, this type of coat, cut away just above the waistline and with tails, would have been described as a 'dress-coat'.[3] Although the terms 'breeches' and 'pantaloons' are often now used as synonyms, in the 1820s, breeches were used to describe a garment for the lower body ending at the knee, with pantaloons ending at the calf or above the ankle.[4] These two impeccably tailored garments represent key pieces in a man's dress ensemble from that time, and will be analyzed in relation to the archetype of the dandy in the first part of the nineteenth century. As poet and literary critic J. A. Barbey d'Aurevilly (1808–89) observed: "A Dandy may spend ten hours a day dressing, if he likes, but once he is dressed, he thinks no more about it. It is for others to notice that he is well dressed."[5]

OBSERVATION

Tailcoat

The case study wool tailcoat is double-breasted, cut away at the waist, and has tails (Figure 6.2).[6] The coat features a high rolled collar of brown silk velvet with notches that form two overlapping points (known as a 'lark's tongue' or 'thrush's tongue') in the revers (Figure 6.3).[7] The coat has two rows of gilt brass buttons and long sleeves with a small, gathered head. The black-silk lined cuffs flare out at the wrist and have working buttonholes with three silk-covered buttons. The back of the coat is shaped to create a long lean line and includes two non-functional pocket flaps and two decorative gilt brass buttons at the centre back waist (Figure 6.5). The tail of the coat measures 14.6 inches (37 cm) across and 19.7 inches (50 cm) long. The vent has double inverted kick pleats with two gilt brass buttons close to the hem and there are two concealed pockets, one in the lining (Figure 6.4) and the other, a 'bottle pocket', accessible from the left side seam of the tail (Figure 6.5). The coat has been partially lined with wool and the hem of the tail has been left unfinished.

OPPOSITE: Figure 6.2.
Detail of coat body.

Figure 6.3. Collar detail.

Figure 6.4. Inside the coat, showing stitching in front and inside pocket of tail.

Figure 6.5. Detail showing concealed pocket.

This coat has been tailored to fit a man with a chest size of 35 inches (88.9 cm) and a waist of 31 inches (78.4 cm). The centre back of the coat (from top of the collar to the hem of the tails) measures 39.5 inches (100.3 cm). The coat has a thick layer of canvas and red wool or felt padding that shapes the shoulders and front chest; this has been secured at the chest area with parallel rows of stitching visible on the inside of the garment (Figure 6.4).[8] The high rolled 'horse' collar has been heavily stiffened, likely with buckram and/or canvas.[9] The two-piece sleeves, which measure 32 inches (83 cm) in length, are lined with unbleached cotton for the sleeve heads and arms. The topstitching on the coat has been rendered in two colors of thread – a dark blue/black thread that matches the color of the wool, as well as a golden yellow color thread used to accentuate the buttonholes (Figure 6.4). The coat is entirely hand-sewn with small even stitches. There is no tailor's stamp or label, but there are two small black ink marks on the lining near the underarm which may be tailor's marks.

The body, tails and sleeves of the coat are made of a dark blue plain weave wool. The quality of the wool is such that the hem of the tails and the edges of certain seams have been left unfinished. The collar of the coat is made of a saddle-brown silk velvet with a short nap. The sleeves are lined with an unbleached cotton and the cuffs are finished in black silk.

This coat shows signs of wear, with evidence of some minor rubbing visible in the wool especially at the mid-back and near the concealed inside pocket (Figure 6.5). The back of the velvet collar also has signs of rubbing, and there is a small cut in the fabric on one side close to the top edge. The black silk twill used for the cuffs is torn on the left side and the cotton lining of the sleeves is stained at the sleeve head. There are several small areas that have been stitched with golden yellow thread, but it is not obvious when such repairs were made.

Pantaloons

The flat-front pantaloons which have been paired with the tailcoat are constructed from a cream-white-colored silk crepe (Figure 6.6).[10] The pantaloons have a high, wide waistband with a small slash pocket lined with cotton on the proper right that measures 3.625 inches wide and 6.25 inches deep (9.2 cm x 15.875 cm). There are seven self-covered buttons (0.8 inches or 2 cm in width) at the front flap closure. The front flap and waistband are lined in white cotton. The pantaloons measure 29 inches (73.7 cm) at the waist, 36 inches (91.4 cm) at the hips, and 24.25 inches (61.6 cm) at the inseam. This garment was hand-sewn with a single color of thread that matches the color of the silk crepe.

Figure 6.6. Pantaloons.

There is ease at the back of the pantaloons further accentuated by the slight gathering of fabric at the back waistband. The centre back of the waistband has a cotton gusset to provide ease at the waist if needed. The pantaloons are tapered to the mid-calf and the inseam measures 24.25 inches (62.2 cm). The leg openings are reinforced with a band of cream-colored silk, with closure by means of lacing the four small round stitched holes. The cord for the right leg closure is missing, and it is not obvious whether or not the cord in the left closure is original to the garment or a replacement.

These pantaloons, which are made of a delicate silk crepe, show signs of wear and use; the seat has been stretched out, and the fabric appears soiled in places, especially at the waistband. There are also several dark colored stains of unknown origin on the back of the garment at the waistband and seat. There is no evidence of insect damage, repair or conservation work.

REFLECTION

These impeccably tailored menswear garments invoke formality, elegance and status. The delicate silk pantaloons suggest a life of leisure and ease for a man unaccustomed to work. The structure of the wool tailcoat was engineered with shaping and padding, while the drapiness of the silk crepe pantaloons, designed to cling to the body, largely relied on the muscularity of the body underneath to give it form. Such garments must have been worn by an elite man with a lithe, muscular figure who sought to present the aesthetic masculine ideal for that time of broad shoulders, narrow waist, and muscular thighs.[11]

The coat is made of a very high-quality wool that is so tightly woven that the edges of the tail's hem were left raw. The construction of this coat very closely matches Norah Waugh's patterned diagram for a dress-coat from c.1825.[12] As Waugh points out, such a coat was considered appropriate for "all dress occasions, both day and evening, except Court."[13] Illustrations of similar coats in fashion publications from the period point to this type of coat as being relatively static in form (aside from minor variations) from the turn of the century until about 1830, after which time it was supplanted by the frock coat for everyday wear.[14]

To complete the look, a man would also wear a starched white linen shirt, a linen cravat, a waist-length silk or wool vest/waistcoat with a high stand collar, and slim-fitting silk breeches or pantaloons (as it was photographed in Figure 6.1), and accessories including a tall hat, leather gloves, walking stick, watch fob, and footwear that might range from riding boots to evening slippers (Figure 6.7). The man who wore this tailcoat may have opted to wear trousers (or *trowsers* as they were then known)—another fashionable option for daytime (Figure 6.8). During the 1820s, trousers became increasingly popular for both day and evening wear (Figure 6.9).

Figure 6.7.
Costumes Parisiens, 1817.
Victoria and Albert
Museum.

1820. *Costume Parisien.*

(1917.)

Habit à collet de velours, large et haut. Cravate en fichu.
Gilet à schall. Pantalon mélangé. Guêtres écrues.

Figure 6.8.
Costumes Parisiens, **1820.**
Victoria and Albert
Museum.

Figure 6.9.
Costumes Parisiens, **1824.**
Rijksmuseum.

Many museum dress collections have elite menswear garments from the nineteenth century and extant examples of similar coats can be found elsewhere.[15] More tailcoats seem to have survived than breeches or pantaloons, perhaps because the wool coats were more durable than silk or buckskin pantaloons. The Los Angeles County Museum of Art has another man's dress ensemble (tailcoat and trousers) dated to the 1820s in its collection (Figure 6.10). This tailcoat is made of a fine plain weave brown wool with a notched collar of silk velvet.[16]

The Victoria and Albert Museum has a double-breasted coat with a similar cut and silhouette made of blue wool, dated to 1823–30 with British provenance (Figure 6.11).[17] Like the case-study tailcoat, the collar of this coat features an unusual detail in the notch known as the 'lark's tongue'.[18]

Figure 6.11.
Double-breasted coat of blue woollen
broadcloth, c.1823–30, previously dated
to 1815–20, Great Britain.
Victoria and Albert Museum
(T.118-1953).

OPPOSITE: Figure 6.10.
Man's dress ensemble, c.1820, New England.
Los Angeles County Museum of Art.

Although the name of the man who once wore the case study tailcoat has been lost to time, the imprints of his body and life live on in this garment. It is clear that he was a man who took notice of the subtle nuances in men's fashion in the 1820s, such as the 'lark's tongue' notch in the high horse collar, the full, gathered sleeve head, and the narrow and overly long sleeves. These fashionable details of the coat and its exquisite tailoring bring to mind the figure of the dandy. This leads me to ask: how was the figure of a dandy portrayed in the early part of the nineteenth century? And would the man who wore an ensemble like this particular tailcoat and pantaloons have been considered a dandy?

INTERPRETATION

According to the Oxford English Dictionary, the noun 'dandy' originated around 1780 and describes "one who studies above everything to dress elegantly and fashionably; a beau, fop, 'exquisite'."[19] The most notorious and influential dandy of the nineteenth century was the British socialite George Bryan 'Beau' Brummell (1778–1840). The son of a minor equerry at court, Brummell was able to distinguish himself with his wit and his wardrobe in order to become the exemplar of taste and elegance in his dress within elite society for a time.[20] As Christopher Breward noted, Brummell's genius lay in "establishing a rule of taste based on subjective aesthetic criteria and the careful exercise of personal choice, rather than deference to status earned through family lineage or traditional forms of power exchange."[21]

There are very few known portraits of Brummell, which is somewhat surprising given his reputation as a man with handsome countenance, classical physique and elegance in dress.[22] In an 1805 watercolor portrait by British artist Richard Dighton (1790–1880), Brummell stands in 3/4 profile wearing his "customary morning attire": an expertly tailored dark blue wool dress-coat with gold buttons, spotless white linen shirt, a buff waistcoat, close-fitting light-colored pantaloons, and polished riding boots (Figure 6.12).[23] The sleek lines of his clothing in combination with his regal posture and demeanour convey both refinement and ease.

Tales of Brummell's fastidious attention to his dress, particularly in terms of his achieving perfection in the artful tying of his cravat, served as inspiration for the book *Neckclothitania,* published in 1818 by an anonymous author who described himself as 'One of the Cloth'.[24] Several other authors in the nineteenth century were inspired by Brummell's life and influence, including the well-known novelists Honoré de Balzac (1799–1850) and J. A. Barbey d'Aurevilly (1808–89), as well as the lesser known military men turned biographers Captain Reese Howell Gronow (1794–1865) and Captain William J. Jesse (dates unknown).[25] Writing with reverence, these accounts celebrated Brummell's wit and sartorial elegance. In 1830, Balzac wrote: "Brummell was quite right to view CLOTHING as the culmination of elegant living; for it governs opinions, it determines them,

Figure 6.12.
Richard Dighton,
Watercolor Portrait
of George 'Beau'
Brummell, 1805.
Art Images via Getty
Images.

it reigns!"[26] Balzac explained that in relation to clothing, "elegance consists of an extreme refinement in the details of the outfit; it is less the simplicity of luxury than a luxurious simplicity."[27] Jesse argued that Brummell "most assuredly was no dandy," since he did not seek "glaring extravaganzas in dress" but rather aimed to produce "a perfectly elegant general effect."[28] Jesse further argued that: "There was in fact nothing extreme about Brummell's personal appearance but his extreme cleanliness and neatness, and whatever time and attention he devoted to his dress, the result was perfect."[29] Even though Brummell has over time come to be known as the exemplar of the dandy, according to these nineteenth century authors, Brummell was not "a slave of fashion", but instead achieved elegance through careful management of his wardrobe.[30]

To achieve the perfect fit, Brummell relied on the skillful work of his tailor, but reportedly "scorned to share his fame" with him.[31] Nonetheless, Brummell's tailor was unmasked as "a Mr. Weston of Old Bond Street"—a "superior genius" who helped Brummell to execute "his sublime imagination" when it came to his dress.[32] By the early nineteenth century, English tailors had become renowned for their skills in shaping wool, molding with heat and steam, and concealing imperfections of the figure with padding to help achieve the fashionable ideal.[33]

The development of the tape measure and the square rule also encouraged a more scientific approach to tailoring (Figure 6.13). Such innovations led to the publication of numerous tailoring guides, including *The Tailor's Friendly Instructor* by J. Wyatt (second edition) published in 1822, which included detailed instructions on how to measure a man for a tailcoat and patterns for various tailored garments.[34]

Figure 6.13.
Jos. Trentsensky, *Der Schneider (The Tailor),* **c.1825.**
Colored lithograph. Imagno/Getty Images.

For the winter season of 1824–25, a man and his tailor could seek guidance on fashionable dress in periodicals such as *The Cyclopedia of the British Costume, which contains the most Fashionable Make and Cut, also the most prevailing Colors and Patterns from the various Manufactories.*[35] In issue 4, a suitable dress-coat for that winter season was described as a well-fitting coat with square cut lapels, very full shoulder heads and closely fitting sleeves with a long slit at the wrist—features that are very similar to the case study coat.[36] Of particular note is that the coat was "to be cut across the small of the waist, so as to cause them to set without the least appearance of any wrinkles and cut rather too small at the bottom of the lapel, so as to cause the coat to be rather on the stretch when buttoned, which, if properly managed, will cause an excellent fit round the small of the waist".[37] Such a coat was to be worn with dress breeches or pantaloons that were "tight to the shape of the knee band" and without fullness "across the top of the front."[38] This description, which closely matches the case study tailcoat as depicted on the dressed mannequin (Figure 6.1), implies that the desirable silhouette for a man—broad shoulders and chest with a narrow waist—could be achieved, in part, with tailoring.

Given the associations of dandy with a man who paid excessive attention to his dress, satirical prints from that period provide visual clues as to what was considered excessive or immoderate. As art historian Diana Donald has argued, satirical prints from this era served to convey fashion information to the wider public, often in terms of what not to wear and the extremes to be avoided.[39] An elite man was expected to pay attention to his dress, but too much attention was also equally problematic, and as I have argued elsewhere, the difference between an ensemble considered elegant and a slovenly one could sometimes come down to the finest of details.[40] In spite of Brummell's infamy, he seems to have escaped the sharp eye of British satirists like James Gillray (1756–1815) and Thomas Rowlandson (1757–1827).[41] Nonetheless, there are innumerable satirical prints from the period that mock the extremes of fashion and the figure of the dandy.

In "The Dandy's Coat of Arms" published on March 28, 1819, George Cruickshank (1792–1878) equated the dandy to an inanimate dress form with donkey ears (Figure 6.14). Two liveried monkeys present the dandy's wardrobe, consisting of a tall black hat, a face-framing cravat, waist-cinching stays, a blue tailcoat with a broad chest and narrow waist, white gloves, buff-colored breeches, high riding boots, gloves and various bottles of perfume and rouge. At the heart of the form, within the lining of the coat, there is a half-man, half-woman shape. The hand-written caption reads: "*The Sexes impaled improper between two butterflies.*" Cruikshank's satirical print suggests that the dandy's singular pursuit of fashion in the extreme was odiously effeminate and indecorous.

In the satirical print *Lacing a Dandy,* published on January 26, 1818, a dandy is shown in the act of dressing, and his shoulders, thighs and calves have been padded (Figure 6.15). Aided by his servant and a French hairdresser, the dandy is being tightly laced into a corset and he has instructed his aides to pull as hard as they can on the lacing. In reply, the French hairdresser mocks his master's "John Bull Belly" – a reference to the character-type of a well-fed plain-speaking British man.[42] This satire mocks the dandy's pursuit of fashion using extreme artifice.

Although Brummell was renowned for his elegance, fastidiousness and pursuit of perfection, he did not condone extremes in fashion. The famous Regency courtesan Harriette Wilson (1786–1845) recounted in her memoirs that Brummell had once said: "If John Bull turns round to look after you, you are not well dressed; but either too stiff, too tight, or too fashionable."[43] This oft-repeated adage by Brummell underlines his belief in tasteful restraint in dress.

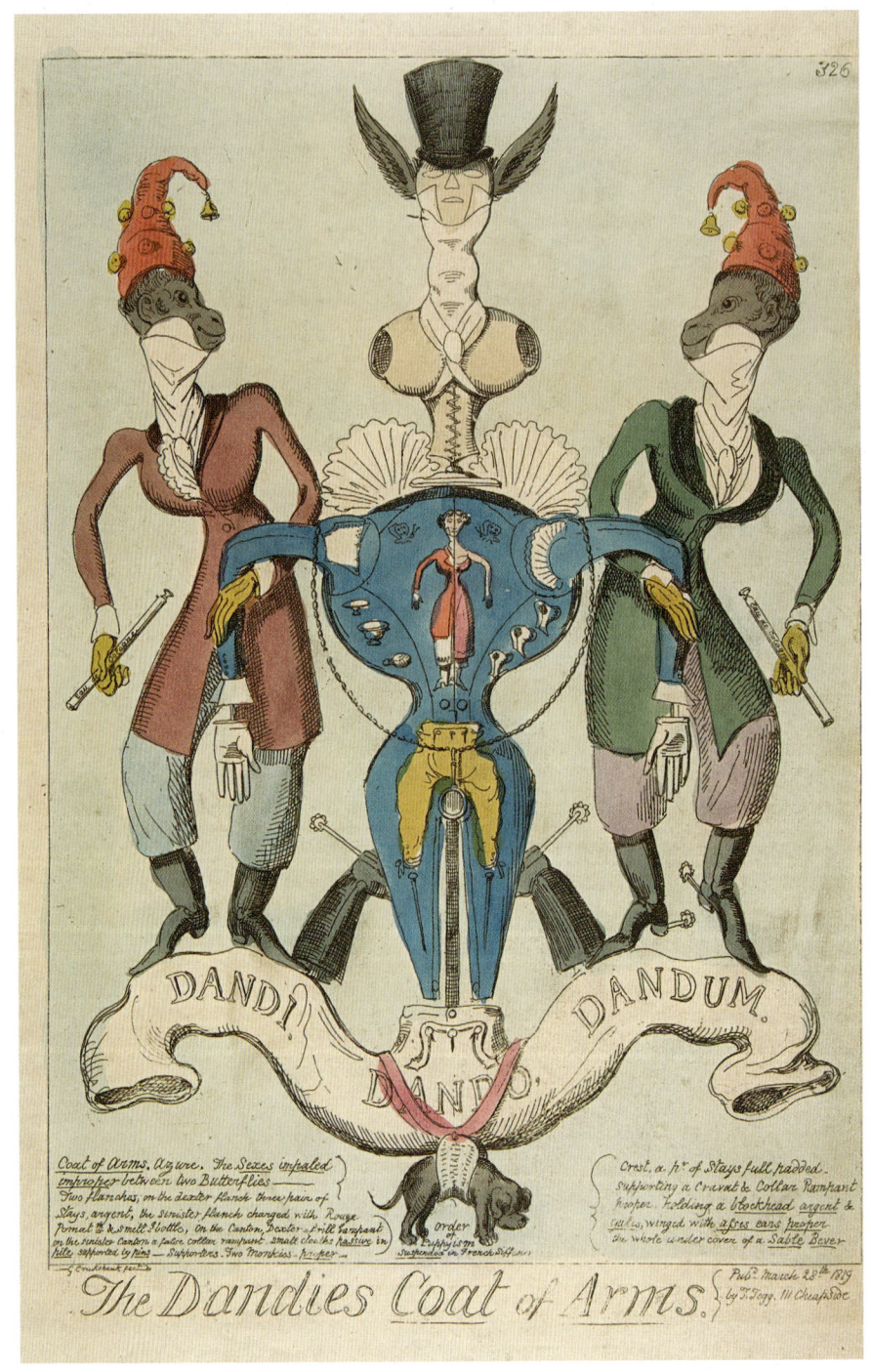

Figure 6.14.
George Cruikshank, *The Dandies Coat of Arms*, published by Thomas Tegg, March 28, 1819.
Metropolitan Museum of Art (1970.541.256).

Figure 6.15.
Anonymous, *Lacing a Dandy*, published by Thomas Tegg, January 26, 1818.
Metropolitan Museum of Art (69.524.35).

Summary

The case study man's dress ensemble of tailored wool tailcoat and silk pantaloons embodies the highest quality tailoring from the early nineteenth century. These garments were made to order, cut and sewn by hand using the finest wool and silk. And although the garments as illustrated on the dressed mannequin did not come from the wardrobe of one man, together they serve to illustrate the desired and fashionable silhouette for the 1820s: broad shoulders, narrow waist and well-defined legs and calves. And while certain details suggest a close attention to fashionable nuances, it is impossible to tell how these items were actually worn in real life. Perhaps the man who wore this tailcoat also donned a corset to exaggerate a close fit across his chest and waist. He may have worn his pantaloons with added padding underneath to suggest more muscular thighs and calves, or he may have instead worn slim trousers. As this analysis has shown, it was not the specific elements of a man's wardrobe that defined the figure of the dandy, but rather the way in which a man put the components together (including the type of underwear, the accessories, the perfumes and makeup); and, moreover, the attitude and bearing of the man donning them. As the poet, essayist and art critic Charles Baudelaire (1821–67) eloquently argued in 1863, "Dandyism is not even, as many other thoughtless people seem to believe, an immoderate taste for dress and material elegance. For the perfect dandy these things are only a perfect symbol of the aristocratic superiority of his spirit."[44]

ENDNOTES

1   Sharon Sadako Takeda et al., *Reigning Men: Fashion in Menswear, 1715–2015* (Prestel Publishing: Los Angeles County Museum of Art & DelMonico Books, 2016), 170–175. See also Norah Waugh, *The Cut of Men's Clothes: 1600–1900* (New York: Routledge, 1964), 112–150.

2   Joanne Begiato, *Manliness in Britain 1760–1900: Bodies, Emotion, and Material Culture* (Manchester: Manchester University Press, 2020), 41.

3   See Waugh, *The Cut of Men's Clothes*, 112.

4   *Ibid.*

5   J. A. Barbey d'Aurevilly, *Of Dandyism and of George Brummell*, translated from the French by Douglas Ainsley, (London: J.M Dent & Sons, 1897), 73.

6   The coat has been cataloged by the museum as follows: Man's Tailcoat, probably England 1825–1830. LACMA (AC 1993.127.1) Credit: Costume Council Curatorial Discretionary Fund.

7   Lucy Johnson, *Nineteenth-Century Fashion in Detail* (V&A Publications, 2005), 138.

8   The layer of wool and canvas is only partially visible if the fabric is lifted near the armhole.

9   'Horse' collar is the term used by Norah Waugh to describe a similar collar for a dress-coat c.1825. Waugh, *The Cut of Men's Clothes*, 124.

10 This garment has been cataloged as follows: Man's Breeches (Pantaloons), Scotland, 1820. LACMA M.2007.211.1076. Purchased with funds provided by Suzanne A. Saperstein and Michael and Ellen Michelson, with additional funding from the Costume Council, the Edgerton Foundation, Gail and Gerald Oppenheimer, Maureen H. Shapiro, Grace Tsao, and Lenore and Richard Wayne.

11 As Begiato points out, this ideal was inspired by the classical bodies of Greek statues of antiquity. Begiato, *Manliness in Britain 1760–1900*, 36–37.

12 Waugh, *The Cut of Men's Clothes*, 124. The only discernable difference between the pattern and the case study tailcoat is at the cuff; the case study tailcoat has three buttonholes instead of a single buttonhole.

13 *Ibid.*, 112.

14 See for example V&A Museum E.22396:68-1957 and V&A Museum E.22396:91-1957. Also see Lydia Edwards, *How to Read a Suit* (London: Bloomsbury, 2020), 76.

15 See also Man's coat of brown wool with velvet collar from the V&A Museum, T.683-1913; Man's wool tailcoat from The Met 2014.501; Man's blue silk tailcoat from The Met 1981.210.4.

16 This brown wool tailcoat's accession number is AC1993.127.5.

17 The gilt brass buttons on this coat were stamped "Hammond Turner & Sons, Extra Superfine." According to research on the history of this button maker, the company was known as Hammond Turner and Sons during the early 1820s. See History, accessed July 23, 2024 at https://hammond-turner.com/history/

18 See the detail photo of the 'lark's tongue' notch in Johnson, *Nineteenth-Century Fashion in Detail*, 138. At the time the 'M' notch style was more common.

19 "Dandy," Oxford English Dictionary online, accessed July 26, 2024 at https://www.oed.com/dictionary/dandy_n1?tab=meaning_and_use#7429392

20 By 1816, Brummell had lost favor with the Prince Regent and was heavily in debt, and fled in disgrace to France.

21 Christopher Breward, "Redressed," in *Fashioning Masculinities: The Art of Menswear*, edited by Rosalind McKever & Claire Wilcox with Marta Franceschini (London: V&A Publishing, 2022): 168.

22 As described by Captain [William J.] Jesse, *The Life of George Brummell, Esq. Commonly Called Beau Brummell* (London: Saunders and Otley, 1844), 48.

23 Jesse, *The Life of George Brummell*, 62.

24 See *Neckclothitania, or Tieatania: Being an Essay on Starchers* by One of the Cloth (London: J. J. Stockdale, 1818).

25 Aside from the work of these authors, there are a myriad of books, films and scholarly publications that include Brummell, and they are far too numerous to list here. Most contemporary books draw on these three nineteenth-century sources. See for example, James Laver, *Dandies* (London, Ebenezer Baylis & Son, Limited: 1968) and Ian Kelly, *Beau Brummell: The Ultimate Dandy* (Edinburgh: Hodder & Stoughton, 2005). Rather than relying on the interpretations of others for my analysis, I have read and referenced the nineteenth-century texts by Balzac, d'Aurevilly and Jesse.

26 Honore de Balzac, *Treatise on Elegant Living*, [first published in *La Mode* October–November 1830], translated by Napoleon Jeffries (Cambridge: Wakefield Press, 2010), 68. Emphasis in original.

27 Balzac, *Treatise on Elegant Living*, 72.

28 Jesse, *The Life of George Brummell*, 59.

29 *Ibid.*, 69.

30 See for example Jesse, *The Life of George Brummell*, 62.

31 D'Aurevilly, *Of Dandyism and of George Brummell*, 71–72.

32 Rees Howell Gronow, *The Reminiscences and Recollections of Captain Gronow: Being Anecdotes of The Camp, Court, Clubs and Society* 1810–1860, vol. 1 (London: John C. Nimmo, 1892), 45.

33 Waugh, *The Cut of Men's Clothes*, 112.

34 See J. Wyatt, Plate 1: Pattern for Man's Coat in *The Tailor's Friendly Instructor*, second edition (London: J. Hariss, 1822).

35 My thanks to curator Clarissa Esguerra for alerting me to this rare volume in the collection of the LACMA Research Library.

36 *The Cyclopedia of the British Costume, which contains the most Fashionable Make and Cut, also the most prevailing Colors and Patterns from the various Manufactorie no. 4,* Winter Season of 1824 and 1825 (W. Hearn Publisher: London), 121–122.

37 *Ibid.*

38 *Ibid.*, 123.

39 Diana Donald, *Followers of Fashion: Graphic Satires from the Georgian Period* (London: Hayward Gallery Publishing, 2002), 8–9.

40 Ingrid E. Mida, "Fashion and Satirical Prints in 1799: James Gillray and *Elegance Democratique*", *Costume* 58, no. 2 (2024): 159–179.

41 Both the British Museum and the Lewis Walpole Library at Yale University house a large collection of the work of British satirists. Although both collections include a large number of prints related to the figure of the dandy, Brummell does not appear to have been made the subject of such satire.

42 John Bull is an invented character who represented an honest and plain-dealing Englishman, and whose stout figure represented prosperity "in an age where rosy cheeks and plump faces were a sign of good health." See Ben Johnson, "John Bull," Historic UK, accessed December 27, 2023 at https://www.historic-uk.com/CultureUK/John-Bull/

43 Harriette Wilson, *The Memoirs of Harriette Wilson* (London: Eveleigh Nash, 1909), 47.

44 Charles Baudelaire, "The Dandy," in *The Painter of Modern Life and Other Essays*, translated and edited by Jonathan Mayne (London: Phaidon Press, 2010 [1964]), 29.

7

FASHION & GENDER

A Boy's Cashmere Frock, circa 1855

During the Victorian era, the traditional roles for men and women were strictly upheld with clear demarcations between masculine and feminine attire. A notable exception was the clothing of young boys and girls, who were typically dressed alike until about age five. From a practical standpoint, having young children wear petticoats or frocks until they were fully toilet-trained made sense, since doing laundry was a lengthy and tedious process. The term 'breeching' described a rite of passage when a boy donned his first pair of breeches or trousers, and, as dress historian Anne Buck explains, this occasion, which marked the transition of the child from the domain of the feminine to masculine, was often planned for and celebrated by the family.[1] The age at which a boy put on his first breeches or trousers ranged from about four to eight years.[2] The timing of this transition was largely a matter of parental preference and that decision was influenced by whether or not the boy was toilet trained, his height, and the family's socioeconomic class. Not surprisingly, fathers were typically more "eager to see their sons out of frocks and into breeches."[3] The first tailored outfit for a boy might consist of a tunic or coatdress worn over light-colored trousers followed by a gradual progression towards a tailored suit at about age fifteen.[4] Around the turn of the century, there was a marked shift in societal attitudes that resulted in a more explicit expression of masculine identity in infant boys' clothing and a notable restriction in the clothing options available to boys, such that by about 1920, young boys were no longer wearing dresses, nor wearing pastel shades such as lilac or pink.[5]

This case study considers a child's frock with an English provenance dated to circa 1855 from the collection of the Los Angeles County Museum of Art (Figure 7.1).[6] According to the dealer from whom the museum purchased the frock, it was likely worn by a boy, and the frock was cataloged as such. This garment provides material evidence of the practice of boys and girls wearing similar styles of dresses in the mid-nineteenth century, and as Anne Buck observed, such a garment also "bears the imprint not only of the child who wore it, but also, of part of a way of life."[7]

OBSERVATION

Construction

This English boy's frock features a round neckline, short sleeves, and a double-tiered full skirt. There are ten silk buttons and silk tassels at the centre front as well as a button and silk tassels on each oversleeve (Figure 7.2). The neckline and waist are finished with piping. The frock closes at the back with eight metal hooks and thread loops concealed under a placket. The overall length of the garment is 19.7 inches (50 cm) and the waist measures 26.7 inches (68 cm). The circumference of the skirt hem measures 38.1 inches (97 cm). The frock was handsewn using a cream-colored thread.

Figure 7.2.
Detail of sleeve on boy's frock.

Close examination of the interior reveals numerous small, irregular pattern pieces used in the skirt and sleeve construction.[8] Although not readily visible, this piecing is more noticeable at the seams and in the interior, and the underside of the upper skirt front includes a small, rounded piece of fabric that has been folded under rather than being cut off, with the shape of this particular piece resembling a sleeve head. This evidence indicates that the frock was constructed from another garment.

Textiles and Materials

The frock is made of a lightweight fine cream-colored cashmere twill woven in Kashmir, India, and this luxurious soft cloth with its sumptuous, embroidered design motif was often used to make Kashmir shawls. The fabric for the bodice, sleeves, and parts of the skirt is lavishly embellished with embroidery in a stylized floral motif with curved tips called *buta* (Figure 7.3). This embroidery incorporates fine silk cord that has been couched to the cashmere cloth with silk embroidery thread. The bodice and sleeves are lined with unbleached white cotton.

Figure 7.3.
Detail of the embroidery and silk tassels on skirt.

Use, Alteration and Wear

In terms of use and wear, the boy's frock was likely worn more than once since the white cotton bodice lining shows general soiling with dirt smudges at the neckline. The cream-colored cashmere also appears slightly darker towards the lower part of the skirt. There are no signs of insect damage, repair, or conservation treatment. As noted earlier, the extensive piecing of this boy's frock indicates it was made from another garment, but there is no sign of subsequent alterations to the boy's frock. There are no marks of identification by a tailor or the former owner.

REFLECTION

The overall impression of this frock is one of refinement and elegance—an effect produced by the high quality of the cashmere cloth, the ornate embroidery motif, and the luxurious silk tassels. Although the frock has been pieced together from another garment—perhaps from a woman's unfitted jacket like that shown in Figure 7.4—this work was undertaken with much care and considerable skill. [9] The irregular pieces have been put together so that the recycling of another garment is barely perceptible, and the beauty of the embroidery pattern has been used to best advantage. The survival of the boy's frock suggests that the original garment and/ or the frock held deep sentimental value to the mother of the boy that once wore it, even though their names have been lost to time.

Figure 7.4.
Woman's Jacket (Paletot), cashmere twill with silk embroidery, c.1865, India (Kashmir) for the English market. Los Angeles County Museum of Art (M.2007.211.193).

The sumptuous cashmere used in the case study frock seems to be an unusual choice for a child, and it is unclear as to what distinguishes this as a boy's frock. LACMA has two other examples of boy's frocks in their collection, including a boy's cotton frock with broderie anglaise (Figure 7.5) dating to circa 1855, as well as a seaside or croquet cotton frock and cape dating to the 1860s (Figure 7.6). These cotton frocks are similar in length to the case study frock, measuring about 20–22 inches (50.8–55.9 cm) in length, and the length of all three garments suggests that they were likely worn by boys around three years old. However, the cotton frocks would have been easier to launder and in this way more practical for a young boy than one made of fine cashmere.

Figure 7.5.
Boy's cotton frock with broderie anglaise, c.1855.
Los Angeles County Museum of Art (M.2007.211.89).

Figure 7.6.
Boy's Seaside or Croquet Frock and Cape (cotton), c.1860.
Los Angeles County Museum of Art (M.2007.211.93a-b.).

Fashion plates of the period often depicted boys with props such as swords, hoops, drums, dogs or boats (Figure 7.7). In the absence of a label or prop that identifies the child as a boy, the child's gender in such images may be ambiguous.

There are numerous photographs from the mid-nineteenth century that include young boys dressed in elaborate frocks, including the daguerreotype portrait of Francis Alofsen from 1855 (Figure 7.8).

Figure 7.7.
Le Moniteur de la Mode, June 1857.
Metropolitan Museum of Art.

Figure 7.8.
Brady & Co., Daguerreotype portrait of Francis Alofsen, 1855.
Metropolitan Museum of Art (2015.400.77).

In an undated portrait in cabinet card format, brothers Sidney and Edward Stoddard were dressed in short-sleeved frocks with full skirts (Figure 7.9). Had the names of the boys not been written in ink in the album, the elaborate nature of their full-skirted frocks might have created some ambiguity as to their gender. The same could be said of the ornate short frock and curled hair of Elmer E. White captured in an undated carte-de-visite (Figure 7.10). Such photographs confirm that in the mid-nineteenth century, young boys were often dressed in elaborate frocks.

Figure 7.9.
Unknown photographer, Portrait of Sidney and Edward Stoddard, undated cabinet card.
The Image Centre, Toronto Metropolitan University.

Figure 7.10.
Unknown photographer,
Portrait of Elmer E.
Witte, undated carte
de visite. Courtesy of
Drs. K. and B. Bohleke.

The case study frock offers additional material evidence of the practice of elite young boys wearing dresses during the mid-nineteenth century. The opulent nature of the textile and its embellishment are distinctive, and the recycling of another garment to make this into a child's frock is unique. And yet in the absence of specific information that links this garment to a named boy, there is some ambiguity as to what distinguishes this particular garment as a boy's frock. In her study of age-related clothing codes for boys in Britain between 1850 and 1900, Clare Rose observed published texts aimed at middle-class women assumed "a shared understanding of the norms for young boys' dresses without needing to spell out what these were or how they differed from girls' dresses."[10] The material qualities of this boy's frock point to the following research questions: Does this frock conform to fashionable norms for boys in the 1850s? And if so, what distinguishes this frock as being suitable for a boy? What guidance was given to mothers regarding the dressing of their young children during the mid-nineteenth century?

INTERPRETATION

Fashion is closely associated with gender—the cultural construction of identity that distinguishes man from woman, and boy from girl. To modern [western] eyes, there is a high correlation between a dress and feminine attire, such that a mid-nineteenth century child's dress—like this boy's frock—might at first glance be assumed to be a girl's dress. However, as Judith Butler has argued, the concept of gender is not fixed but rather exists as "a relative point of convergence among culturally and historically specific sets of relations".[11] In Daniel Thomas Cook's historiography of children's dress, he argues that "it is not the dress that makes the child, but rather the (stated or unstated) view of childhood that makes the meaning of the dress."[12]

The survival of extant dress worn by children generally privileges garments that were worn by the elite. The Victoria and Albert Museum has an ivory-colored silk frock dated to 1843 that is comparable in both color and cut to the case study frock (Figure 7.11). This frock was worn in 1843 by Albert Edward, Prince of Wales (1840–1910), Queen Victoria's first son and second child. After the artist Franz Xaver Winterhalter (1805–1873) painted a portrait of the young prince at age three wearing this dress (Figure 7.12), Queen Victoria noted in her journal on August 24, 1843 that the portrait "was the most spirited & beautiful likeness of the Boy, imaginable".[13] In 1846, Winterhalter painted another portrait of Queen Victoria and her family, and the second son Alfred (who was three at the time) wore a similar dress.[14]

Figure 7.11.
Boy's dress of ivory-colored silk, worn by Albert Edward, Prince of Wales; English, c.1843. Victoria and Albert Museum (T20.1933).

Figure 7.12.
Franz Xaver Winterhalter, Portrait of Edward VII (1841–1910) when Albert
Edward, Prince of Wales, was a child, 1843.
Oil on canvas (128.3 x 102.8 cm). Royal Collection Trust.

Given the English provenance of the case study frock, the clothing worn by
Queen Victoria's sons represents a notable fashion precedent. Although the case
study frock lacks a waist sash and is made of cashmere rather than silk, the cut
and silhouette with its wide neckline, short sleeves, and full skirt are similar to the
frocks worn by Queen Victoria's young sons. Several decades later in 1888, Queen
Victoria's young grandchildren—Prince Arthur and Princess Patricia—were dressed
identically in short frocks with frilled necklines and waist sashes (Figure 7.13).

Figure 7.13.
Queen Victoria with two
of her grandchildren,
Prince Arthur of
Connaught and Princess
Patricia of Connaught,
c.1888.
Photo by Hulton Archive/
Getty Images.

The Metropolitan Museum of Art has several children's dresses made of wool and silk that might have been worn by a boy or a girl in the 1850s, but only one is comparable in style to the case study frock.[15] A child's dress made with a creamy yellow wool, its short sleeves, open neckline, and full skirt have been richly embellished with silk embroidery in a manner that calls to mind the Hussar uniform (Figure 7.14). Such a dress might have been worn by either a girl or boy.

Figure 7.14.
Child's dress, c.1855. Metropolitan Museum of Art (2009.300.686a, b).

In terms of general advice on children's dress published in the mid-nineteenth century, the readers of *Godey's Lady's Book* and *The Englishwoman's Domestic Magazine* were cautioned against dressing children in fine clothes.[16] For example, in the July 1850 issue of *Godey's Lady's Book,* the anonymous author argued that children "are not puppets, made for display of fine clothes; or Paris dolls, to be tricked out in the extravagance of the latest fashion."[17] This advice was later echoed by Mrs. Merrifield in an article titled "Some Thoughts on Children's Dress" published in two parts in the May and June 1853 issues of *Godey's Lady's Book.* In her columns, Merrifield maintained that children's clothing has been subjected to the whims of fashion rather than being governed by convenience and common sense.[18] She commented at length on the type of textile, indicating that it should be "light and warm, sufficiently warm to shield the child from the effects of the cold but not too warm as to elevate greatly the temperature of the body"; Merrifield further advised that flannel (which at that time was made from wool) was preferable to linen or calico, since the former "never strikes cold to the skin" even when saturated with perspiration."[19] In part II of the article, Merrifield advocated for simplicity in the dress worn by children, "especially in the ornamental part, and that the most appropriate kind of decoration is embroidery, either in silk, worsted, or braid."[20] Merrifield also noted that "light colors in general are well adapted to children; light drabs give beauty and freshness to the complexion."[21] An almost identical version of this article appeared a few years later in *The Englishwoman's Domestic Magazine.*[22]

Although children's fashion was not the primary focus of *Godey's Lady's Book* and *The Englishwoman's Domestic Magazine*, both journals published numerous illustrations of dresses labelled as children's dresses (typically described as petticoats) in the 1850s.[23] Other journals, including *Le Moniteur de Mode* (Figure 7.15), also published similar illustrations.

The transition of young boys out of petticoats was viewed as a somewhat awkward stage. In August 1859, *Godey's Lady's Book* noted: "Every mother knows the difficulty in arranging the dress of youngsters at this period, so as to distinguish them from their sisters on the one hand and from monkeys on the other."[24] During this transition, the dresses worn by a young boy often resembled a tunic or a long-skirted frock coat.[25] This style of frock conformed with the recommendations of Joseph Couts (dates unknown), who in his 1850 treatise *A Practical Guide for the Tailor's Cutting Room* suggested that the first tailored garment for a boy of age six be "a jacket with a skirt to come down mid-thigh made of cotton velvet".[26] The boy in blue in the illustration below (Figure 7.16) wears such a garment.

Figure 7.15.
Le Moniteur de Mode, **February 1853.**
Metropolitan Museum of Art

Figure 7.16.
Journal de Modes, **1857.** Metropolitan Museum of Art.

Often the nuances between a boy's dress and a girl's dress were slight. Many children's dresses from this period look like they could be worn by either a boy or girl. For example, in volume 5 of *The Englishwoman's Domestic Magazine* (1855–56), the dress pattern featured a wide neckline, short sleeves, and double-flounced skirt with a single tassel at the centre-front waist, and the accompanying text indicated that the dress was suitable for "a boy up to the age of six or seven years of age."[27] The style of this dress, especially the fitted waist, flounced skirt and beribboned shoulders, differs markedly from the tunic or coat-dress style recommended by Couts for a boy of age six, which suggests that a mother had considerable flexibility in selecting clothing for her young son.

In the 1850s, the materials considered appropriate for children's dress included cambric, linen, lawn, silk, flannel (wool), and cashmere. Although instructions for the recycling of adult clothing into children's garments were not found in the pages of these journals, there was a notable mention of this practice which read: "When a mother has worn a dress as long as she can, it will be strange if there is not enough which is pretty good left in the skirt, which will make a frock, or perhaps even two, for a little girl."[28]

In the mid-nineteenth century, middle-class and elite mothers had considerable leeway in how they dressed their young sons. This analysis has confirmed that the specific features that distinguished a young girl's dress from that of a young boy were somewhat ambiguous. Boys might wear a tunic or coat-dress style as their first tailored garment at age four, or they might wear a velvet-trimmed dress until age seven. As Daniel Cook concluded in his historiography of studies of children's dress: "At every point when a mother dresses her young children or considers the kind of garments thought suitable for them—from fancy fashionable dress to everyday play wear—she is aware that it is her motherhood that is on display."[29]

Summary

The case study frock embodies one particular mother's preferences. She took a beautifully embroidered woman's cashmere jacket and had a tailor or skilled seamstress construct a frock for her young child. This frock, although luxuriously embellished with embroidery and silk tassels, fits within the fashionable norms for young boys during the mid-nineteenth century. Notably, the material qualities of the frock—a light-colored, lightweight textile that was warm to the skin and ornamented with embroidery—aligned with published advice on suitable materials and embellishment. To modern eyes, the dress might appear overly fussy and unsuitable for a young boy, but at the time, it signalled the parent's wealth and class. Perhaps the frock was worn by a young boy when he accompanied his mother during social calls or during children's hour when his elite parents spent an hour with him outside of the nursery. It might even have been worn for a family portrait or photograph. Although the specific details of provenance have been forever lost to time, this child's frock represents an embodiment of the cultural values of the time and place in which it was made and worn.

ENDNOTES

1   Anne Buck, "Breeching," in *Clothes and the Child: A Handbook of Children's Dress in England 1500–1900* (New York: Holmes & Meir, 1996), 150–153.

2   Noreen Marshall, *Dictionary of Children's Clothes* (London: V&A Publishing, 2008), 16.

3   Buck, *Clothes and the Child,* 151.

4   A detailed description of age-related clothing codes for boys from age six and up can be found in Joseph Couts, *A Practical Guide for the Tailor's Cutting Room; being a treatise on measuring and cutting clothing in all styles, and for every period of life from childhood to old age* (Edinburgh and London, Blackie and Son, 1850), 5–55.

5   Jo Paoletti, *Pink and Blue: Telling the Boys from the Girls in America* (Bloomington: Indiana University Press, 2012).

6   Boy's Frock, Los Angeles County Museum of Art (M.2007.211.88). Purchased with funds provided by Suzanne A. Saperstein and Michael and Ellen Michelson, with additional funding from the Costume Council, the Edgerton Foundation, Gail and Gerald Oppenheimer, Maureen H. Shapiro, Grace Tsao, and Lenore and Richard Wayne.

7   Buck, *Clothes and the Child*, 15.

8   The piecing of the garment that was observed during my visit to collection storage in October 2023 was later confirmed with curator Clarissa Esguerra, who indicated that a pattern for the frock had been documented as part of the LACMA Costume and Textiles Pattern Project. The pattern for the boy's frock can be accessed at https://www.lacma.org/sites/default/files/FF_patterns_M.2007.211.88.pdf

9   My thanks to Clarissa Esguerra for pointing out the resemblance between the textile for the child's frock and the woman's jacket ca. 1865 in LACMA's collection (M.2007.211.193).

10 Clare Rose, "Age-Related Clothing Codes for Boys in Britain, 1850–1900," *Critical Studies in Men's Fashion* 2, nos. 2&3 (2015): 127.

11 Judith Butler, *Gender Trouble: Feminism and The Subversion of Identity* (New York and London: Routledge Classics, 1990), 14.

12 Daniel Thomas Cook, "Embracing Ambiguity in the Historiography of Children's Dress," *Textile History* 42, no. 1 (May 2011): 15.

13 Queen Victoria, qtd. in the notes to the Portrait of Edward VII (1841–1910) when Albert Edward, Prince of Wales was a Child, at Royal Collection Trust, accessed November 15, 2023 at https://www.rct.uk/collection/401411/edward-vii-1841-1910-when-albert-edward-prince-of-wales

14 See Franz Xaver Winterhalter, *Portrait of Queen Victoria and family*, 1846, Royal Collection Trust.

15 See also Child's Wool and Silk Dress, 1850–55, The Met (2009.300.927) and Child's Wool and Silk Dress, 1850–55, The Met (2009.300.667).

16 I studied issues of *Godey's Lady's Book* published between 1850–59 and issues of *The Englishwoman's Domestic Magazine* published between 1852–59. All issues were digitized and are accessible online. I also examined bound copies of *Godey's Lady's Book* for 1855 and 1860.

17 *Godey's Lady's Book*, July 1850, 55.

18 Mrs. Merrifield, *Godey's Lady's Book*, May 1853, 446.

19 *Ibid*., 447.

20 Mrs. Merrifield, *Godey's Lady's Book*, June 1853, 541.

21 *Ibid*.

22 Mrs. Merrifield, "On Children's Dress," *The Englishwoman's Domestic Magazine*, 1856–57, 310–314.

23 Both journals were aimed at middle-class women and included articles on fashion as well as a variety of other topics in their pages. See for example, Illustration of Children's Dresses, *Godey's Lady's Book*, July 1850, 54.

24 *Godey's Lady's Book*, August 1859, 191.

25 Illustration of "The Fashions", *The Englishwoman's Domestic Magazine*, May 1854–April 1855, 17. Also see "Pattern for a Boy's Dress", *Godey's Lady's Book*, July 1853, 83.

26 Joseph Couts, *A Practical Guide for the Tailor's Cutting Room*, 40.

27 "Boy's Dress," *The Englishwoman's Domestic Magazine*.1855–56, 338.

28 "Remaking and Mending", *Godey's Lady's Book*, May 1852, 421.

29 Cook, "Ambiguity in the Historiography of Children's Dress," 17.

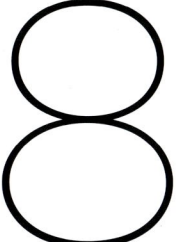

8

CREATIVE PRACTICE

A 1927 Wedding Dress

Wedding dresses are often worn once and then stored away to honor the memory of a celebration of love and commitment. As time passes, memories fade and textiles decay, such that a wedding dress may not only lose its luster but also yield to the inevitable processes of decomposition. And yet, even when a wedding dress has disintegrated beyond repair, there is tender poignancy that make these totems of memory difficult to discard. As curator and dress historian Amy de la Haye observed, a dress belonging to a loved one may hold "physical traces of the wearer's life, become imbued with their scent and/or have been stretched to echo their body contours" and, in that person's absence, the dress "can serve as a surrogate".[1] The emotional resonance of wedding dresses and other special occasion garments is evidenced by their high survival rate in women's wardrobes, as well as in museum and study collections.[2]

This case study focuses on a silk taffeta calf-length wedding dress worn by Evelyn Normand Wilkie (1902–69) for her wedding to William Douglas Howard (1899–1981) at St. James United Church in New Glasgow, Nova Scotia on November 15, 1927. Over the course of almost a century since the couple's union, both the dress and the veil have yielded to the processes of decay (Figure 8.1), and the once creamy white silk has yellowed, and the net used in the veil has become brittle and dark. Stored for decades in a cardboard box by the family, by 2016 when it was mailed to me at Toronto Metropolitan University (formerly Ryerson University), the delicate silk of the wedding dress crumbled with the softest of touch (Figure 8.2).[3] Normally a garment in such an advanced state of decay would not have been accepted into a museum or study collection, and yet I was reluctant to discard the dress and veil, especially since the family had donated other garments belonging to Wilkie and her mother, along with photos and other contextual material. This presented me with a conundrum as to what might be done with this dress and other objects that are too fragile to be handled. This case study draws on that experience to illustrate both theoretical and practice-based modes of creative interpretation.

Figure 8.2.
Wilkie wedding dress, back. Photo by Victoria Hopgood.

OBSERVATION

This flapper-style silk wedding dress is in extremely fragile condition. With each touch, the silk shatters, producing fragmentary traces of the metallic salts used to treat the silk, and once this type of degradation has begun, it cannot be reversed with conservation treatment. During this study, care was taken to minimize further damage to the dress. The embroidered bridal veil, with its delicate wax orange blossoms, was discolored, brittle, and heavily crumpled and could not be handled at all (Figure 8.3).

**Figure 8.3.
Detail of Wilkie
wedding veil.** Photo by
Victoria Hopgood.

Construction

This sleeveless calf-length silk taffeta wedding dress features a rounded wide neckline, a dropped waist, and a softly gathered skirt (Figure 8.4). There is an extended shawl collar that circles the neckline and extends to the waist attaching to a circular ornament, five inches (12.7 cm) in diameter, that contains three satin ribbon rosettes with centers that mimic the pistils of flowers (Figure 8.5). The collar measures 7.8 inches (29 cm) at its widest point, with four rows of top stitching. The collar is edged with narrow, scalloped silver trim that creates diagonals that lead the eyes to the central rosette. The seam attaching the bodice to the skirt is piped. Towards the hem of the skirt, there are three bands of top stitching with five rows in each band, 0.4 inch (1 cm) apart. The back collar is accented with a small bow with long tails that measure 33.5 inches (85 cm) in length. The dress is mostly machine stitched and unlined, except for a wide band of lightweight creamy-white cotton that lines the hem. There are no pockets.

**OPPOSITE: Figure 8.4.
Pencil sketch of Wilkie wedding dress by author.**

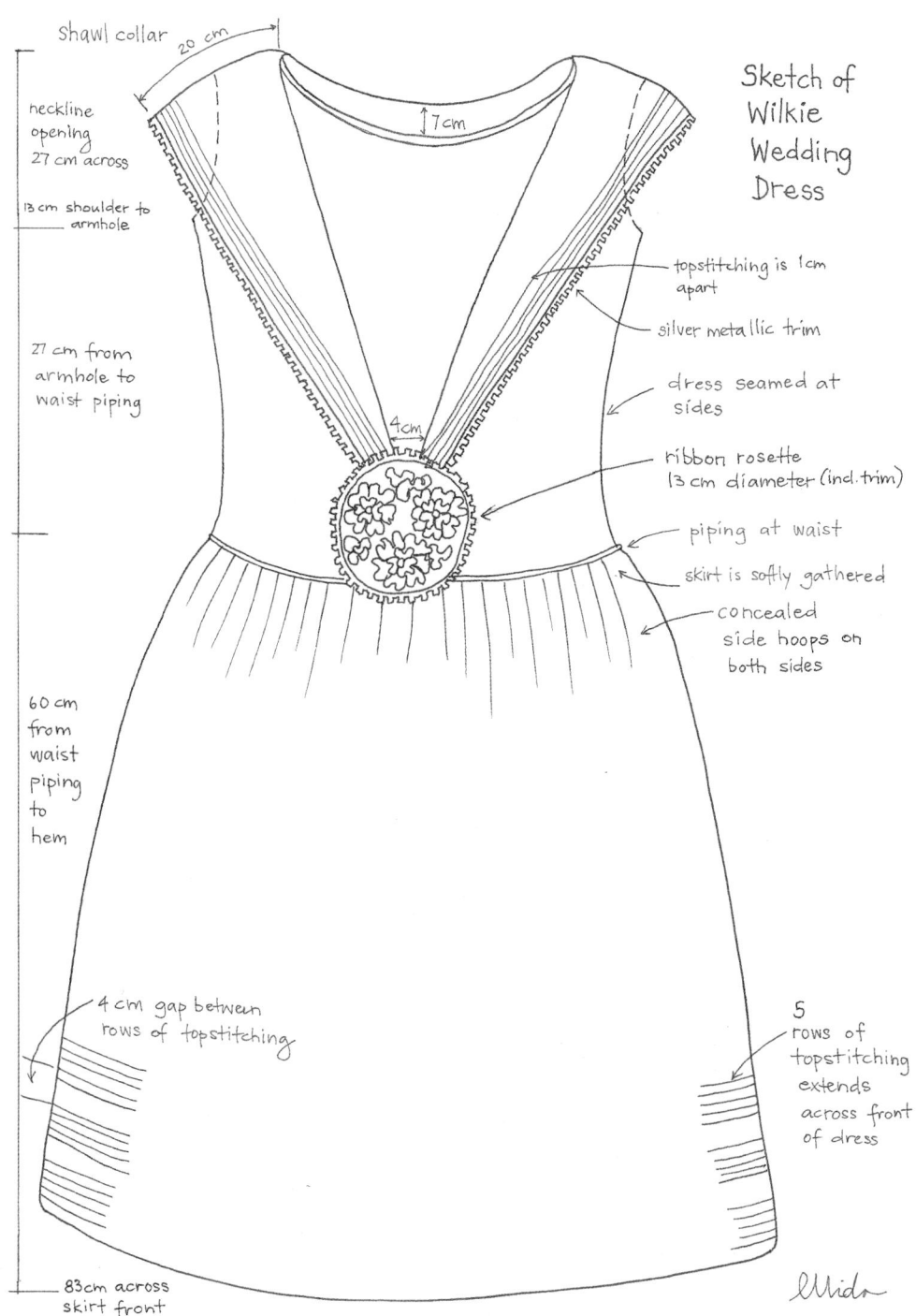

shawl collar

20 cm

neckline opening 27 cm across

13 cm shoulder to armhole

27 cm from armhole to waist piping

7 cm

Sketch of Wilkie Wedding Dress

topstitching is 1cm apart

silver metallic trim

dress seamed at sides

4 cm

ribbon rosette 13 cm diameter (incl. trim)

piping at waist

skirt is softly gathered

concealed side hoops on both sides

60 cm from waist piping to hem

4 cm gap between rows of topstitching

5 rows of topstitching extends across front of dress

83 cm across skirt front

Figure 8.5.
Detail of rosettes. Photo by Victoria Hopgood.

The dress measures 41.7 inches (106 cm) from back neckline to hem. The bust measures 31 inches (78.7 cm) and the dropped waist is 33.5 inches (85.1 cm). The width across the back is 16.5 inches (41.9 cm). These measurements are subject to error since the extreme fragility of the dress precluded handling.

Small hoops on either side of the skirt give slight emphasis to the hips. Two rectangular pieces of loose-weave linen about 10 inches (25.4 cm) long by 9 inches (22.9 cm) wide are attached at the inner waist seam on either side and contain narrow 3/8-inch (.95 cm) bands of unknown material in the shape of a U. A trade name (possibly reading *Earthstone)* is visible on one of the hoops but the letters in script are obscured in the casing.

Textiles and Materials

The dress is made from a glazed cream-colored silk taffeta. The hem of the skirt is partially lined with plain cotton as noted above. The hoops are of an unknown flexible material and are attached to a piece of loosely woven linen. The trim used to ornament the dress likely includes silver.

Marks, Labels and Logos

There are no labels visible, but it was not really possible to closely examine the inside of the dress for other maker marks.

Use, Alteration and Wear

There is soiling along the front and back of the neckline as well as perspiration stains under the arms of the dress. The silk fabric has yellowed and has shattered in various places, likely due to the presence of metallic salts in the silk and the untreated stains of wear. The most notable areas of decomposition are the area under the arms (Figure 8.6) and the large gaping hole at the back of the dress (see Figure 8.2). The narrow silver trim has tarnished.

Figure 8.6.
Close up of soiling and damage at underarm area. Photo by Victoria Hopgood.

Supporting Material

The dress and veil were sent to me in a cardboard department store box that included a handwritten note in pencil that reads: "Nanan's wedding gown (Evelyn Wilkie) Nov. 15/27." The family also provided several related documents including a family tree that traces Evelyn Wilkie's roots back to the 1780s. Copies of several undated photos of Evelyn and her husband William Douglas were also shared, but none featured the bride wearing her wedding dress. However, an undated copy of her wedding announcement published in the local paper provided a wealth of related details. The announcement read in part: "The bride, who was given away by her father, wore a period gown of white taffeta with touches of silver. The bridal veil was caught in a cap fashioned to the head with orange blossoms, and her bouquet was of sweetheart roses."[4] The maid of honor, Miss Ruth MacMillan of Halifax, "wore a dainty gown of yellow georgette with a large black picture hat and carried a sheaf of orchid chrysanthemums."[5] The flower girl, who was dressed in "orchid crepe de chine" carried a basket of rose petals, and another young girl "frocked in white canton" carried the bride's train belonging to the veil.[6] For the reception, the bride changed into a gown of "black georgette and silver" with a "corsage bouquet of pink roses."[7] The survival of the wedding dress and veil, as well as several items of her lingerie, is a testament to the love and affection Wilkie's family had for her memory.[8]

REFLECTION

When Evelyn Wilkie married in 1927, she was twenty-five years old. And although no photos of her wearing the wedding dress are known to exist, several other undated black and white photos of Wilkie show her to have been a slim, youthful looking woman with dark hair cut into a chin-length bob (Figure 8.7). In the 1920s, the fashionable silhouette for a bride was "flat-chested, slim-hipped and athletic,"[9] and the bust and hip measurements of Wilkie's dress indicate that she fit this profile.

Wilkie conformed to fashionable norms by selecting a knee-length dress with a round neckline and dropped waist, accessorized with a long translucent wedding veil that trailed on the ground and pooled at the feet (Figures 8.8 and 8.9). Although a fashionable bride in 1927 might opt to wear a full-length gown instead, the shorter, below-the-knee length style of dress that Wilkie selected was considered youthful and modern.[10] Whether short or long, a key part of the ensemble was a long transparent tulle veil that trailed behind the bride "to create a shimmering haze of light around her."[11] Wilkie's long veil, capped with its crown of artificial orange blossoms, would have created just such an effect.

Figure 8.7.
Unknown photographer, Portrait of Evelyn Wilkie, c.1920s. Courtesy of Dougald O'Reilly (grandson).

Figure 8.8.
The new Mrs. Hampton wearing a wedding dress with a long lace train and embroidered headdress, June 23, 1927.
Photo by Sasha/Hulton Archive/Getty Images.

Figure 8.9.
The wedding of Anthony Ashley-Cooper, Lord Ashley to model and actress Sylvia Hawkes at St Paul's, Knightsbridge, London, February 3, 1927.
Photo by Central Press/Hulton Archive/Getty Images.

Although Wilkie's wedding attire aligned with the fashions of 1927, the dress—as a homemade garment made by Wilkie, her mother or a local seamstress—was not considered valuable or unique from a curatorial perspective. The collection already housed several other wedding dresses from the 1920s in better condition, including a wedding dress from the Paris couture label Jenny, similar in appearance to a dress from the collection of the Chicago History Museum (Figure 8.10).[12] As well, the advanced state of decay and fragility of the Wilkie wedding dress and veil made them ill-suited to the handling that typically occurs in a university study collection.

Are only pristine garments worth saving? Budgetary constraints related to staffing and conservation and the limitations of collection storage space suggested that the Wilkie wedding dress and veil did not belong in the collection.[13] And yet, it might also be asked: whose stories are worth telling? The dress is an embodiment of memory, and the inevitable decay associated with time. Given that the dress cannot readily be studied in a conventional manner, nor can it be easily exhibited, what purpose might such a garment serve? To answer such questions, this case study explores the *thingly* presence of Wilkie's wedding dress as inspiration for creative practice by a curator, a contemporary artist, and a maker.

Figure 8.10.
Wedding dress in silk satin, chiffon, rhinestones and glass beads by Blum's Vogue, Chicago, 1927.
Photo by Chicago History Museum/Getty Images.

INTERPRETATION

Many garments in museum and study collections suggest the spectral presence of their former owners. The poignant traces of wear—perspiration stains under the arms, dirt at the back of the neckline, a tear in an oft-used pocket, a waistband that has been let out to accommodate weight gain, the footprints in a shoe—provide evidence of a personal history in the garment's biography and call to mind the absent presence of the person who wore it. To me, this material evidence of the former owner can be as potent, if not more so, than the representation of that person in a photograph, especially since scents can linger in worn shoes and clothing. Sometimes as I handle a garment with heavy traces of wear and use, I become aware of a vibrant energy or *thingly presence* that acts as a gravitational pull that draws me in. [14]

As I placed the Wilkie wedding dress and veil in an archival box and packed the cavity of the dress with tissue, it took on the slender shape of Evelyn Wilkie herself (Figure 8.1). She was there in the sweat stains under the arms; she was there in the hand stitching of the bow at the nape of the back neckline; she was there in the creases and the folds of the dress, and she was there in the scrap of paper on which someone had penciled: "Nanan's wedding gown." The dress had become a *thing* that pulled me closer and drawn me into its field.

Thing theory acknowledges the in-between state that exists in objects, and allows us to articulate the stories and ideas that arise from the encounter between humans and things. The distinction between objects and things is not always easy to articulate and may depend on the person, and my acknowledgement of a *thingly* presence might not be felt by someone else. In his seminal essay 'Thing Theory', cultural scholar Bill Brown explains that an object is transformed into a thing when there is a "changed relation to the human subject" such that the "thing really names less an object than a particular subject-object relation."[15] Brown notes that the word *thing* is often used to describe a state of ambiguity that hovers between "the nameable and unnameable, the figurable and unfigurable, the identifiable and unidentifiable."[16] He suggests that we become most aware of the power of things when they "stop working for us" and/or assert their "power and presence" as can happen when we trip over a toy, cut a finger, or the car stalls.[17] Brown does not mention clothing in his essay, but to me the Wilkie wedding dress had stopped 'working' when its intended purpose—as a garment donated for study—was thwarted by its advanced state of decomposition. And yet, as Brown points out, it is not the toy, the car, or thing itself, but what ideas it represents and what actions it inspires that are worthy of analysis.

Brown suggests that we can unlock the underlying narratives between the thing and ourselves by probing our relationship to such objects.[18] For me, the *thingly* presence of Evelyn Wilkie's wedding attire was not sinister or threatening, but poignant. The imprints, marks and signs of decay enacted what philosopher Roland Barthes has described as *punctum*, that aspect or detail which draws notice and "pricks me" and "also bruises me, is poignant to me."[19] The material traces of Evelyn Wilkie in her wedding dress became compelling totems of memory and mortality as well as a potent reminder of the fragility of life. As artist and material culture researcher Ellen Sampson so eloquently writes about the relationship of garments to memory: "Grief is contained within the object."[20]

Drawing as a form of Creative Interpretation

The Wilkie wedding dress—stuffed with tissue and laid out like a body in its coffin-like archival box—offered ripe provocation for the creative practice of artist Sarah Casey, who sees clothing as a metaphor for the ephemerality of human presence. During her career, Casey has created and exhibited drawings of the undergarments of Queen Victoria, bonnets and garments made of lace in the collection of the Bowes Museum, clothing worn by polymath and art critic John Ruskin, as well as objects of clothing found in the glacial fields of Switzerland.[21] Her life-size drawings meticulously capture the minute details of each garment, and her choices of materials for each series echoes the inevitable processes of decay and disintegration that occur in textiles with the passage of time.

In 2016—when the family mailed the dress and veil to me—Casey and I were working on a collaborative project titled *Exquisite Corpses*.[22] I presented Casey with the Wilkie wedding dress as well as several undergarments worn by her, and Casey made, over the course of several visits to the facility, full-scale drawings with a pencil on sheets of graph paper, drawings of the wedding dress and other related garments worn by Wilkie. After a period of discussion and reflection, Casey created, in her studio, life-sized drawings that aimed to capture the haunting absent presence of Wilkie that clings to these garments. For this series, Casey's method of drawing echoed that of a dressmaker by using a sewing needle to inscribe the surface of the paper—sheets of folded newsprint that had she coated with wax (Figure 8.11). She explained her choice of materials in her artist statement:

> I chose to transcribe these drawings onto newsprint, thinking of the garments that many of us may have inherited in our own families and stored folded up … I coated the newsprint with wax, thinking of it as a medium for preservation, for sealing up specimens … Wax is vulnerable to heat and if not protected, the marks inscribed upon it will melt away, as ephemeral as a breath or a memory. Just as the garments are aging, the acids in the newsprint will discolour it to deep yellow, taking on a patina of age.[23]

Figure 8.11.
Sarah Casey in her
studio, drawing the
wedding dress with a
dressmaker's pin.
Photo by author.

In Casey's finished drawings, Wilkie's dress and select undergarments were depicted like spectral forms, seemingly on the cusp of appearing and disappearing. Her choice of paper—plain newsprint on paper coated with wax—was as fragile as the garments themselves. As Casey reflected on this project, she recalled that as she "viewed the clothing belonging to Wilkie laid flat in their storage boxes," she was "reminded of fairy tale princesses, a Sleeping Beauty, lying in repose."[24]

In 2019, the Wilkie wedding dress and veil and related objects were presented alongside Casey's drawings (Figures 8.12 and 8.13) in the exhibition titled *Absent Presence: A Wedding Dress and the Drawings of Sarah Casey* (May 9 – July 5, 2019) at the MLC Gallery in Toronto.[25] In Casey's drawings of these garments, viewers were encouraged to reflect on the inevitable passage of time and the forces of decay, and acknowledge the absent presence of the slender, vibrant young woman that once wore these lovely things.

Figure 8.12.
Sarah Casey, *Absent Presence (Wilkie wedding dress, back)*, 2018–19. Drawing wax on paper (70 x 99 cm).
Photograph by Mark Bentele.

Figure 8.13.
Sarah Casey, *Absent Presence (Yolande)*, **2018–19. Drawing wax on paper (70 x 99 cm).** Photograph by Mark Bentele.

Reproducing Historic Dress as a form of Creative Interpretation

Given that the Wilkie wedding dress could not be displayed on a mannequin in the exhibition, the making of a replica of the dress became a compelling alternative. Lacking the time to make such a dress myself, Olivia da Cruz, a fourth-year fashion design student at the time, was invited to make the replica. Da Cruz was not able to handle the dress but used my drawings and measurements to supplement her observation of the Wilkie dress in its archival storage box.

As is common with the historic reproduction of garments, the sourcing of materials of comparable quality turned out to be very challenging. With pressing time constraints, a modest budget, and limited options available in local fabric shops, I selected a creamy white silk and a decorative trim that approximated but did not match the original; other compromises included the omission of hoops and artificial floral centers in the rosettes. In accordance with her brief, Da Cruz first created a muslin toile for my approval and then used the supplied materials to create a beautiful replica for exhibition (Figure 8.14).

Figure 8.14.
Replica Wilkie
wedding dress in silk,
by Olivia da Cruz.
Photo by Victoria
Hopgood.

When the reproduction was dressed on a mannequin, certain details of the design became more readily apparent. The dress skimmed the body—alluding to but not revealing the shape of the body underneath. The wide neckline was big enough to pull the dress over the head without the hassle of fastenings. It was in the process of remaking that the careful work needed to properly execute the evenly spaced rows of topstitching in the skirt and collar were more fully appreciated (Figure 8.15).

Although the challenges of finding comparable materials meant that the reproduction dress was not an exact match, the creation of a replica helped to animate the dress—allowing it to be photographed on a mannequin and displayed within the exhibition. In this way, visitors could more readily envisage Evelyn Wilkie as she might have looked while wearing the dress.

Figure 8.15.
Detail of collar and bow at back neckline of replica wedding dress by Olivia da Cruz.
Photo by Victoria Hopgood.

Curation as a form of Creative Interpretation

In telling the story of Evelyn Wilkie's delicate and disintegrating wedding dress in an exhibition format, I sought to highlight the spectral presence of Wilkie in the gallery (Figure 8.16). Her wedding dress, stuffed with acid-free tissue in the form of her body, was presented in a coffin-like archival box elevated on a table. Along the walls, Casey's exquisite and delicate life-sized drawings hung on clips so that each time the gallery door to the street was opened, the drawings moved slightly with the breeze, almost as if Wilkie's ghost had made a brief appearance. Replica photographs of Wilkie were displayed nearby and issues of *Vogue* (New York) from the 1920s with articles about wedding dresses and silk were also displayed in the glass display cases. The text panels that accompanied the exhibit "invited visitors to reflect on the processes of memory, time and disintegration", and also consider "the politics of preservation, namely whose stories are told in our collections and who decides?"[26]

In posing these questions, the exhibition presented viewers with a dilemma that faces curators on a regular basis, since storage and budgetary constraints mean that not all objects of dress are deemed worthy of preservation. And for a short period of time, the exhibition—as a collaborative effort between a team that included artist Sarah Casey, maker Olivia da Cruz, photographer and curatorial assistant Victoria Hopgood, and gallery staff and volunteers—highlighted the poignant story of a young middle-class woman who was born and married in Nova Scotia, and whose once pretty wedding dress and veil had become a totem of memory.

Figure 8.16.
Installation view of exhibition "Absent Presence: A Wedding Dress and the Drawings of Sarah Casey." MLC Gallery, Toronto Metropolitan University (May 10 – July 5, 2019).
Photo by Victoria Hopgood.

Post-script to the Exhibition: Wearing as Experiential Learning

In 2024, while revisiting Wilkie's dress to write this chapter, I also explored wearing as a research methodology. As Ellen Sampson has powerfully argued, wearing allows the researcher to position themselves as a participant rather than observer in order to fully access the bodily sensations and affects of wear.[27] Although I was familiar with Sampson's work, I was initially reluctant to consider wearing as a methodology myself. I found it challenging to overcome a key tenet of my curatorial training that had taught me that garments in museum and study collections must never be worn.[28] Eve Townsend, Director of the TMU Fashion Research Collection, encouraged me to reconsider using the muslin toile as a simulacra for the real thing, since this toile—created by Olivia da Cruz to test the pattern for the dress—was never intended to be exhibited or accessioned.

The following is an extract of my wearing diary, recorded on December 3, 2024 while on site:

> I feel like I am doing something illicit as I remove my clothes and set them aside on a stool nearby. The floor is cold on my feet, and I wish I had worn stockings and brought shoes suitable to wear with a wedding dress. As I close the door [to the back room in the collection facility], I notice the sign I had posted years ago that reads 'Garments are VALUABLE ARTIFACTS and are not to be tried on' and I laugh.

> I hold the dress in my hands and study it for a moment. I wonder if I am slim enough, and I gently pull the dress over my head. I need to shimmy my shoulders a little, but otherwise the dress fits well. It skims my torso and falls to just below the knee. The skirt is wider than I realized—even without hoops. The shawl collar is stiff and sticks out way too much because it is made of muslin rather than silk. I twirl around and feel the long tails of the bow twirl with me. I feel giddy.

Wearing the replica was a form of experiential knowledge—inducing feelings and sensations quite unlike other museum encounters. The dress fit differently than I had anticipated, with a slight curvature along the torso that did not conceal the body underneath, and with a skirt that was fuller than it appeared when laying flat. By trying on the muslin toile, I gained a deeper appreciation for the close fit and the subtle details of construction of Wilkie's wedding dress. And while the extended shawl collar felt stiff and unattractive, it was easy to imagine the way the silk collar of Wilkie's actual dress would have softly draped over the shoulders. In the act of wearing, I also discovered that I was probably about the same height and that my body's measurements were very similar to Evelyn Wilkie's. The dress seemed to fit like it was made for me.

During this experience, I felt a strange mix of sensations and initially found it difficult to fully articulate what I felt during the brief interval that I wore the muslin toile. On the one hand, I felt somewhat giddy because I had done something I had been taught never to do in museum work. On the other, I felt an inexplicable connection to a person who I had never met, but whose once pretty, but now yellowed and decaying silk wedding gown had become the focus of my attention. In the act of wearing, the *thingly* presence of Wilkie's wedding gown had become tangible to me—both in "bodily sensation and psychic mingling."[29]

Summary

The homemade silk taffeta dress worn by Evelyn Wilkie for her wedding in 1927 was lovingly saved by her family for decades but had disintegrated to the point where it could no longer be safely handled. Although the dress would normally not be accepted into a museum or study collection, the spectral and '*thingly*' presence of Wilkie asserted itself into my consciousness, leading me to retain the dress within the collection. As this case study has documented, this dress served as inspiration for creative practice, generated new knowledge, and became the focus of an exhibition in 2019. Artist Sarah Casey's delicate drawings in wax emphasized the uncanny absent presence of Wilkie and highlighted the fragility of life itself. The reproduction of the dress by Olivia da Cruz, initially as a muslin replica and then in silk, facilitated a better appreciation for the inherent challenges of reproducing historic dress, and furthered an understanding of the ease inherent in this deceptively simple style of dress. In engaging in wearing as a research methodology, I was able to appreciate the subtle details of fit and the dimensions of Wilkie's body in relation to my own. And within a broader discussion about the politics of preservation, this case study illustrates that garments in an advanced state of decomposition, like Wilkie's wedding dress, can become compelling objects for artistic inspiration. Not only is there abundant beauty in decay, but there are many rich opportunities for interpretation.

ENDNOTES

1 Amy de la Haye, "A Critical Analysis of Practices of Collecting Fashionable Dress," *Fashion Theory* 22.4–5 (2018): 395–396.

2 See Amy De la Haye, "Objects of Passion," in *A Family of Fashion, The Messels: Six Generations of Dress*, ed. Amy de la Haye, Lou Taylor and E. Thompson (London: Philip Wilson, 2010), 128–51. See also Maura Banim and Ali Guy, "Dis/continued Selves: Why do Women Keep Clothes they no Longer Wear?" in *Through the Wardrobe: Women's Relationships with their Clothes*, ed. Ali Guy, Eileen Green and Maura Banim (New York: Berg, 2001), 203–219.

3 At that time, the university was known as Ryerson University but has since changed its name to Toronto Metropolitan University (TMU) in order to distance the institution from the colonial legacy associated with Egerton Ryerson.

4 Photocopy of undated wedding announcement published in an unidentified Canadian newspaper after the wedding in November 1927.

5 *Ibid.*

6 *Ibid.*

7 *Ibid.*

8   The donation to TMU also included four related pieces of silk lingerie that had once belonged to Wilkie (a peach-colored silk knee-length slip, a peach silk and lace tap pants set, and a cream silk teddy, and a peach silk bed jacket with ostrich trim). The first three garments listed here include the label Yolande, Paris & New York.

9   Edwina Ehrman, *The Wedding Dress: 300 Years of Fashions*, (London: V&A Publications, 2011), 109.

10   See for example, a knee-length Jean Patou wedding gown made of white tulle with a dropped waist and frothy layered skirt, worn with a long tulle veil that extends behind the bride like a train, in "Tulle Fashions a Wedding-Gown of Youthful Charm," *Vogue (New York),* April 1, 1927, 59. Photograph by George Hoyningen-Huene.

11   *Ibid.*

12   See Sleeveless silk wedding dress by Jenny, 1921. Gift of Jane Dowsett, Toronto Metropolitan University, FRC2001.02.002.

13   For some institutions whose collection mandate is to preserve and display garments of exemplary quality, condition and provenance, as is the case with the Costume Institute Collection at The Met.

14   Other scholars who have acknowledged this type of *thingly* presence include Martin Heidegger, "The Origin of the Work of Art," in *Basic Writings From Being and Time to the Task of Thinking,* ed. David Farrell Krell (London: Harper Perennial, 2008 [1950]), 139–212; Marlis Schweitzer, "'Nothing but a String of Beads': Maud Allan's Salomé Costume as a choreographic thing," in *Performing Objects and Theatrical Things,* ed. Marlis Schweitzer and Joanne Zerdy (New York: Palgrave, 2014), 36–48; and Jane Bennett, *Vibrant Matter: A Political Ecology of Things* (London: Duke University Press, 2010).

15   Bill Brown, "Thing Theory," *Critical Inquiry* 28, no. 1 (2001): 4.

16   *Ibid.*, 5.

17   *Ibid.*, 3–5. Robin Bernstein likewise suggests that the power of a thing can be felt when we manipulate or shake it "to see what meaningful gestures tumble forth." See Robin Bernstein, "Dances with Things: Material Culture and the Performance of Race," *Social Text 101*, 27 no. 5 (2009): 90.

18   Brown, "Thing Theory", 9.

19   Roland Barthes, *Camera Lucida* (New York: Hill and Wang, 1980), 27.

20   Ellen Sampson, *Worn: Footwear, Attachment and the Affects of Wear* (Bloomsbury, 2020), 169.

21   See Sarah Casey's website for a listing of her drawing projects, accessed November 23, 2024 at https://www.sarahcasey.co.uk/about

22   This project was funded by a grant from the British Council. For more information on this project, see related The British Council Blog posts, accessed November 23, 2024 at https://design.britishcouncil.org/blog/2018/may/01/canada-exquisite-corpses-1/ https://design.britishcouncil.org/blog/2018/may/01/canada-exquisite-corpses-2/

23   Sarah Casey, "Drawn from Life: The Absent Presence of Drawing," in *Absent Presence: A Wedding Dress and the Drawings of Sarah Casey,* exhibition catalog edited by Ingrid Mida, 2019, 4.

24   *Ibid.*

25   This chapter expands on my previous published analysis. See *Absent Presence,* ed. Ingrid Mida, 2019. Also see Ingrid E. Mida, "On Objects and Things: The Wilkie Wedding Dress and the Drawings of Sarah Casey", *Museum & Society* 17.3 (2019), 295–300.

26   Ingrid Mida, "Curatorial Statement," in *Absent Presence,* ed. Ingrid Mida, 2019, 3.

27   Sampson, *Worn,* 37.

28   For more on the history of wearing extant clothing and the prohibition against wearing of dress artifacts in museum collections, see Ingrid Mida, "Animating the Body in Museum Exhibitions of Fashion and Dress," *Dress* 41, no. 1 (2015): 37–51.

29   Sampson, *Worn*, 41.

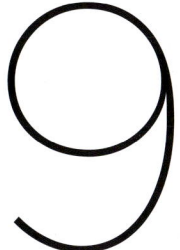

9

FASHION & GLAMOUR

A Dress Ensemble from Christian Dior Paris, Fall/Winter 1958–59

OPPOSITE: Figure 9.1.
Yves Saint Laurent, Green wool dress ensemble (*Tramway*), Dior Paris, fall/winter 1958–59.
Seneca College Fashion Resource Collection. Photo by Cole Bangia, Gezellig Studios.

Many dress collections contain examples of couture garments that are valued for their aesthetic beauty, innovative construction, exquisite embellishment, exemplary design, and/or monetary value. Such garments, especially those designed by Christian Dior (1905–57) and his successors at the house of Dior, are often highly prized by their former owners, both in terms of the financial investment required, and the prestige associated with wearing couture. The fashioning of an ultra-feminine shape in Dior's inaugural collection on February 12, 1947, which came to be known as *The New Look,* took inspiration from the restrictive silhouettes of historic fashions that had emphasized a woman's curves. Although subsequent collections explored alternative silhouettes (including the H-line of fall/winter 1954-55 and the A-line of spring/summer 1955), the name of Dior continues to be associated with sophisticated, elegant luxury and heightened femininity. Examples of original Dior garments and couture copies (a system of fashion diffusion, which Dior did much to promote) can be found in many institutional (Figure 9.2) and private collections around the world.

Figure 9.2.
Christian Dior,
Eggplant-brown
mohair dress ensemble,
spring-summer 1955.
Texas Fashion Collection,
College of Visual Arts
and Design, University
of North Texas
(1938.001.320).

The wool dress suit examined here (Figure 9.1) with its rounded shoulder line, nipped-in waist, and wide full skirt, exemplifies the feminine silhouette so often associated with the house of Dior.[1] It is one of many garments and accessories donated to Seneca College Fashion Resource Collection in Toronto by a woman who headed a major consumer products company and sat on the corporate board of a Canadian bank at a time when few women held such posts. This case study will consider this dress suit in relation to its former owner's wardrobe and biography, since clothing plays a significant role in the construction and presentation of self.

OBSERVATION

This hunter green wool dress ensemble by Christian Dior Paris from fall/winter 1958-59 is composed of three parts: a dress, a matching bolero jacket, and a self-fabric leather-lined belt with fringe (Figure 9.1).

Construction

This Dior dress has a bateau neckline, dropped shoulder line, short sleeves, and full pleated skirt that falls to just below the knee (Figure 9.3). The bodice is shaped to fit close to the body with two bust darts and a wide band of fabric encircling the waist that is slightly wider at the middle and measures 5.75 inches (14.6 cm) at the centre front and 5.5 inches (14.0 cm) at the sides. There is a canvas interlining in the dress neckline that adds support and structure to the bodice. The attached pleated skirt illustrates the complexity of construction so often associated with couture; the circumference at the hem of the skirt measures 50 ¼ inches (127.6 cm) but the fullness of the pleated skirt has been minimized at the waist with the clever use of 24 darts measuring 6 7/8 inches (17.5 cm) long and 3/4 inches (1.9 cm) wide (Figure 9.4). The dress closes at the back with a 24.5-inch (62.2 cm) metal zipper that extends 9.5 inches (24.1 cm) beyond the opening, and with two hook & eye closures, one at the back neckline and one at the mid-back waist. Like many designer garments, the dress incorporates a mixture of machine-stitched seams and hand-finishing; large seams have been machine stitched, while hand stitching has been used for the hem and at the waistband, to affix the interfacing, and to finish edges of select seams. Three colors of silk thread chosen to match the fabrics used in the dress—green, black and beige—have been used. There are no pockets in the dress.

Figure 9.3.
Dior dress and belt shown without jacket.
Photo by Cole Bangia, Gezellig Studios.

Figure 9.4.
Detail of the darts in the
Dior skirt pleats.
Photo by author.

The short bolero-style jacket is boxy in shape with a dropped shoulder line, elbow-length sleeves, and a rolled collar, and closes with a single hook and eye at the throat (Figure 9.5). Constructed of relatively few pieces, the jacket is fully lined.

The matching green wool leather-lined belt measures 28 inches (71.1 cm) long and 3 inches (7.6 cm) wide. The belt has a 4-inch (10.2 cm) wide fabric-covered buckle, and the other end is finished with 2 ¾-inch (7 cm) long fringe. The belt closure consists of three rows of concealed hooks and eyes allowing the wearer to adjust the waist to measure 26, 27 or 28 inches (66, 68.6, or 71.1 cm).

Figure 9.5.
Detail of Dior jacket and belt. Photo by Cole Bangia, Gezellig Studios.

Textiles and Materials

The bolero jacket, knee-length dress, and matching belt are made of a high quality, heavy-weight plain weave wool that has been dyed hunter green. The quality of this wool is such that the edges of the fabric have been left raw in places, including the shoulder seams, skirt darts, and hem.

The dress has been partially lined with a delicate, beige-colored silk organza and a heavier weight of plain weave green silk (near the neckline) and a black silk (near the hem). The jacket has been fully lined in a lightweight plain weave hunter green silk. The belt has been lined with a lightweight, beige-colored leather.

Marks, Labels and Logos

The jacket has two labels that have been hand-sewn to the lining at the centre back near the collar (Figure 9.6). The larger label reads: AUTOMNE–HIVER 1958/ Christian Dior/PARIS, and the smaller label sewn to the lower edge reads: MADE IN FRANCE, printed in red. The stitching has been rendered in black thread.

Figure 9.6.
Label and lining of Dior jacket. Photo by author.

The dress has three labels. A light-brown silk label identifying the retailer, Holt, Renfrew & Company Limited, has been sewn into the dress lining on the back, close to the zipper closure with green thread (Figure 9.7). The designer label reads: AUTOMNE–HIVER 1958/Christian Dior/PARIS, with MADE IN FRANCE printed vertically in a smaller font along one edge. There is a trace of the couture numbering sequence on this label, but the numbers have faded and are barely discernable (and may possibly read 96988). A smaller label affixed to the bottom edge of the designer label reads: MADE IN FRANCE printed in red. The labels appear to be authentic. There are no care or size labels in either the dress or jacket, which is normal for couture garments.

Figure 9.7.
Store label in Dior dress bodice. Photo by author.

Use, Alteration and Wear

Both dress and jacket are in good condition, and there are no signs of alteration. In the dress, most of the wear is evident near the waistband of the skirt, with fraying and small tears in the green silk, especially near the zipper closure at the back (Figure 9.8). Some of the bands of silk concealing the skirt seams have separated. There is also some tearing of the lining near the underarms of the dress. There are slight perspiration stains under the arms, and the small gray silk underpads in the underarms of the dress are creased. The jacket shows no adverse traces of use or wear.

Figure 9.8.
Signs of wear in Dior dress skirt near waist closure. Photo by author.

Provenance

The Dior green wool dress ensemble was one of many garments and accessories donated to the Seneca College Fashion Resource Collection by Mona Campbell in May 1991.[2] Other garments donated by her at the same time included (ordered here in chronological sequence):

1. 1939 Black taffeta evening gown with short, puffed sleeves and back bow of red and gray striped silk, label Marcel Rochas Paris
2. 1953 Red and black brocaded silk strapless evening gown, identified by donor as Victor Stiebel (Figure 9.9)
3. 1955 Grey, black and red beaded silk satin sleeveless sheath dress (Figure 9.10). Matching evening coat with fur collar, label Guggenheim of Rome (not shown)
4. 1956 Burgundy red velvet sleeveless V-front cocktail dress with crystal rhinestones, label Guggenheim of Rome
5. 1957 Claret red wool coat with attached scarf and bracelet length gusset sleeve, label Christian Dior (Figure 9.11)
6. 1957 Claret red silk shantung sheath dress with matching jacket with ¾ length kimono-style sleeves, label Christian Dior, *Rubris*, spring/summer 1957
7. 1957 Gold brocade sleeveless evening gown, missing label
8. 1958–63 Brown and black checked wool skirt suit, label Victor Stiebel (see Figure 9.16)
9. 1958–63 Raspberry red and black checked wool skirt suit, label Victor Stiebel (Figure 9.12)
10. 1960 Moss green day dress, missing label
11. 1962 Grey wool knit sleeveless empire-waist evening gown with petal hem with matching stole, labels Pattuloo-Jo Copeland and Joan Rigby Toronto
12. 1963 Cherry red velvet empire-waist sleeveless long gown with matching bustier and large floral bow at centre front, labels Nina Ricci Boutique, Paris and Simpsons
13. 1969 Pink, turquoise, green, orange and cream cotton caftan, lined in blue silk, label Geoffrey Beene.

Campbell also donated several accessories at the same time, including: six pairs of 1960s pumps; an alligator clutch bag (from the early 1930s–40s); and a 1950s snakeskin handbag. Selected items from Campbell's donation have been photographed and are accessible online.[3]

Figure 9.9.
Victor Stiebel,
Sleeveless floor length
evening gown, 1953.
Seneca College Fashion
Resource Collection.
Photo by Cole Bangia,
Gezellig Studios.

Figure 9.10.
Guggenheim of Rome, Grey, black and red beaded silk satin sleeveless sheath dress, c.1955.
Matching evening coat not shown.
Seneca College Fashion Resource Collection. Photo by Cole Bangia, Gezellig Studios.

Figure 9.11.
Christian Dior Paris,
Claret red wool coat with
attached scarf, c.1957.
Seneca College Fashion
Resource Collection.
Photo by Cole Bangia,
Gezellig Studios.

Figure 9.12.
Victor Stiebel, Raspberry red and black checked wool skirt suit, 1958-63.
Seneca College Fashion Resource Collection. Photo by Cole Bangia, Gezellig Studios.

REFLECTION

The case study dress ensemble was designed by Yves Saint Laurent (1936–2008) as part of the fall/winter 1958–59 collection for the house of Dior. For this collection, his second as creative director, Saint Laurent took inspiration from Renaissance architect Andrea Palladio (1508-80). The collection was titled "*Line Courbe— Silhouette en Arc*" (Curved Line—Arched Silhouette), and the show notes describe the translation of the curves of Palladio's arcades into a "definitive curve of the well-marked rounded shoulder line" and "the softened curves of skirts."[4] The collection received effusive coverage in the press, with *Vogue* (New York) reporting in the September 1958 issue that:

> *The fact is that while the Dior skirts are longer than the rest of the Paris Collections clothes, their new look is not in the length alone, but in a new and elegant proportion. What M. St. Laurent sets out to do (and we think he has done it) is to elongate the whole feminine figure by means of high heels, narrow shoes, narrow skirts, tall hats, and the higher waistline. This proportion is the newest look in Paris.*[5]

Garments from this popular collection were also shown elsewhere. At the presentation in November in London, England (Figure 9.13), Princess Margaret (a faithful Dior client) apparently declared she "had never seen so beautiful a collection."[6]

Figure 9.13.
Designer Yves Saint Laurent with Dior models at reception, Westbury Hotel, London, November 11, 1958.
Photo by Bob Hope/ Mirrorpix/Getty Images.

The design of *Tramway* (as this dress and jacket combination was called)—with its striking combination of a short bolero jacket and a dress with a fitted waist panel and full skirt—produced the illusion of a small waist and emphasized the wearer's femininity. However, unlike prior collections at Dior, the volume of the skirt was not supported by layers of tulle.[7] This dress and jacket combination differs from the comparatively narrow, hip-hugging skirts of several other dress suits from this collection, including *Transat, Djebel, Baroud, Paris,* and *Frileuse*.[8] The design for *Tramway* shares notable similarities to designs from the two previous fall collections, for which Saint Laurent had acted as design assistant to Christian Dior. For example, the wool tweed dress and jacket called *Virevolte* from fall/winter 1955–56, and the wool dress suit called *Ritz* from fall/winter 1956–57, share this same full-skirted silhouette.[9] Images of similar full-skirted dress suits by other designers appeared in *Vogue* (New York) that year (Figure 9.14), including a dress suit in a gun-check wool (Figure 9.15) by American designer Vera Maxwell (1901–95).

Figure 9.14.
Vogue **(New York), August 1, 1958. Model wearing a dress suit in orange wool and nylon tweed by Milliken.** Photo by Karen Radkai/ Condé Nast via Getty Images.

Figure 9.15.
Vogue (New York), August 1, 1958. Model in a British gun-club check wool suit by Vera Maxwell with earrings and bracelet by Cartier. Photo by Horst P. Horst/Conde Nast via Getty Images.

On the 15th of September 1958, the Canadian department store Holt Renfrew organized an event at the Royal Ontario Museum in Toronto with models wearing garments from the latest collections from Dior, Balenciaga, Lanvin-Castillo, Pierre Balmain, and Jacques Griffe. In attendance at the gala evening presentation with proceeds going to support "the Museum's costume department" were "several hundred women, many themselves mink clad." [10]

What is perhaps most interesting about the case study dress ensemble is the woman who wore it, Mona Louise Morrow Campbell (1919–2008). Campbell was born to a prominent Toronto family, and aspects of her life have been documented in the press such that it is possible to consider her biography in relation to her donated clothing. Two questions come to mind. How does this dress suit compare to other garments in her wardrobe? What aspects of her personality and presence can be gleaned from the material evidence of her wardrobe?

INTERPRETATION

When a donor makes the decision to part with objects that have significant value or personal meaning, they generally want to ensure that these things are given to a person or organization that is willing to care for them and in so doing help ensure their preservation. [11] In 1975, Mona donated two couture gowns to the Royal Ontario Museum, including a rose pink silk satin gown called *Rose France,* as well as a dove gray silk satin evening gown called *Saadi* from Christian Dior Paris for fall/winter 1947–48. [12] Mona had a long-standing relationship with this museum, and in making this donation she had the comfort of knowing that her couture pieces would be cared for in perpetuity. [13]

In 1991, Campbell decided to donate the case study dress suit from Christian Dior Paris along with other selections from her wardrobe to the newly founded study collection at Seneca College. [14] At the time she was 72 years old and recently widowed. Unlike Mrs. John Chambers Hughes, who donated her Dior *Tramway* green wool dress suit to the Metropolitan Museum of Art in 1960—only a few years after it was the height of fashion—Campbell waited thirty-three years. [15] In a 1979 interview published in the *Toronto Star*, Mona said "I've loved clothes all my life and I wear them for years." [16]

A wardrobe is part of the extended self, embodying memory in material form, and in parting with these items from her wardrobe in 1991, Campbell acknowledged that she would no longer wear these garments. Measurements from the donated items indicate that Mona had a bust of 34 inches (86.36 cm), waist of 25 inches (63.5 cm), and hip of 37 inches (93.98 cm), and wore a size 8 1/2 shoe. At the time of donation, some of the items might not have flattered her figure as her body had aged, or perhaps she no longer attended as many glamourous social events. As Julia Twigg has observed in her study of dress in relation to aging, many women keep items of clothing that they no longer wear but hold significant meaning (such as a wedding dress), and the decision to discard such garments invokes reflection on the changes wrought by time and age.[17]

Campbell was born Mona Louise Morrow on the 3rd of February 1919. As the only daughter of Mr. and Mrs. Frederick K. Morrow of Wychwood Park in Toronto, she lived a life of upper-class privilege. In 1937, when she was seventeen, Mona attended finishing school in London, and it was during that trip that she was first introduced to couture by her mother, making her first purchase from the London couturier Olive Todd (dates unknown).[18] Mona was presented at Court on the 6th of May 1937 "to their Majesties" (King George VI).[19] Upon her return to Toronto in September 1937, her debut was announced in *The Globe & Mail* (Canada's national newspaper).[20] The debut presentation and ball took place on the 29th of October 1937 and Mona wore a "handsome presentation frock of white net embroidered in daisies with sequin centres, a little belt of the net" and a "corsage of mauve orchids".[21]

Mona Louise Morrow married 'the dashing' naval officer John Turnbull Band on the 5th of October 1939. Mona's wedding gown of antique ivory lame was "after a Balenciaga model in the new draped bustle-back style" with a long square train over the full, circular skirt; her wedding veil was made of the "sheerest ivory silk ninon" and "held by a halo of mother-of-pearl encircling her fair hair".[22] Her mother wore a "handsome gown of silk crepe in rich petunia tone, a French model by Jane Duverne" and the five bridesmaids wore matching gowns of eggshell faille and brown velvet that were "copies of a Maggy Rouff creation."[23] For her going-away outfit, Mona wore a Molyneaux wool coat of "airway blue trimmed with blue fox and full-skirted frock of beige crepe" with a pillbox style blue hat with bows, blue gloves and brown suede shoes.[24]

Given that Mona had been introduced to couture by her mother in 1937 while attending finishing school, it is notable that she and her bridesmaids wore gowns that had been copied from designs by Balenciaga and Maggy Rouff.[25] The decision to engage in copying may have been influenced by the rising tensions in Europe in the months that preceded the outbreak of WWII on September 1, 1939 or perhaps her parents thought it financially prudent for garments that would be only worn once. Either way, the practice of copying Parisian couture was by this time widespread in North America, as historian Mary Lynn Stewart has documented in her study of the marketing of haute couture during this time period.[26]

Following the death of Mona's father in 1952, she took his place as the majority stockholder of Dover Industries, a flour-milling company that also made ice cream cones, straws and paper products. In 1954, Mona stepped up to run the operation, even though her father had once told her that women should not be "doing this sort of thing."[27] Lacking business training, she later recounted that she initially drew on her experiences with volunteer organizations in "dealing with budgets, scrounging for money."[28] Mona learned on the job and ultimately transformed the company from a modest operation into one of the largest Canadian-owned flour-milling companies.[29]

In 1955, Mona and John divorced acrimoniously even though they had "cut glamourous figures in society and had three children".[30] In this light, it is interesting that she kept her black and red silk Marcel Rochas gown from 1939—the year of her marriage to John. This full-length gown featured short, puffed sleeves, a deep V-neckline, fitted waist, long full skirt and an extravagant back bow in a dove gray and cherry red striped silk.[31] In donning such a feminine gown, perhaps for her pre-wedding celebrations, Mona embraced the romantic styles that dominated women's fashions in the 1930s. And in keeping the gown for many years, she held onto her happy memories of that time. This was the only black gown in Mona's surviving wardrobe, which is consistent with her belief that one should only wear black at age eighteen since "beyond that, it ages you."[32]

In Erving Goffman's book *The Presentation of Self*, the sociologist reflects upon how individuals manage their appearance and manner in performing certain roles for a given audience.[33] Goffman points out that setting is highly relevant to how an individual negotiates their performance, especially when stepping into a new role or an unfamiliar setting. When Campbell became CEO of Dover Industries, she had to negotiate societal expectations that at that time precluded women from positions of power. In such settings, formality prevailed, especially for a woman, and the conservative styling of the boxy jackets and knee-length skirts of Mona's two suits (Figure 9.12 and 9.16) by the "quintessentially English designer" Victor Stiebel (1907–76) seem better suited to the corporate environment.[34]

Figure 9.16.
Waist detail of brown checked wool Victor Stiebel suit, 1958-63.
Seneca College Fashion Resource Collection. Photo by Cole Bangia, Gezellig Studios.

Based on the surviving garments donated to institutional collections, Campbell had an obvious affinity for Dior. Apparently, Mr. Dior once told her "the classic lines never go out of style."[35] Imbued with glamour, Campbell's cherry red Dior *Rubris* dress and jacket from 1957, and her hunter green Dior *Tramway* dress and jacket from fall/winter 1958–59 seem more appropriate for cocktail hour rather than the boardroom. When Mona acquired these two ensembles from Dior, she was single and may have been dating, given that she remarried in 1960. Alternatively, she may have worn these chic outfits to the theater, the ballet or social events at the Royal Ontario Museum (where she would later chair the board of directors). Whatever the occasion, her investment in couture at this time in her life may have reflected her desire to dress in an explicitly feminine manner in certain settings.

In Efrat Tseelon's study of femininity, she explains that femininity is a constructed identity that can be "donned, like masquerade," to disguise the pursuit of power.[36] In dressing in these sophisticated dress suits that not only emphasized the feminine form but also embodied glamour and sophistication, Campbell concealed the parts of herself that did not fit the norms for upper class women in Toronto society at that time. As a working woman and a divorced mother, she defied the expectations for her gender and her place in elite society.[37] Her selection of eye-catching figure-hugging couture garments, including many garments made of textiles in shades of red, point to a woman who was comfortable in the spotlight. Cultural historian Stephen Gundle has argued that glamour can be used as "a weapon and a protective coating, a screen on which an exterior personality can be built to deceive, delight and bewitch."[38] In this light, Campbell's many glamourous outfits may have served as a fashionable shield as a woman who had stepped outside of societal norms of the time.

In 1967, not long after Mona's second marriage ended in divorce, she married Colonel Kenneth Campbell.[39] She was still active in the corporate sector, and Mona said in a 1979 interview that she often wore tailored suits or a simple wool dress with gold jewelry for business meetings and board meetings for the Toronto Dominion Bank, where she was the only woman on the 37-member board.[40] After her third husband's death in 1990, Mona did not remarry. Mona died in 2008 and in her obituary, her entrepreneurial spirit and financial savvy was lauded. Not only had she raised money for many charitable organizations, but it was noted that she had been ranked "among Canada's top CEOs".[41]

The garments Mona donated to the Seneca College Fashion Resource Collection in 1991 spanned thirty years of her life: from 1939—the year she was first married at age twenty—to 1969; the year she turned fifty. Although these garments represent only a fraction of her wardrobe, their survival marks their embodiment of memory as markers of significant moments in her life. It seems plain that she preferred shades of red and had an affinity for couture even though she sometimes economized on lesser-known labels or copies. Mona was tall, slim and stylish, as evidenced by the various published images of her attending glamourous events like the pre-opening gala of Holt Renfrew's new store in support of the Royal Ontario Museum in 1979 (Figure 9.17).[42] And according to her daughter, Mona was "fastidious about her appearance" and "every thread on her had to be perfect."[43]

Summary

The *Tramway* dress suit by Yves Saint Laurent for Christian Dior fall/winter 1958-59 that inspired this case study seems like an unusual choice for a divorced woman who was in the early years of her tenure as CEO of Dover Industries. Not only was the suit made of a thick wool that would have been suitable only during cold winter months, but the short jacket and fitted waist and full skirt of the dress emphasized her femininity. Mona yielded power in the boardroom, but she was also a woman "who loved men".[44] Perhaps she used this dress suit to don the masque of femininity, disguising her ambition and power with glamourous clothing in order to fit in when the situation demanded it.

OPPOSITE: Figure 9.17.
Toronto style: Mona Morrow
Campbell, March 19, 1979.
Photo by Erin Combs/Toronto Star via
Getty Images.

ENDNOTES

1   Yves Saint Laurent for Christian Dior, Green wool dress, bolero jacket and belt, fall/winter 1958-59. Seneca College Fashion Resource Collection, Gift of Mona Campbell, 1-958-15-00936.

2   Mona Campbell's May 1991 donation record at the SCFRC indicates 1953 as the assigned year for her garments designed by Victor Stiebel. However, in 1953 Stiebel was working for Jacqmar and did not design under his own label until 1958 (and his final collection was in summer 1963 when he was forced to retire due to poor health). Accordingly, I have revised the assigned date of origin for the suits by Stiebel to 1958-63 since these garments include labels associated with his post-Jacqmar career: "Victor Stiebel, 17 Cavendish Square, W1 London.' The gown lacks a label but in an oral history interview with Alexandra Palmer, the gown was apparently worn to the Ballet Ball in 1953. See Alexandra Palmer, Couture & Commerce: The Transatlantic Fashion Trade in the 1950s (Toronto: UBC Press in association with Royal Ontario Museum, 2001), 273.

3   Selected garments from the Campbell donation have been photographed and can be accessed at https://digitalrepository. senecapolytechnic.ca/s/sfrcollectiononline/item?fulltext_search=%22Mona%20 Campbell%22

4   Alexander Fury, Dior Catwalk (New Haven: Yale University Press, 2017), 114.

5   Jessica Daves, "Paris Report, Hemline debate: waistline decisions; the details in the charm," Vogue (New York), September 1, 1958, 210.

6   Alexander Fury, Dior Catwalk, 114.

7   Harold Koda notes this change first occurs with the Ritz suit from fall/winter 1956-57. See Harold Koda, Christian Dior (New York: Metropolitan Museum of Art Publications, 1996), 180.

8   A photocopy of the original sketches from this collection was provided to the study collection by the house of Dior but cannot be reproduced here.

9   Examples of the Virevolte suit, Christian Dior, fall/winter 1955-56 can be found in the collection of The Met (2009.300.443a-d) and ASU FIDM Museum (81.443.1A-C). See also Ritz suit, fall/winter 1956-57, The Met (C.I.62.52.2a-c).

10   Holt Renfrew ad for the "Presentation of Exclusive Couture Models and furs by Christian-Dior Paris" at the Royal Ontario Museum, The Globe and Mail, September 15, 1958, 17.

11   See Susan Pearce, Museums, Objects and Collections (Leicester: Leicester University Press, 1992), 63–65.

12   Christian Dior, Silk satin evening gown (Saadi), fall/winter 1947–48, Royal Ontario Museum (975.297.1a, b), gift of Mrs. [Mona] Kenneth Laidlaw Campbell. Christian Dior, Silk satin evening gown (Rose France), fall/winter 1947–48, Royal Ontario Museum (975.297.2), gift of Mrs. [Mona] Kenneth Laidlaw Campbell. See also Alexandra Palmer, Christian Dior: History and Modernity 1947–1957 (Toronto: Royal Ontario Museum, 2018), 104–111.

13   Mona Campbell was a long-term supporter of the Royal Ontario Museum and was chairman of their capital campaign in 1978. See Ron Csillag, "Obituary, Mona Campbell, 89 Chief Executive Officer," The Globe & Mail, June 28, 2008, S12. See also "And the Walls Came Tumbling Down," Toronto Star, May 10, 1978, A3. In the photo accompanying the Toronto Star article, Campbell was identified as the Chairman of the ROM Capital Campaign and is wearing a suit very similar to the case study dress suit ensemble.

14   "Show Traces Fashion History," Toronto Star, June 6, 1991, F4.

15   See Christian Dior wool dress suit donated by Mrs. John Chambers Hughes, 1960. Metropolitan Museum of Art C.I.60.44.2a–c.

16   Stasia Evansuk, "She dresses like a president," Toronto Star, March 25, 1979, D2.

17   See Julia Twigg, Fashion and Age: Dress, the Body and Later Life (London: Bloomsbury, 2013), 75–78.

18   Alexandra Palmer, Couture and Culture: The Transatlantic Fashion Trade in the 1950s (Vancouver: UBC Press and Royal Ontario Museum, 2001), 43.

19   "Young Toronto Women in England," The Globe and Mail, May 7, 1937, 14.

20   "Will Make Debut," The Globe and Mail, September 3, 1937, 14.

21   "Society to Welcome Debutantes of 1937: Formal Presentation of Lovely Daughters at West Creche Ball," The Globe and Mail, October 29, 1937, 12.

22   "Oak-Panelled Living Room Becomes Wedding Chapel," Toronto Daily Star, October 6, 1939, 26. See also the announcement of the wedding accompanied by a photo of the bride published in The Globe and Mail, October 11, 1939, 8.

23   Ibid.

24   Ibid.

25   See Palmer, Couture & Commerce, 43.

26   Mary Lynn Stewart, Dressing Modern Frenchwomen: Marketing Haute Couture, 1919–1939 (Baltimore: Johns Hopkins University Press, 2008), https://dx.doi.org/10.1353/book.60338.

27   Csillag, "Obituary: Mona Campbell", S12.

28   Ibid.

29   When Mona took over Dover Industries in 1954, revenues were $10 million and in 2007 (the year prior to her death), the revenues were $228 million. See Csillag, "Obituary: Mona Campbell", S12.

30   *Ibid.*

31   This gown is not in good condition and cannot be mounted for photography.

32   Evansuk, "She dresses like a president," D2.

33   Erving Goffman, *The Performance of Self in Everyday Life* (New York: Anchor Books, 1959), 22–27.

34   See Amy de la Haye, "Gilded Brocade Gowns and Impeccable Tailored Tweeds: Victor Stiebel (1907–76) a Quintessentially English Designer," in *The Englishness of English Dress*, ed. Christopher Breward, Becky Conekin and Caroline Cox (London: Berg 2002), 147–157.

35   Evansuk, "She dresses like a president," D2.

36   Efrat Tseelon, *The Masque of Femininity: The Presentation of Woman in Everyday Life* (London: Sage Publications, 1995), 37–38.

37   Mona's financial acumen was mentioned in various articles in the press, including "High finance won't go to her head," *Toronto Star*, February 26, 1977, F1 and "The Women [of Bay Street]", *Toronto Star*, July 23, 1978, E20.

38   Stephen Gundle, *Glamour: A History* (Oxford: Oxford University Press, 2008), 4.

39   Csillag, "Obituary: Mona Campbell", S12.

40   Evansuk, "She dresses like a president," D2.

41   *Ibid.*

42   Stasia Evansuk, "Fashion Plates on Menu at New Store's Gala," *Toronto Star*, March 14, 1979, C8.

43   Daughter Vicki qtd. in Csillag, "Obituary: Mona Campbell", S12.

44   *Ibid.*

10

FASHION & IDENTITY

A 1976 CN Tower Uniform

A uniform is a specialized form of functional clothing, typically designed with a certain role or setting in mind and, as cultural historian Jennifer Craik has pointed out, "uniforms shape who we are and how we perform our identities."[1] The word uniform comes from the Latin *unus*, meaning one, and *forma*, meaning form. In adopting a specific form of dress for military, academic, religious, corporate or other setting, a uniform creates a sense of distinct identity and belonging to a particular group. Sometimes this may create an internal dilemma for the wearer, who feels the pressure to fit in while still wanting to assert their personality in how they wear the uniform.

This case study considers a jumpsuit-style uniform (Figures 10.1 and 10.2) featuring a custom-designed print that includes a motif of the CN Tower from the Fashion Research Collection at Toronto Metropolitan University in Canada.[2] As cultural historian Jane Tynan has observed, there is a complex and "ongoing dialogue" between fashion and uniforms.[3] The case study jumpsuit, with its unique textile design, was designed in 1976 by Pat McDonagh (1934–2014) and it is a material artifact associated with a very particular place and time in the history of Toronto. What story does it tell?

OBSERVATION

Figure 10.2.
CN Tower jumpsuit uniform (back).
Photo by Jazmin Welch.

Construction

This one-piece jumpsuit for female employees of the CN Tower has been designed for mass production and consists of a short-sleeved bodice attached at the waist to trousers. The uniform has an open shirt-style collar, cuffed short sleeves, a removable coordinating necktie and a centre-front zippered opening (Figure 10.1). The garment is semi-fitted with side seam bust darts, 1-inch-wide (2.5 cm) elastic at the back waist, and ties attached to the side seams at the front waist. There is one horizontal welt pocket on the left side of the bodice and two vertical welt pockets, one on each side of the hips. The pant legs are cut straight with a slight flare towards the hem (Figure 10.2). The 19-inch (48.2 cm) orange nylon zipper begins just above the crotch level and zips up to the open collar.

Machine stitching with burnt orange color thread has been used throughout. Fusing has been applied to the facing of the collar. The seams have been machine serged. The garment is unlined.

The jumpsuit measures 59.5 inches (151.1 cm) from collar to hem. The bust measures 34 inches (86.3 cm), the adjustable waist (with the ties open) measures 28 inches (71.1 cm) and the hips 34 inches (86.3 cm). The inseam measures 30.5 inches (77.5 cm). The sleeves are 9.5 inches (24.1 cm) long with a cuff of 2 5/8 inches (6.7 cm). The necktie is 76 inches (193.0 cm) long and measures 2.5 inches (6.35 cm) at its widest point.

Textiles and Materials

The jumpsuit is made of a poly-cotton blend (65% polyester, 35% cotton). This custom-printed textile is distinctive in incorporating the CN Tower motif (Figure 10.3). Narrow stripes of burnt orange alternate with stripes of light blue-gray and white, and every other burnt orange stripe contains the CN Tower motif.

Figure 10.3.
Detail of textile with CN Tower motif.
Photo by Jazmin Welch.

This fabric was likely screen printed on white fabric, since some of the blue used to create the CN Tower motif is slightly overprinted into the adjacent burnt orange stripe. In the construction of the jumpsuit, the fabric is oriented vertically except for the pockets and waist ties where the fabric is in a horizontal orientation.

Marks, Labels and Logos

There are two labels inside the jumpsuit, sewn into the back neckline (Figure 10.4). A cloth label reads "Career tex. For Career Wear, By Sainthill Levine, Division of Sanlee, Ind. Ltd." A second label reads CA 000777 (identifying the manufacturer), the fabric content (65% Polyester, 35% Cotton), the style (CW708), and size 10. There is no care label. The jumpsuit does not include a name tag or other identifying mark indicating the name of the employee who wore this garment.

Figure 10.4.
Labels inside back neckline.
Photo by Jazmin Welch.

Figure 10.5.
Detail of collar showing signs of laundering. Photo by Jazmin Welch.

Use, Alteration and Wear

The jumpsuit is in good condition but appears to be somewhat faded from laundering (Figure 10.5). There are minor signs of wear at the inside neckline and under the arms, and there are some loose stitches near the crotch seam and just below the zipper that suggest strain. There are marks along the hem of the pant legs that may have come from contact with the floor or top of a shoe. As well, there is a horizontal line of fading about 2 ½ inches (6.35 cm) above the hem which suggests the trouser legs were at some point let down and this altered hem has been secured with small running stitches using white thread.

REFLECTION

The jumpsuit, a full-body garment consisting of a top and pants that are attached at the waist, has come in and out of fashion at various times since its origins in the early twentieth century.[4] Depending on the context, this type of garment has also been described as a flight suit, siren suit, boilersuit, overalls, coveralls, or onesie.[5] The term 'jumpsuit' is linked to the wearing of this type of garment by pioneering parachutists like the famous English "Parachute Diver" Sylva Boyden (dates unknown, born c.1899–1902) who was one of the first women to jump out of a plane with a parachute in 1919 (Figure 10.6).[6] The one-piece design of this garment protected the jumper's body from the colder temperatures of higher altitudes and from being entangled in various cords of the parachute. The practical design of the jumpsuit led to its adaption for other purposes such as factory workers, especially during World War II (Figure 10.7).

One of the first designers to co-opt the jumpsuit into everyday wear was Elsa Schiaparelli (1890–1973), who in the early 1930s created a wide-legged sleeveless version in silk.[7] Several American designers, including Vera Maxwell (1901–95) and Bonnie Cashin (1908–2000) also experimented with the jumpsuit (Figure 10.8). Nonetheless, this garment was largely considered only appropriate for sportswear until the mid-1960s.[8] In the September 1964 issue of *Vogue (New York)*, the jumpsuit was elevated into high fashion with Irving Penn's photo of a brown-wool jersey jumpsuit designed by Guy La Roche (1921–89).[9] When other designers, including Hubert de Givenchy (1927–2018), Oscar de la Renta (1932–2014), and

Figure 10.6.
British pioneer parachutist Sylva Boyden, July 1920.
Photo by Topical Press Agency/Hulton Archive/ Getty Images.

Figure 10.7.
Wartime Fashion,
March 26, 1942. Photo
by Bettman/Getty Images.

Yves Saint Laurent (1936–2008) (Figure 10.9) experimented with jumpsuits as fashion in the 1960s, this garment came to be associated with the youthful spirit of rebellion associated with that time.[10]

This uniform with its CN Tower motif is linked to a very specific place and time in Canada's history. When the CN Tower opened in Toronto to the public on the 26th of June 1976, it became the tallest freestanding structure in the world, at 1815 feet (553 metres).[11] Although another tower has since surpassed that record, it remains a much-loved tourist attraction and a centre of telecommunications for Toronto.

In 2013, this garment was found in this university study collection and its provenance remains unknown.[12] There is another CN Tower uniform in the collection (also from an unnamed donor)—a silver nylon jumpsuit with a nametag attached that reads 'Karen'—and this style of uniform, which alludes to space, was worn by elevator operators.

The case study uniform—with its jaunty textile and feminine flourishes—seems to project an aesthetic of ease, fun, and femininity, which seems somewhat unusual in the context of a corporate uniform. How does this aesthetic align with fashions of the period and with the work of the designer, Pat McDonagh? And given that uniforms are intended to create a sense of belonging, is it possible to discern anything about the young women who wore such uniforms in 1976? To answer these questions, my interpretation will incorporate archival research as well as reference the recollections of several women who shared their memories of wearing such a uniform with me in 2015.

Figure 10.8.
Bonnie Cashin,
Jumpsuit, 1963.
RISD Museum
(80.171.8).

Figure 10.9.
A fashion model wearing black flare trousers crepe jumpsuit by Yves Saint Laurent, Paris, France, August 19, 1968. Photo by Reg Lancaster/Daily Express/Getty Images.

INTERPRETATION

As Jennifer Craik explains in her book *Uniforms Exposed*, "The rationale of uniforms is highly specific to an institution, organization or group because it embodies precise calculations designed to distinguish members of that uniformed group."[13] The distinctive textile motif of the case study jumpsuit makes an obvious reference to the CN Tower and could only have been worn by an employee who worked there.

Prior to the opening of the CN Tower in June of 1976, the uniforms worn by hostesses were described in detail in an article published in the *Toronto Star* newspaper:

> *Hostesses will have sienna jumpsuits, safari jackets, and skirts and gray striped T-shirts emblazoned with a Tower print. They'll also have sienna and gray sweaters with a Tower print and sienna pants and sienna and gray scarves. They'll be issued with storm coats – gray rubber with sienna piping – that are reversible to become sienna coats piped with gray. The uniforms for all staff were designed by Pat McDonagh of Toronto, who also designed those worn by guides at Ontario Place and the Ontario Legislature.*[14]

The word 'hostess' connotes hospitality and entertainment and, in 1976, hostesses at the CN Tower acted as cashiers and guides, in a role that would likely be described as guest service representatives today.[15] Male hosts wore a shirt made of this fabric, as did male and female security guards.[16] The uniforms worn by hostesses, hosts, and security guards, made with this distinctive textile motif, would have made these employees easy to identify among the crowds of visitors who wanted to visit the observation decks or restaurant at the CN Tower. Although this article refers to a wardrobe of sorts for hostesses, the other items—the safari jackets, the skirts and gray striped T-shirts—are not known to have survived. The focus of this analysis will be on the jumpsuit, and it is notable that in the published images of CN Tower employees from this time, hostesses are dressed in jumpsuits, perhaps because the distinctive textile branded the employee with corporate identity from shoulder to ankle.

When the CN Tower initially advertised for positions in the spring of 1976, more than 1200 applicants lined up for jobs as hosts and hostesses, elevator operators and other operating personnel.[17] The rules of conduct for CN Tower staff were based on Disney World operations and included the following stipulations: "All visitors are 'guests' and must be treated as such; Tower staff must be made to feel like part of a team and everyone will work on a first-name basis; Staff must be pleasant in appearance and personality, able to cope with any problem without losing their cool."[18] Such rules of conduct suggest that the corporation sought out employees who were friendly, at ease with strangers, and happy to be of service.

In Craik's definition of a uniform, she articulates that this particular form of clothing is "employed to announce a particular type of identity that acts both as a shorthand of the kind of behaviour exhibited by the wearer and expected by the observer."[19] The staff of the CN Tower had a set code of behaviour which expected them to be "pleasant in appearance and personality" and their uniform—with its distinctive textile—appears to have been designed to create a unique identity associated with this tourist attraction.

The designer of the first uniforms worn by CN Tower employees was Manchester-born Pat McDonagh (1934–2014). McDonagh, who never intended to become a fashion designer, attended the University of Manchester and the Sorbonne to study romance languages, and as a student, she turned to modelling to supplement her income. In the early 1960s, McDonagh opened clothing shops in Manchester and London and also designed costumes for the Beatles as well as Dianna Rigg (who played the character Emma Peel in the original Avengers television series). After moving to Toronto in 1966 with her husband and children, McDonagh opened a boutique featuring her own creations called 'The Establishment' and, after her business grew, she sold the shop and opened a factory. Her clothing designs were sold in stores across North America, including Bloomingdales and Henri Bendel in New York.[20] During her career, she won numerous awards (Figure 10.10) including the World Bureau award (1975), the New York Times award for design excellence (1982), the Judy Award for her contributions to the Canadian fashion industry (1992), the Matinee International Award (2002), and the Lifetime Achievement Award by the Fashion Design Council of Canada in 2003.[21] During her career, McDonagh was widely known for her "sense of youthful romanticism," and her designs were worn by celebrities around the world, including singer Ella Fitzgerald (1917–96) and Diana, Princess of Wales (1961–97).[22]

Figure 10.10.
Pat McDonagh with her Judy award.
Photo by Reg Innell/Toronto Star via Getty Images.

McDonagh was a versatile designer, designing a range of clothing including special occasion wear, costumes, sportswear, and uniforms. In 1971, McDonagh designed the uniforms worn by employees at Ontario Place, another prominent Toronto tourist attraction, event venue, and park on the shores of Lake Ontario. A photo published in *The Globe and Mail* a few days prior to the official opening of Ontario Place on the 22nd of May 1971, shows a lithe, young Black model wearing a cropped zippered long-sleeved jacket made of a quilted material in shades of brown, worn with short shorts, dark tights, and knee-high boots.[23] This uniform—with its hot pants—projects a youthful spirit and aligns with the fashions of the early 1970s. According to Canadian dress historian Caroline Routh, hot pants were somewhat slow to catch on in [conservative] Canada, but in 1971, the pages of the women's magazine *Chatelaine* featured a design by McDonagh headlined as "the zippy new leg-baring short pants for summer."[24] McDonagh's Ontario Place uniforms were fashionable and functional, and this experience would have been helpful when she received the CN Tower uniform commission.

Fashions for spring 1976 were all about ease. The editors of *Vogue* (New York) explained that "it's about clothes that are so easy in and of themselves and give off such a feeling of ease, they relax every gesture."[25] Many of the looks by American designers featured in *Vogue* that year had simple lines and figure flattering cuts; and the prevailing colors were blue, beige, cream, or small prints.[26] Similarly, reports from Paris indicated that "Marc Bohan's collections for Dior were inspired by sportwear" and "the newest [look] appearing in the collections is the jumpsuit, a Paris revival."[27]

In 1976, the jumpsuit embodied this celebrated spirit of ease and was considered fashionable for day and evening.[28] Extant examples from the 1970s exist in various museum and study collections including The Met, the Philadelphia Museum of Art, and the Texas Fashion Collection (Figures 10.11 and 10.12). A woman wearing a jumpsuit in the 1970s looked put together without a lot of effort and was able to go about her day in clothing that was elegant and comfortable. As fashion show producer Dorothy Smythe noted in 1976: "Jumpsuits are really big this year. They're so practical."[29]

Many fashion articles and ads from 1976 refer to the stylish ease of the jumpsuit and feature tag lines like "Come—jump on the fashion bandwagon … get yourself a jumpsuit."[30] A jumpsuit that bears a remarkable similarity to the case study jumpsuit was featured in a display ad for the department store Simpsons in May 1976; this zip-front jumpsuit with shirt collar, open neck, short sleeves with mock cuffs and a tie belt was available in dark brown, powder blue, coral (pale orange) or beige, and was made of "easy-care, fun-to-jump-in polyester that will flatter and fit any figure type."[31]

Figure 10.11.
Geoffrey Beene, Jumpsuit of cream wool knit.
Designer label: "Beene/Bazaar" c.1970s.
Texas Fashion Collection, College of Visual Arts and
Design, University of North Texas (1985.004.003).

Figure 10.12.
Domonic Rompollo, Lounging jumpsuit of orange
polyester with peplum and tie half-belt/sash, c.1970s.
Texas Fashion Collection, College of Visual Arts and
Design, University of North Texas (1980.006.024).

These examples make it clear that McDonagh's designs for the CN Tower jumpsuit uniform aligned with fashion trends of 1976. Her choice of fabric—an easy-to-care-for polyester-cotton blend fabric—was practical in that it allowed employees to launder their uniform at home and forgo the expense of dry cleaning. The slight fading of the textile, especially in areas that might have been subjected to the heat of an iron, such as the collar and pant legs, is consistent with laundering. The minor signs of wear and the faint lines that indicate where the hem was let down offer further evidence that this garment was worn.

What is difficult to discern with any certainty is how hostesses wore the necktie. In 1976, thin scarves were an important accessory. An article published that year noted that: "There is a certain knack to accenting your neck with a scarf."[32] This article mentions a scarf 72 inches (182.9 cm) in length, which is the same length as the necktie for the case study uniform; and the article suggested (and illustrated) folding the scarf in the middle, tying it into a loop, and draping loosely around the neck, with or without a clip.[33] In styling the uniform for photography, the necktie was tied in a bow under the collar, but in studying published photographs of the uniform, it appears that the scarf could be tied in different ways, including in a bow at the neck inside the collar or left off altogether (Figure 10.13).[34] At an event held at the Royal Alexandra Theatre in advance of the opening of the CN Tower in June 1976, selected staff modelled their uniforms for the rest of the employees and the caption for a photo indicates that hostess Angie Turcotte is "helping Sue Ross adjust her scarf" even though the scarf is not actually visible in the photo.[35] The wording of the caption and the staging of such an event suggests that it was important to the corporate entity that employees wear their uniforms in a certain way. Perhaps the necktie was the one aspect of the uniform that hostesses were allowed to express their personality in a small way—by opting to tie it in a bow or loop, or perhaps even choosing to leave it off altogether.

There is a powerful link between clothing and memory. In March 2015, within hours of posting a watermarked image of the case study uniform on social media, I received a message from a woman who had once worked as a hostess/cashier and guide at the CN Tower. After corresponding with her, she and several of her former coworkers visited the study collection and fondly recounted their experiences to me. As Craik points out in her book, "most people recall vivid experiences with uniforms and these encounters are often highly memorable."[36] Although I did not record a formal oral history with these women, their affection for each other was plain to me at the time, as were their recollections of the jumpsuit uniform and happy memories of their work decades prior. There was much laughter about their inability to wear such figure-revealing jumpsuits any longer, and one former hostess recalled that back in 1976 female staff were "blatantly hired for their looks—mostly modelling or fashion or flight attendant graduates and mostly tall and slim."[37]

Figure 10.13.
Megan Hutchinson, a hostess at the CN Tower for the summer. Published in *Toronto Star***, August 17, 1976.**
Photo by Erin Combs/Toronto Star via Getty Images.

The measurements of the case study uniform confirm that the hostess who wore this jumpsuit to work at the CN Tower in 1976 was, in fact, relatively tall and slender—approximately 5'4 to 5'8 inches tall with a bust of 34 inches (86.3 cm), waist of 24–28 inches (61–71.1 cm), and hips of 34 inches (86.3 cm). Although the uniform was thoughtfully designed by McDonagh to lengthen the figure with vertical stripes and also accommodate minor changes in waist size, these hourglass measurements represent a socially constructed model of normative femininity. In dressing the hostesses in a fashionable jumpsuit uniform like this, the corporation encoded oppositional messages that blended what Craik identifies as being unique to the history of women's uniforms with "familiar messages about uniforms—regulation, restraint, discipline, practicality" encoded with "certain attributes of femininity—tailored modesty, neatness, demureness —but not others—loose morals, sexiness, slovenliness or precociousness."[38] This aligns with the CN Tower uniform for hostesses in 1976, which McDonagh designed to be fun, functional, fashionable and feminine but not overtly sexy or improper.

Summary

This CN Tower uniform represents a unique artifact linked to Toronto's history. The playful textile design with its vibrant coloration and tower motif is distinctive in creating a visual connection to a particular time and place. The aesthetics of this jumpsuit style of uniform correlate to the prevailing fashions of the mid-1970s and also fit with the corporate identity of the CN Tower at that moment in time. Employees were expected to be attractive and personable, and this uniform designed by Pat McDonagh created a uniform aesthetic for female employees that was crisp, tailored, fashionable and feminine. The decades long friendships and the memories of women who wore such uniforms confirm the sense of belonging and unity that had been fostered by their experiences as CN Tower hostesses in wearing such a uniform.

ENDNOTES

1   Jennifer Craik, *Uniforms Exposed: From Conformity to Transgression* (London: Berg, 2005), 3.

2   Pat McDonagh, CN Tower Jumpsuit, 1976. Toronto Metropolitan University Fashion Research Collection (2013.99.003). Donor unknown.

3   Jane Tynan, "Utility Chic: Where Fashion and Uniform Meet," in *Uniform: Clothing and Discipline in the Modern World*, ed. Jane Tynan and Lisa Gordon (London: Bloomsbury Visual Arts, 2019), 221.

4   For a comprehensive history of the jumpsuit, see Yuniya Kawamura, "Rompers and Jumpsuits," in *Berg Encyclopedia of World Dress and Fashion*, Volume 3: The United States and Canada, ed. Phyllis G. Tortora (Bloomsbury Academic, 2010).

5   *Ibid.*

6   Sylva Boyden, "Girl Parachute Diver from Airplanes: What It Feels like to Leap into Space from a Machine Flying One Hundred Miles an Hour a Thousand Feet Up," *New York Times*, September 28, 1919, SM6.

7   An extant example is in the collection of The Met. See Elsa Schiaparelli, Silk Jumpsuit, c.1930–35, Metropolitan Museum of Art (1974.181.3).

8   See Kawamura, "Rompers and Jumpsuits." Also see extant examples of jumpsuits in the collection of The Met, including Vera Maxwell, Short-sleeved jumpsuit in wool, 1945, Metropolitan Museum of Art (2009.300.116) and Bonnie Cashin, Orange jumpsuit in wool, 1962–63, Metropolitan Museum of Art (1979.431.39).

9   See "Fashion: Paris," *Vogue (New York)*, September 15, 1964, 110. This article focuses on variations of fashionable pants as seen in the latest collections, and includes the jumpsuit by Guy Laroche, lace knee-length pants by Jacques Heim, and 'pantboots' by Roger Vivier.

10 See for example, Givenchy's yellow jumpsuit in *Vogue (New York)*, November 15, 1967, 83; Oscar de la Renta's daisy-patterned silk evening jumpsuit in *Vogue (New York)*, February 1, 1969, 152, and also a black and white windowpane silk jumpsuit in *Vogue (New York)*, April 15, 1969, 68–69.

11 "The CN Tower Story," CN Tower. Accessed November 15, 2024 at https://www.cntower.ca/history

12 In 2012–13, I cataloged all FIC (found-in-collection) items in what was then known as the Ryerson Fashion Research Collection. This study collection had been dormant for almost a decade and with a corrupted database, there were a substantial number of garments that predated my tenure and had little or no provenance information. I revisited the collection in November 2024 to double check my measurements and notes related to this artifact.

13 Craik, *Uniforms Exposed*, 6.

14 Michael Hanlon,"Corned beef caper ends in a fare-thee-well," *Toronto Star*, April 1, 1976, B1.

15 Author's email correspondence with former hostess, March 31, 2015.

16 *Ibid.*

17 Paul Dalby, "1,200 job-seekers ready to move up in world," *Toronto Star*, April 23, 1976, A8.

18 *Ibid.*

19 Craik, *Uniforms Exposed*, 4.

20 The Canadian Press, "Pat McDonagh, award-winning designer, dead at age 80," CBC News, June 1, 2014. Accessed November 15, 2024 at https://www.cbc.ca/news/canada/toronto/pat-mcdonagh-award-winning-designer-dead-at-age-80-1.2661377

21 "Pat McDonagh," The Canadian Encyclopedia. Accessed November 15, 2024 at https://www.thecanadianencyclopedia.ca/en/article/pat-mcdonagh

22 *Ibid.*

23 See Dennis Robinson's photo of the unidentified model wearing the Ontario Place uniform, titled "A Short Look at Fall Futures," *The Globe and Mail*, May 18, 1971, 12.

24 Caroline Routh, *In Style: 100 Years of Canadian Women's Fashion* (Toronto: Stoddart Publishing, 1993), 149–150.

25 "Fashion: Spring Collections, American Style '76—the Word is Ease," *Vogue (New York)*, February 1, 1976, 125.

26 See the February 1976 issue of *Vogue (New York)*.

27 Stasia Evasuk, "A fashionable way to dress," *Toronto Star*, September 10, 1974, E2. See also "Shapes pared down for fall," *Toronto Star*, September 11, 1976, E3.

28 "Paris [Fashion]," *Toronto Star*, September 11, 1975, E30.

29 Dorothy Smythe qtd. in "Fashions men love featured at show," *Toronto Star*, April 9, 1976, E9.

30 Also see for example, the jumpsuits featured in Stasia Evasuk, "Spring's coming and skin is IN," *Toronto Star*, February 26, 1976, E1, and the jumpsuits advertised for sale by Eatons in the *Toronto Star*, March 6, 1976, L28.

31 Simpsons Department Store ad for Jumpsuits, *Toronto Star,* May 29, 1976, J11.

32 Marilyn Brooks, qtd. in Stasia Evasuk, "Scarves can steal the show," *Toronto Star,* June 30, 1976, E2.

33 *Ibid.*

34 See the cover of the CN Employees Newsletter, "Keeping Track," 11, no. 6 (July 1976). A photo of the cover was supplied to me by a former CN Tower employee.

35 Photo by Barrie Davis, "A Special Showing," *The Globe & Mail*, June 14, 1976, 16.

36 Craik, *Uniforms Exposed*, 3.

37 Email correspondence with author, dated March 31, 2015.

38 Craik, *Uniforms Exposed*, 8.

11

THE LANGUAGE OF THE KIMONO

An Edo-period Kimono (*Uchikake*)

The rich symbolism and cultural significance of the Japanese kimono extends far beyond its translation as 'something to wear.' Variations of the kimono can be worn by a man, woman, or child as everyday wear and for formal occasions including weddings and festivals. Although this garment appears deceptively simple in its construction, a kimono can be fitted to the wearer with extra fabric concealed in the seam allowances, or with folds hidden under the waist sash.[1] Worn with the left side lapped over the right and fastened with an *obi* or another form of sash at the waist, the kimono encircles the body with fabric from neck to ankle such that the natural curves of the figure underneath largely disappear from view.

In the west, there has been a long-standing misconception—perhaps originating from the reopening of Japan with the landing of the ships led by American Commodore Matthew C. Perry in Tokyo Bay in 1853—that the kimono was a static form and outside of fashion.[2] However, this T-shaped garment has a long and complex history that has included various shifts in proportions, sleeve styles, and design motifs over time.[3] And as curator Monika Bincsik points out, "not only did Japan have fashion trends; it had an apparatus for the design, production, promotion, and sale of fashion every bit as complex as the west."[4] There is now a much better appreciation that the forces of fashion are reflected in kimono through the textile itself, such that various colors, patterns, and decorative techniques can be linked to specific periods in history.[5]

During the Edo period (1615–1868)—a relatively peaceful period in Japan's history—there were distinct stratifications of society, with samurai class at the top of the social stratum and farmers, artisans, the merchant class, and others ranking below.[6] Although sumptuary laws sought to uphold these rigid social demarcations, such regulations were largely ineffective, and the increasing wealth of the artisan and merchant classes led to a consumerist mentality and the flourishing of the arts.[7] Fashion became a form of conspicuous consumption, and the kimono became a kind of canvas on which to display one's aesthetic preferences, taste, and wealth.[8]

The *uchikake* is a type of outer kimono that was worn unbelted over other garments for formal or ceremonial occasions such as weddings, festivals, and celebrations.[9] Initially adopted by court ladies and high-ranking samurai women, this highly decorative garment was also worn by elite women from the wealthy merchant class, courtesans, and male actors playing women in the kabuki theater.[10]

This case study will consider a white figured silk uchikake with red silk lining and padded hem dated to the mid-nineteenth century from the collection of the Textile Museum of Canada (Figure 11.1).[11] Like many garments that have been donated to museums, this uchikake represents a formal raiment worn by an elite woman whose name has been lost to time. As art historian Terry Satsuki Milhaupt notes: kimono represent "snapshots of a specific time and place—a frozen moment of history visible in the material from which they are woven and decorated, the designs that adorn them, the form in which they are constructed and their mode of presentation."[12] The nuances of textile choice, color, the length of sleeves, and the forms of embellishment offer a myriad of clues as to the wearer's age, marital status and social position.[13] What then might be discerned about the young woman that wore this uchikake?

OBSERVATION

This striking white figured silk satin uchikake has a red silk lining, padded hem, and long hanging sleeves (*furisode*). It would have been worn as an outer layer over one or more *kosode* (robe with small wrist openings), and without a sash so that fabric at the hem draped to create a beautiful circle of fabric around the wearer's feet. This uchikake is richly ornamented with pine, bamboo, plum blossoms, cranes, tortoises, and water motifs (Figures 11.1 and 11.2).

Figure 11.2. Uchikake back.

Construction

The body of the uchikake is constructed according to the normal conventions for a basic kimono. The outer layer has been cut from a single bolt of fabric into two body panels (*mihaba*), two sleeves (*sode*), two front overlapping panels (*okumi*), and a neckband (*eri*). The most notable variations from a basic kimono are this garment's long sleeves (*furisode),* its soft padded hem, and its red silk lining. The long hanging sleeves measure 39.4 inches (100 cm) in length (from shoulder to sleeve end) and 12.4 inches (31.5 cm) wide. The sleeves are open along the side closest to the body, with the opening for the hands measuring 9.2 inches (23.3 cm). The padded hem, which extends beyond the red silk hem, includes about 4.7 inches (12 cm) of silk wadding.

The measurements of the widths of textile panels used for the sleeves and body (excluding the seam allowances) fall within the traditional 12 to 14-inch width (30.5–35.6 cm) associated with Japanese kimono textiles from this period. The length of the fabric—from front hem to back hem—used to create the body panels measures about 126 inches (320 cm), and the neckband measures 35.4 inches (90 cm) long and 5.1 inches (13 cm) wide.

Textiles and Materials

Figure 11.3.
Detail of uchikake back.

The outer layer of the uchikake is made of a creamy white figured silk satin called *rinzu*. This fine textile is not only lustrous, but has sufficient density to support the extensive embroidery across the body of the garment. The kimono is fully lined in a bright red silk that is visible at the neckline, the sleeve openings, and the hem. The hem and sleeve openings are padded with silk wadding. The entire surface of this formal garment, both front and back, has been embellished in some way using a combination of embroidered and stencilled motifs. The colorful ornamental motifs include pine, bamboo, plum blossoms, mandarin oranges and nandina berries, as well as cranes and tortoises. Both the front and back of the uchikake feature long bamboo stalks rendered either with stencilled imitation tie dye or couched silver wrapped threads (Figure 11.3). Silver accents on selected bamboo stalks and body parts of the tortoises were created with couched silver gilt paper threads wrapped around a silk core. The stenciled motifs—used for certain bamboo stalks, leaves, and tortoise bodies—imitate the expensive and time-consuming tie-dye process of *kata kanoko shibori*.[14]

There are seven embroidered cranes situated in the upper part of the garment, all rendered in silk thread using satin stitch (Figure 11.4). There are three cranes on the front: a pair on either side of the neckline and one on the proper left front sleeve. On the upper back of the uchikake, each pair of cranes is oriented as if they are flying towards each other.

Figure 11.4.
Detail of crane.
Photo by author.

Towards the padded hem, the design is grounded by an abstracted landscape of embroidered green hills and stylized embroidered waves. There are five tortoises with long tails swimming in the waves of water on both front and back, and each tortoise swims in a slightly different orientation. Of the three tortoises swimming on the front, two have stenciled bodies and the body of the third tortoise is embroidered using padded satin stitch (see Figure 11.3). The back of the uchikake features two tortoises swimming towards each other on either side of the centre back seam.

Marks, Labels and Logos

There are no maker's marks or labels inside this garment. The textile design does not incorporate a family crest.

Use, Alteration and Wear

There is some evidence of wear at the inside neckline, small tears in the fabric on the right sleeve (Figure 11.5), and signs of rubbing on the hem near the padding (Figure 11.6). There are some pulled threads at the back of the kimono, likely from wear, and there are two small, stabilized holes in the fabric on the bottom of the padded hem that have had conservation treatment. Minor damage may have occurred when this garment was first worn or at some later date. The uchikake is otherwise in very good condition, especially given its age. There are no signs the uchikake has been altered.

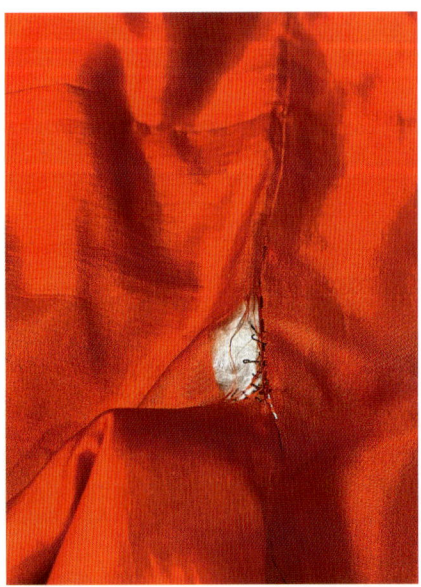 

Figure 11.5.
Tears in the silk lining of the right sleeve.
Photo by author.

Figure 11.6.
Stabilized hole in padded hem.
Photo by author.

REFLECTION:

The exquisite workmanship of this beautiful uchikake suggests that much care was taken in its creation. It is a wearable work of art, and as Dale Gluckman and Sharon Takeda explain in the introduction to their book *When Art became Fashion: Kosode during Edo-period Japan*, no distinction was made between the fine and decorative arts during the Edo period.[15] And thus, artisans approached the ornamentation of the "clean, straight lines and unbroken surfaces" of the kimono in a manner "akin to a painter approaching a blank surface."[16] Some of the leading artists of the time, such as Ogata Korin (1658–1716) and Sakai Hoitsu (1761–1828), even painted directly on kimono.[17]

A pivotal moment in the history of the kimono took place when the country was forced to open its borders to foreigners in the 1850s after nearly two hundred years of isolation. The resultant exposure to western clothing had a profound impact on the wearing of the kimono. Japanese men were quick to don western style clothing, which was seen as modern and progressive, while women—who at the time generally led more cloistered lives—adopted western fashions more slowly. In 1886, the Empress Shōken appeared in public wearing a western-style gown for her husband's birthday celebration, and in the following year, she issued an imperial memorandum encouraging women to adopt western fashions made with domestic textiles.[18]

The beauty of Edo-period kimono captivated many in the west, and these garments often appeared in western paintings after the opening of the borders of Japan in the latter part of the nineteenth century.[19] Fashionable dresses made from panels of kimono textiles or from dismantled kimonos also started appearing in Paris and London in the 1870s (Figure 11.7).[20]

The sumptuous and colorful uchikake of the Edo period were much sought after in the west, and many found their way into many private and museum collections (Figures 11.8, 11.9 and 11.10). And while many extant uchikake in museums appear to be similar, it is rare to find matching sets. Typical floral motifs included bamboo, pine trees, cherry blossoms, chrysanthemums, and peonies. Common animal motifs included cranes, ducks, tortoises, and butterflies. Other popular design motifs from that time included fans and books.

Figure 11.7.
Day dress, Misses Turner, Figured-silk satin, hand-painted with stencil imitation tie-dyeing and embroidery in silk and gold-wrapped silk threads, probably Kyoto 1800–60; tailored in London, 1876–78.
The Kyoto Costume Institute, (AC8939.93.28.1ab). Photo © Richard Haughton.

Figure 11.8.
Woman's Outer Robe (Uchikake) with Long-Tailed Birds in a Landscape, second half of eighteenth century, Japan.
Photo by Sepia Times/Universal Images Group via Getty Images.

Figure 11.9.
Woman's Outer Robe (Uchikake) with Scenes of Filial Piety, late eighteenth–early nineteenth century, Japan.
Photo by Sepia Times/Universal Images Group via Getty Images.

Figure 11.10.
Woman's Outer Robe (Uchikake) with Books and Mandarin Orange Branches, first half of the nineteenth century, Japan.
Photo by Sepia Times/Universal Images Group via Getty Images.

In interpreting the complex symbolism embodied in the beautiful uchikake that is the focus of my case study, I am sensitive to the need to take due care, especially given my stance as an outsider, and for this reason I sought the counsel of a colleague with the relevant background and expertise.[21] To enhance my material understanding of such garments, I also examined several uchikake with furisode sleeves and padded hems in various collections.

An opulent white silk uchikake with padded hem and furisode sleeves dated to the late Edo period from the collection of the Los Angeles County Museum of Art (Figure 11.11) offered an interesting comparable. Like the case study uchikake, this robe is made of creamy white figured silk satin ornamented across the entire surfaces of the front and back with stenciled imitation tie-dye motifs, as well as motifs embroidered with silk thread. The most prominent design element of this uchikake is a stylized cloud pattern. Embroidered motifs include the flowers associated with spring: cherry blossoms, peonies, chrysanthemums, hollyhock leaves, and wisteria, rendered in a harmonious palette of orange, pale pink, light greens, mid-greens, and dark purples, balanced with motifs in neutral browns. The couched gold gilt-wrapped silk threads on select motifs across the body of the garment add sparkle even in the relatively dim light of the storage facility. There is evidence that this uchikake was once worn, since there was slight soiling at the neckline and the red lining. The hem has three patches of wear that have been stabilized with conservation treatment, and the silk at the hem has become a faded orange rather than bright red with the passage of time. I also observed that the pattern no longer aligns at the seams for the sleeves, however, this misalignment most likely occurred after the garment was dismantled and then stitched back together after cleaning.[22]

Figure 11.11.
Young Woman's Samurai-Class Outer Kimono (Furisode, Uchikake) with Cherry Blossoms, Chrysanthemums, Hollyhock Leaves, Peonies, Wisteria, and Stylized Cloud Pattern, Late Edo period (1615–1868), early nineteenth century. Los Angeles County Museum of Art (AC1999.177.2). Photo © Museum Associates/LACMA.

Like the case study uchikake, the ornamentation of the LACMA uchikake has been exquisitely rendered. The main difference, aside from the specific motifs rendered in embroidery or stencil, is the strong diagonal orientation to the design. It was in comparing the measurements of the two robes that it became obvious to me that these uchikake were tailored to fit specific individuals.

	TMC Uchikake	LACMA Uchikake
Center back length	66 inches (167.6 cm)	72 inches (182.9 cm)
Shoulder Width	48.8 inches (124 cm)	47 inches (119.4 cm)
Sleeve length	39.4 inches (100 cm)	35.4 inches (89.9 cm)
Sleeve width	12.2 inches (31 cm)	13 inches (33 cm)
Padding depth	4.7 inches (11.9 cm)	7.9 inches (20.1 cm)
Estimated textile width	13 inches (33 cm)	13 inches (33 cm)

Upon reflection, this case study raises several questions: Given that social status and identity are conveyed through the design of the uchikake, what does the case study uchikake reveal about the young woman that first wore it? What can be learned about how such garments were worn?

INTERPRETATION

The opulent design and colors of the case study uchikake suggest that this outer kimono was worn as part of a bridal ensemble during the late Edo period. As Masami Yamada explains, the wedding ceremony rituals for the samurai class during this period were staged over several days and included a procession from the bride's house to the groom's house, a sacred ceremony, and a banquet.[23] For weddings, the preferred and most auspicious colors for uchikake were white, red, and black, which were sometimes worn in sequence.[24]

Uchikake were made to order. Depending on where the family lived, the family's requirements might be conveyed by letter to stores in Kyoto (where the majority of the artisans were located during the Edo period). A sketch artist created an initial design, and often several iterations of the design were necessary. When the design had been finalized, the work of various artisans, including spinners, weavers, dyers, shibori artist, and embroiderers, was orchestrated by a *shikkaiya* (a type of production co-ordinator) or kimono merchant.[25] For special occasion garments like an uchikake, the process of procurement might take up to a year.[26] Such garments were very costly, and in donning such an expensive outer garment, the wealth of the family was on display for all to see.[27]

As a wedding garment, the case study uchikake reflects a family's hopes and dreams for their daughter as she transitioned to a married woman, and each of the floral and animal motifs on this uchikake would have been chosen for their auspicious significance.[28] Perhaps the bride and her mother studied pattern books in making their selection of motifs, as is illustrated in the 1716 woodblock print *Order Book of Kosode Patterns* (Figure 11.12).

Figure 11.12.
Order Book of Kosode Patterns (Chūmon no hiinagata/Hiinagata chūmon chō), Edo period (1615–1868), 1716, Woodblock-printed book; ink on paper. Image: 9 3/4 × 7 1/16 in. (24.8 × 18 cm). The Metropolitan Museum of Art, Gift of Betty and Paul Nomura, in memory of Nomura Shōjirō, 2018 (2018.954.8a).
Image copyright © The Metropolitan Museum of Art. Image source: Art Resource, New York.

As a wearable work of art, the design of the uchikake can be considered in terms of line, color, space, composition and style. And as was explained to me, a kimono is 'read' from top to bottom.[29] There are embroidered cranes in flight near the shoulders, with two on either side of the front opening, two on either side of the centre back seam, and one on each shoulder. The eye is drawn to the elements rendered in red embroidered thread, including select plum blossoms, leaves, and nandina berries, but a balance between light and dark has been achieved by rendering some elements in brown stencil or embroidered silk thread. The delicate arcs of branches of plum trees and red pine trees create a sense of dynamic movement across the field and also serve to connect the colorful red plum blossoms and mandarin oranges. There are no straight lines in the design aside from the straight lines of the bamboo stalks. Tall stalks of bamboo rise from the landscape on both left and right fronts, and this is echoed at the back on the right of the centre back seam. Curved branches or vines wrap around the bamboo stalks and lead the eye upwards. Tortoises with long curvaceous tails swim in the waves, their bodies twisting toward each other—like a bride and groom—at the front and back. The design is grounded by the wave patterns near the padded front and back hems. Although the opulent asymmetrical design covers the entire surface of the garment and leaves no empty space, or *ma* (the Japanese philosophical concept of space between the edges), the overall visual effect is one of balance and harmony.

There is a language to the kimono, in that each design element has an associated meaning. And thus, my reading of the case study uchikake draws on the work of Roland Barthes in linking semiology to fashion, whereby every sign is composed of two elements—namely the signifier and the signified.[30] In this case, the signifiers include the length of the sleeves, the color and type of fabric, and each of the motifs that ornaments the surface of this garment. Each of these material elements has an associated cultural meaning in terms of what is being signified. As anthropologist Lisa Dalby has observed, every kimono embodies a visual language that takes "into account distinctions on each of the following dimensions: Life/ Death; Gender; Formality or Occasion; Season; Age; Taste or Class."[31]

The long *furisode* sleeves of the case study uchikake were not limited to uchikake, but this length of sleeve was considered appropriate only for young, unmarried women. The red silk lining and padded hem were signifiers of glamour, and the glimpses of red that appeared when the long hanging sleeves moved with the wearer would have created an impression of seductive allure. The dye used to create red—which comes from safflower (*benibana*)—was very costly but often faded quickly. And thus became symbolic of passionate but transient love."[32]

The nuances of the seasons were also factored into the selection of motifs and colors for this uchikake, since certain colors and patterns were considered appropriate at different times of the year.[33] In this case, the auspicious grouping of pine trees, bamboo stalks, and plum blossom were known as the "Three Friends of Winter" (*shochikubai),* and this suggests that the wedding ceremony may have taken place around the New Year.[34] The ornamental motifs signified the family's hopes for a long and happy marriage for their daughter and her new husband. Long stalks of bamboo were considered symbols of resilience and vitality. Tortoises were considered auspicious symbols of longevity and happiness.[35] Cranes were symbols of good luck and felicity, and pairs of cranes are considered symbols of "perpetuating a family line."[36] The wave patterns in the landscape connoted youth and vigor.[37]

A design incorporating similar motifs, including stalks of bamboo, pine needles, a crane and a tortoise can be found in the 1670 *Kosode Pattern Book* (*On-Hiinagata*). Although this design (Figure 11.13) emphasized asymmetry and large-scale motifs (characteristics associated with the kosode of the early part of the Edo period), it is clear that the complex layers of meaning associated with these design motifs endured across the centuries.

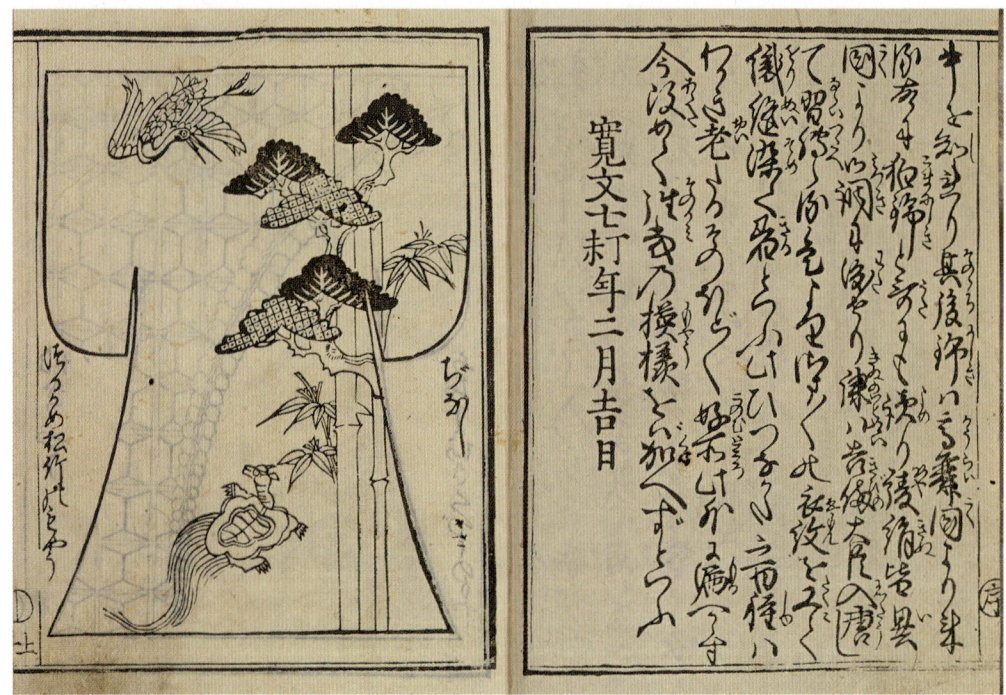

Figure 11.13.
Kosode Pattern Book (On-Hiinagata) Vol. 1, Japan, plate 2, 3, Edo period (1615–1868), 1667, One of a set of two woodblock-printed books; ink and red color on paper, H. 7 in. (17.8 cm); W. 5 in. (12.7 cm); D. 1/4 in. (0.6 cm). The Metropolitan Museum of Art, Gift of Betty and Paul Nomura, in memory of Nomura Shōjirō, 2018 (2018.954.5a). Image copyright © The Metropolitan Museum of Art. Image source: Art Resource, New York.

It was customary for the bride to wear white during the sacred part of the ceremony, since the Japanese word for white (*shiro*) "denotes purity."[38] After the sacred ceremony and before the banquet, the couple typically changed into colored garments.[39] This ritual, known as the *ironaoshi* (color alteration), was depicted by artist Utagawa Kuniyoski in a woodblock print dated to 1843–47 (Figure 11.14). In this print, the samurai bride, who is dressed in a white kimono layered over a red kimono and a black obi, is changing clothes after her wedding ceremony in preparation for the banquet. It is evening, since one of her attendants is lighting a candle.

Figure 11.14.
Utagawa Kuniyoshi, Japanese, 1797–1861. Publisher: Iseya Ichiemon, Japanese. *The Bride Changing Clothes after the Wedding Ceremony (Konrei ironaoshi no zu)***, Japanese, Edo period, 1843–47 (Tenpō 14–Kōka 4). Woodblock print (nishiki-e); ink and color on paper. Vertical ōban triptych; 35.8 x 72.9 cm (14 1/8 x 28 11/16 in.).** Museum of Fine Arts, Boston. William Sturgis Bigelow Collection (11.34954a-c).

It was at the wedding banquet that a bride's sumptuous uchikake could be seen to best effect. A bride wore her uchikake like a "cloak with the top shrugged a little way off the shoulders and the front held together by the hand." [40] The couched metallic threads of her uchikake would have sparkled in the candlelight and glimpses of the red lining in her long fluttering sleeves would have drawn all eyes to her. She might even have changed her uchikake at the middle of the banquet and donned a second and possibly even a third uchikake, worn in sequence.[41]

Summary

The material clues and visual language embodied within the case study uchikake tell a story about the bride and her family. During the latter part of the Edo period, a young woman was married in the winter months, possibly around the New Year. Born to a wealthy family from the samurai or merchant class, her family demonstrated their good taste by selecting a design that had stood the test of time, and their hopes for a long and happy marriage were reflected in their selection of auspicious symbols for their daughter's bridal ensemble. The uchikake was probably worn only once, and like many special occasion garments, stored away for many years as a treasured symbol of that happy event. Like many such garments, the name of the bride has vanished to the ravages of time, and yet the survival of this beautiful uchikake not only carries many layers of cultural meaning but also offers a tribute to the personal narrative of a young woman with hopes for a long, happy marriage.

ENDNOTES

1. A bolt of cloth used to make an adult kimono typically measures 12.5 yards long and 14 inches wide (11.43 metres by 35.5 cm). See Lisa Dalby, *Kimono: Fashioning Culture* (London: Random House, 2001), 20.

2. In his journal, Commodore Perry described the dress of Japanese people as follows: "the costumes of the various classes are as unchangeable in fashion, cut, and color as they are unchangeable in their laws and customs, and the rank and condition of the wearer are known by their dress." *The Japan Expedition, 1852–1854: The Personal Journal of Commodore Matthew C. Perry*, ed. Roger Pineau (Washington: Smithsonian Institution Press, 1968), 186.

3. Dalby, *Kimono: Fashioning Culture*, 17–63.

4. See Monika Bincsik, with contributions by Karen Van Godtsenhoven and Arai Masao, *Kimono: Edo Traditions to Modern Design* (New York: The Met and Yale University Press, 2022), 14.

5. There are many recently published books that document the history of kimono. See for example, *Kimono: Kyoto to Catwalk*, edited by Anna Jackson (London: V&A Publishing, 2020). As well, it is also important to note that there were fashions in hairstyles and accessories as well, including the obi, but this is beyond the scope of this chapter. For fashions in obi, see Dalby, *Kimono: Fashioning Culture*, 48–55.

6. Others that fell outside of these categories included actors, courtesans, geisha, and the untouchables (including night-soil collectors and those burying the dead). Jill Liddell, *The Story of the Kimono* (New York: Penguin Books, 1989), 122.

7. For more on the rise of the wealthy merchant class and expenditures on clothing, see Dale Carolyn Gluckman and Sharon Takeda, *When Art Became Fashion: Kosode in Edo-Period Japan* (Los Angeles: LACMA, 1992), 35. See also Liddell, *The Story of the Kimono*, 151, and Dalby, *Kimono: Fashioning Culture*, 57–61.

8. Gluckman and Takeda, *When Art Became Fashion*, 30.

9. *Ibid.*, 339.

10. *Ibid.* Also see Sacico Ito, *The Kimono: History & Style* (Tokyo: Brucke/PIE International/PIE Books, 2011), 11.

11. Silk embroidered kimono (uchikake), mid-19th century. Textile Museum of Canada (T98.0041). Gift of Karen Mulhallen. I examined this garment in storage on August 15, 2022.

12. Terry Satsuki Milhaupt, *Kimono: A Modern History* (London: Reaktion Books Ltd., 2014), 13.

13. Milhaupt, *Kimono: A Modern History*, 43.

14. For more on this process, see Liddell, *The Story of the Kimono*, 151, or Dalby, *Kimono: Fashioning Culture*, 300–301.

15. Gluckman and Takeda, *When Art Became Fashion*, 30.

16. *Ibid.*, 29–30.

17. See Liddell, *The Story of the Kimono*, 146–148. Also see Kosode, Kimono with small wrist openings, autumn flower-plants pattern on twill weave fabric, by Ogata Korin (1658–1716) in the Tokyo National Museum. L147.2 yuki65.1 Accessed September 21, 2024 at https://emuseum.nich.go.jp/detail?langId=en&webView=&content_base_id=100547&content_part_id=0&content_pict_id=0

18. Liddell, *The Story of the Kimono*,185–186.

19. See for example, Claude Monet, *La Japonaise* (Camille Monet in Japanese Costume), 1876, oil on canvas. MFA Boston. Accessible at https://collections.mfa.org/objects/33556. See also James Tissot, *Japonaise au bain*, 1864, oil on canvas. Musée des Beaux-Arts, Dijon. Accessible at https://commons.wikimedia.org/wiki/File:La_Japonaise_au_bain,_by_James_Tissot.jpg

20. See Elizabeth Kramer and Akiko Savas, "The Kimono Craze: From Exoticism to Fashionability," in *Kimono: Kyoto to Catwalk*, 177–179. See also Yuki Morishima and Rei Mii, eds., "Japonism in Fashion" in *Kimono Refashioned*, 47.

21. My sincere thanks to Sharon Takeda, LACMA Senior Curator, for her generosity of spirit in reading through my initial draft of this chapter and helping me understand the nuances of such garments. Any errors remaining in this text are my own.

22. The probable cause of this misalignment in the pattern was pointed out to me by Sharon Takeda. Conversation with author, February 27, 2025.

23. Masami Yamada, "Clothed in Splendour: Bridal Kimono from the Edo Period to the Present Day" in *Kimono: Kyoto to Catwalk*, 103.

24. Yamada, *Kimono: Kyoto to Catwalk*, 106.

25. Anna Jackson and Iawo Nagasaki "Creation and Commerce," *Kimono: Kyoto to Catwalk*, 83.

26. *Ibid.*, 81–98.

27. Jackson and Nagasaki, *Kimono: Kyoto to Catwalk*, 81–101.

28. Anna Jackson, *V&A Pattern Kimono* (London: V&A Publishing, 2010), 4.

29. Sharon Takeda in conversation with the author, February 27, 2025.

30   See Roland Barthes, *The Fashion System,*
     translated by Matthew Ward and Richard
     Howard (Berkeley: University of California
     Press, 1983). Also see Paul Jobling,
     "Roland Barthes: Semiology and the
     Rhetorical Codes of Fashion" in *Thinking
     Through Fashion: A Guide to Key Theorists,*
     edited by Agnes Rocamora and Anneke
     Smelik (London: I.B. Tauris, 2016),
     132–148.
31   Dalby, *Kimono: Fashioning Culture*, 184.
32   Anna Jackson, *V&A Pattern Kimono*
     (London: V&A Publishing, 2010), 5. See also
     Monica Bethe, "Reflections on Beni: Red as
     a Key to Edo-Period Fashion," in *When Art
     Became Fashion,* ed. Gluckman and Takeda,
     133–154.
33   Dalby, *Kimono: Fashioning Culture,*
     234–238.
34   Yamada, *Kimono: Kyoto to Catwalk*, 137. See
     also Dalby, *Kimono: Fashioning Culture,* 237.
35   Nitanai, *Kimono Design*, 297.
36   Keiko Nitanai, *Kimono Design: An
     Introduction to Textiles and Patterns*,
     translated by Leeyong Soo, (Tokyo: Tuttle
     Publishing, 2017), 258.
37   *Ibid.*, 135.
38   *Ibid.*, 104.
39   *Ibid.*, 104.
40   Liddell, *The Story of the Kimono*, 80.
41   Yamada, *Kimono: Kyoto to Catwalk*, 104.
     As Yamada notes, these second or third
     uchikake were worn in sequence. See also
     Bincsik, *Kimono Style*, 105.

Appendix 1: Checklist for Observation

PART I: PRELIMINARY QUESTIONS

1. Identify the object of dress for study. If applicable, record the description provided by the institution and identify the associated collection accession number(s).

2. What decade or general period does the garment or accessory belong to?

3. Why are you interested in this particular object?

4. Does the collection have any other comparable objects of dress from the same period that might be helpful to your study? If so, list them here for follow up.

PART II: AT YOUR RESEARCH APPOINTMENT

General:

5.	What type of dress object is it? Who was this object designed to be worn by? Male, female or gender-neutral? Child, teen, or adult? Was it designed with a specific purpose in mind (wedding, mourning, maternity wear, sportswear, work uniform, or theater costume)?
6.	Does the dress object have multiple parts or removable elements such as an alternate bodice or waistcoat, or detachable collars or cuffs? If so, list the components that make up the ensemble and note whether any parts are missing.
7.	What materials have been used in creating this garment, costume, or accessory?
8.	What are the dominant colors and/or patterns?
9.	What are the most unusual or unique aspects that first attract your attention?
10.	Are there any obvious signs of fragility that require special care in handling?

Construction:

11. Engage in the *Slow Approach to Seeing* to generate a detailed description of the object of dress. You may wish to draw the object and/or specific details to enhance your ability to see. Consider the front, back, side, and/or detail as appropriate.

12. Record relevant measurements for garments in metric and/or imperial measurements in the table below. For accessories, use your judgment to record key measurements. Annotate your drawings as appropriate.

Object Part	Imperial Measurement	Metric Measurement
Overall length		
Chest/Bust		
Waist		
Hip		
Front neck to hem		
Front waist to hem		
Length of zipper or opening		
Size of buttons		
Sleeve length		
Inseam measurement		
Outside trouser leg measurement		
Dress hem circumference		
Trouser leg circumference		
Armhole circumference		
Neck or collar circumference		
Height of collar		
Center back neck to hem		
Back waist to hem		
Width across back		
Underarm to underarm at back		
Other		
Other		
Other		
Other		
Other		
Other		
Other		
Other		
Other		
Other		

13. Does the structure of the garment or accessory give shape to or add emphasis to one part of the body? If so, how does it accomplish this? Consider the use of pleats, darts, placement of seams, and other construction techniques in shaping the body.

14. Was the object made with the aid of a machine, by hand, or incorporate a combination of these methods? What types of stitches have been used? Has the same thread or wool been used throughout? Is the stitching consistent in quality?

15. How is the garment, costume, or accessory closed or fastened? How many closures are there? Are these closures original to the dress object? Document the details such as ornamentation of buttons or manufacturer's stamps, and take measurements of the fastenings if relevant to your research. For a costume, was it made to be worn by different performers?

16. Are there any front, side, flap, or hidden pockets? Are the pockets functional? If the pockets are visible, are they embellished in any way? Have any objects been left inside the pockets?

17. Are the pattern pieces cut straight on the grain? Are there any remarkable features in the construction, such as a bias cut, piecing of fabric, or use of nontraditional materials or structural elements?

18. How are the seams finished? Is the fabric selvedge visible in the seams, and has this been incorporated into the cutting or construction of the garment?

19. Is the object of dress reinforced in any way using interfacing, padding, boning, metal hoops, or wire reinforcements? If so, describe in detail and note how this affects the drape and shaping.

20. Is the dress object fully or partially lined? What materials have been used in the lining? Is the lining original to the garment or accessory?

21. Has any material been subsequently added or removed?

Textiles and Materials:

22. List the textiles and/or materials and their associated colors used in creating this dress object, including the lining (if present). If possible, note whether the materials used in making this object are natural or man-made.

23. Record your perception of the relative quality of the materials. If relevant to your research, note the thread count of the textile.

24. Does the textile or other material incorporate a floral design, stripe, plaid, check, brand logo, family crest, or other form of patterned ornamentation? How has this been created (woven into the fabric, embroidered, stenciled, painted, or by manipulation)? How has the maker dealt with the pattern at the seams?

25. Has the dominant material been subjected to a finishing process, such as block printing, painting, bleaching, pressing, or glazing?

26. Does the object have any form of applied decoration, such as sequins, appliqué, trim, leather, lace, beadwork, fur, decorative buttons, ruffles, pleated bands, bows, or gemstones? If so, describe in detail. Are there signs that any such decoration has been removed or lost?

27. Has any fabric been removed? Are there any parts missing? Has the maker used piecing?

28. Has the textile or other materials faded or otherwise changed in color with the passage of time?

Marks, Labels and Logos:

29.	Is there a marking inside the dress object that indicates the specific owner, such as embroidered or inked initials, a nametag, or a laundry mark?
30.	Is there a maker's mark, label, or brand logo? Note the placement of the logo and/or label, and document any information recorded thereon or related thereto, especially if the label records a couture number or season.
31.	Is there a label or other mark such as a custom stamp that identifies where the garment or accessory originated?
32.	Are there any care or size labels? Have any labels been cut off or removed?

Use, Alteration and Wear:

33.	Is the object soiled in any way (such as dirt or perspiration stains)? Where are these stains located on the garment? Mark the areas of soiling on your drawing(s).

34. Does the object show other signs of use or wear such as friction, splitting, or fraying? Have seams ripped, silk split, or fabric decomposed? Is there evidence of insect or pest damage? Mark these areas of use and damage on your drawing(s).

35. Is there any evidence of alteration, repair, or conservation work? If so, mark this on your drawing or annotated photograph. Where is this evident and how has this impacted the original object? If the garment has been altered or repaired, is the work of the same quality as the original construction?

36. Are there any other indications that the garment or accessory has been altered from its original form? Has the object been dyed to alter its original color? Have trim or other forms of embellishment been unpicked or removed?

PART III: BEFORE YOU LEAVE

Supporting Material:

37. Does the collection have any provenance records or conservation reports related to this object that you might be permitted access to? Has the object been exhibited before? Is the donor a known person?
38. Are there any photographs of this garment or accessory being worn or mounted for display?
39. Does the collection have any other material (including related objects such as garments, tags, or original packaging, letters, or other information) associated with the garment that might aid in your research?

Initial Impressions:

40. What is most notable, unexpected, intriguing, or puzzling about this object of dress? Does anything seem atypical or spark your interest?

Appendix 2: Checklist for Reflection

I. GENERAL

1.	What was remarkable, surprising, strange, or striking about the dress object? What questions come to mind?
2.	Why has this object survived? What does this reveal about the economic or personal value ascribed to this object?
3.	Is the manner of construction consistent with the dating of the dress object? Was the garment or accessory created from another? What is the condition of the object relative to its age? Are there clues that reveal how the garment or accessory was worn, altered, or stored? What might this reveal about the person(s) who wore, owned, or handled this object?
4.	Does the catalog record for this object accurately reflect what was observed? Was anything noted that seems to be inconsistent with the written record?
5.	Does this object come from a culture different than your own or a historically marginalized community? Would it be helpful to engage the assistance of a person from that community in your research?

II. SENSORY REACTIONS

6.	What is most visually striking about this object? Does the color of the textile or the motifs therein have symbolic or cultural meaning? Does the object incorporate stylistic, religious, artistic, or iconic references? Does the garment, costume, or accessory represent a life transition?
7.	Is the garment or accessory stylistically consistent with the period from which it came? Does it seem to reflect the influences of that period or diverge from it?
8.	What is the texture and weight of the cloth or other materials used to construct the garment or accessory?
9.	Would a person wearing this garment or accessory make noise and draw attention to themselves?
10.	Does the garment or accessory emit an odor? Can the origin of the odor be identified?

III. PERSONAL REACTIONS

11.	Does this garment or accessory spark a memory or hold emotional resonance for you?
12.	Would the garment or accessory fit your body? Are you the same gender and size as the person who wore or owned this object? Would you wear this garment or accessory if you could? Is the style and color appealing to you? What would it be like to wear this garment or accessory? Would it be tight or loose on your body? Would it cause any discomfort?
13.	Does the design of the object emphasize status, sexuality, or gender roles? What does this communicate about cultural values of the time in which the object was made and worn?

IV. CONTEXTUAL INFORMATION

14. If you were permitted access to the provenance record for the artifact, what does this information reveal about the owner, and their relationship to the garment or accessory?

15. If the museum, study, or private collection had other garments that are similar, how do these other garments compare to your object of study? If the garment or accessory was worn by a known person, are there other objects from that person's wardrobe that can be accessed for study?

16. Do other museums have similar objects? Can you identify similar objects in online collections of dress? How do these objects compare?

17. Are there any significant historical events that occurred around the time that the object was made that are relevant to the object biography?

18. How are similar garments or accessories represented in fashion plates, photographs, illustrations, paintings, or other forms of visual media? What does this reveal about the social context of the time? How was this object worn and accessorized?

19. Has this object, or others like it, been referenced in documents such as published diaries, letters, magazines, novels, or other forms of written material like inventories, wills, or legal documents? What does this reveal/suggest/convey about the material practices or the cultural beliefs of that time?

20. Are there similar objects (such as fashion dolls) or related ephemera (advertisements, fashion photographs, packaging, and other print material) available for sale on online vintage retailers, auction sites, or eBay? What does this information reveal about the perceived value and rarity of this object?

21. If the designer/maker of the garment or accessory is a known person, what information is available about them? How does this object fit into their oeuvre? Has the designer/maker written an autobiography, recorded an oral history, or been profiled in magazines or journals?

22. Have other scholars written about this type of garment or accessory in scholarly books or peer-reviewed journals? If so, list these sources and assess how this material might be used to interpret this object.

V. NEXT STEPS

23. Consider the cultural values of the time in which the object of dress was made and how these values are reflected in the design, use and survival of the object. How do these values inform your understanding?

24. After studying the object and the related contextual material, what patterns have emerged? What questions remain? What interests you most about this object now?

25. List your anticipated next steps.

Index

Note: Page locators in *italic* refer to figure captions.